Palgrave Studies in European Union Politics

Series Editors

Neill Nugent
Emeritus Professor of Politics Manchester
Metropolitan University, UK

William E. Paterson
Honorary Professor for German and European Politics
Aston University, UK

Michelle Egan
Professor and Jean Monnet Chair of European Integration
School of International Service
American University, USA

Fellow, Wilson Center, USA

Following on the sustained success of the acclaimed European Union Series, which essentially publishes research-based textbooks, Palgrave Studies in European Union Politics publishes cutting edge research-driven monographs. The remit of the series is broadly defined, both in terms of subject and academic discipline. All topics of significance concerning the nature and operation of the European Union potentially fall within the scope of the series. The series is multidisciplinary to reflect the growing importance of the EU as a political, economic and social phenomenon.

More information about this series at
http://www.springer.com/series/14629

Giovanni Faleg

The EU's Common Security and Defence Policy

Learning Communities in International Organizations

Giovanni Faleg
Centre for European Policy Studies
Brussels, Belgium

Palgrave Studies in European Union Politics
ISBN 978-3-319-41305-1   ISBN 978-3-319-41306-8   (eBook)
DOI 10.1007/978-3-319-41306-8

Library of Congress Control Number: 2016917117

Cover illustration: © Ton Koene / Alamy Stock Photo

Printed on acid-free paper

This Palgrave Macmillan imprint is published by Springer Nature
The registered company is Springer International Publishing AG Switzerland

This book is dedicated to my wife, Carolina, and to my son, Alberto.

PREFACE

This book explains how international organisations learn and change, through collaborative practices and knowledge sharing. Specifically, it looks at the evolution of the European Union's Common Security and Defence Policy (CSDP), a dynamic policy area that has witnessed a significant degree of institutional and policy change, especially during operational experience. The book shows that a process of learning, whereby communities of practitioners and experts interact, has not only driven forward the CSDP, but shaped its softer, more civilian character, rather than the military role this policy was initially supposed to fulfil.

Through the creation of new policy frameworks, such as civilian crisis management (CCM) and security sector reform (SSR), the CSDP has gone beyond the military dimension of security. As a matter of fact, the academic literature on European security has not explained why the CSDP has predominantly scaled up civilian activities, instead of military programmes. Although the nature of past errors (namely, policy failure in the Western Balkans) and the lessons learned by the EU have to do with the absence of military means, and despite the St Malo commitment to build up military capabilities, the EU has invested in the development of civilian tools for crisis management. In the field, civilian missions have also overwhelmed military ones.

To account for this outcome, the book provides an original perspective, which draws from theories of institutional learning, policy evolution and the recent "practice turn" in International Relations theory. It shows that the EU has learned to be a security provider thanks to the role of communities of experts and practitioners, who engage in learning by doing—hence the term "learning communities". The creation of a transnational policy consensus on new forms of security cooperation in the late 1990s has triggered policy change in the EU, prompted by like-minded groups of practitioners who are informally as well as contextually bound by a shared interest in learning and applying a common practice.

A sounder theoretical framework on learning bears significant policy implications for international institutions. Learning communities can be used to foster and manage organizational change in international bureaucracies, to support policy innovation, and to create new patterns of cooperation across state boundaries. The structure, composition, preferences, goals, *modus operandi* of communities and networks are highly contextual, and extremely fluid. Each institution has specific rules and behaviours governing its communities, because cultural, ideational and power dynamics vary from one institution to another. To understand how practitioners are connected to each other and how such connections allow them to share knowledge and experiences is a key determinant of success when planning institutional reform and change management processes. In a fast-paced world, it is vital for modern institutions to promptly adapt to changing circumstances. Communities have the power to build fast-track lanes to effective learning.

Washington, DC   Giovanni Faleg
19 August 2016

CONTENTS

List of Abbreviations

ASPR	Austrian Study Centre for Peace and Conflict Resolution
ASSET	Association for Security Sector Reform Education and Training
ASSN	African Security Sector Network
AU	African Union
BASIC	British American Security Information Council
CA	Comprehensive Approach (EU)
CCM	Civilian Crisis Management (EU)
CFSP	Common Foreign and Security Policy (EU)
CHAD	Conflict and Humanitarian Affairs Department (UK)
CHG	Civilian Headline Goal (EU)
CiLMA	Civilian Lessons Management Application (EU)
CIVCOM	Committee for Civilian Aspects of Crisis Management (EU)
CMB	Crisis Management Board (EU)
CMC	Crisis Management Centre
CMPD	Crisis Management and Planning Directorate (EU)
COREPER	Committee of Permanent Representatives (EU)
COREU	Correspondence Européenne Network (EU)
CPCC	Civilian Planning and Conduct Capability (EU)
CPDC	Conflict Prevention and Development Cooperation Network (OECD)
CRCT	Crisis Response Coordination Team (EU)
CRT	Civilian Response Team (EU)
CSDG	Conflict, Security and Development Group
CSDP	Common Security and Defence Policy (EU)
CoP	Community of Practice
DAC	Development Assistance Committee (OECD)

DCAF	Geneva Centre for the Democratic Control of Armed Forces
DDR	Disarmament, Demobilisation and Reintegration
DEVCO	European Commission's Directorate-General for Development Cooperation—EuropeAid
DFID	Department for International Development (UK)
DOD	Department of Defense (US)
DOS	Department of State (US)
DRC	Democratic Republic of Congo
EC	European Commission
ECHO	European Commission's Humanitarian Aid and Civil Protection Department
ECOWAS	Economic Community of West African States
EDA	European Defence Agency
EEAS	European External Action Service (EU)
EGT	European Group on Training (EU)
ELMA	European Lessons Management Application (EU)
EMU	Economic and Monetary Union (EU)
ENP	European Neighbourhood Policy (EU)
ENTRi	Europe's New Training Initiative for Civilian Crisis Management (EU)
EP	European Parliament
EPC	European Political Cooperation
EPLO	European Peace-building Liaison Office
ESDC	European Security and Defence College (EU)
EU	European Union
EUBAM	European Union Border Assistance Mission
EUCAP	European Union Capacity-building Mission
EUFOR	European Union Force
EU ISS	European Union Institute for Security Studies
EULEX	European Union Rule of Law Mission
EUMC	European Union Military Committee
EUMM	European Union Monitoring Mission
EUMS	European Union Military Staff
EUPM/EUPOL	European Union Police Mission
EUSR	European Union Special Representatives
EUSSR	European Union Security Sector Reform Mission
EUTM	European Union Training Mission
FBA	Folke Bernadotte Academy
FCO	Foreign and Commonwealth Office (UK)
FYROM	Former Yugoslav Republic of Macedonia
GFN-SSR	Global Facilitation Network for Security Sector Reform
HQ	Headquarter

HR/VP	High Representative of the Union for Foreign Affairs and Security Policy and Vice President of the Commission (EU)
IGC	Inter-governmental Conference (EU)
IMF	International Monetary Fund
INCAF	International Network on Conflict and Fragility (OECD)
IO	International Organisation
IR	International Relations
ISSAT	International Security Sector Advisory Team
KFOR	Kosovo Force (NATO)
MFA	Ministry of Foreign Affairs
MoD	Ministry of Defence
MS	Member States (EU)
NATO	North Atlantic Treaty Organization
NGO	Non-governmental Organisation
ODI	Overseas Development Institute
OECD	Organisation for Economic Cooperation and Development
OHQ	Operational Headquarters
OMIK	OSCE Mission in Kosovo
OPCEN	Operation Centre (EU)
OSCE	Organization for Security Cooperation in Europe
PMG	Politico Military Group (EU)
PSC	Political and Security Committee (EU)
RELEX	European Commission's Directorate General for External Relations
RFSI	Swedish Council for Peace and Security Initiative
SHAPE	Supreme Headquarters Allied Powers Europe (NATO)
SIDA	Swedish International Development Cooperation Agency
SSG	Security Sector Governance
SSR	Security Sector Reform
SWG	Security Working Group (EU)
TEU	Treaty on European Union (Maastricht Treaty)
UK	United Kingdom
UN	United Nations
UNDAC	United Nations Disaster Assessment and Coordination
UNDP	United Nations Development Programme
UNMIK	United Nations Interim Administration Mission in Kosovo
US	United States of America
USAID	United States Agency for International Development
WEU	Western European Union
ZIF	Zentrum für Internationale Friedenseinsätze (*Center for International Peace Operations*)

LIST OF FIGURES

LIST OF TABLES

CHAPTER 1

Introduction: Ideas that Changed the EU's Common Security and Defence Policy

Ideas change the world. They produce new patterns of cooperation among states, impinging on the formal and informal institutions that were created to foster such cooperation. What is problematic is to determine how ideational factors bear impact on actors' decisions, particularly those leading to the adoption of common policy frameworks. What is also unclear is how these frameworks then result in observable policy outcomes. Take the case of the European Union's Common Security and Defence Policy (CSDP): since the late 1990s, the evolution of this policy has been markedly oriented towards a soft provision of security, involving the build-up of civilian crisis management means rather than sheer military capabilities. Where did the idea of non-military crisis management come from, and why was it so impactful on EU security cooperation? Why didn't the EU develop a military crisis manager instead?

Drawing from the academic debate on institutional learning (Nye 1987; Haas 1990a; b; Hall 1993; Levy 1994; Radaelli 2009), policy evolution (Adler and Haas 1992) and the recent "practice turn" in IR (Adler and Pouliot 2011a, b), this book explains why and how security policies in the European Union have evolved since the creation of the CSDP. It is argued that as new security paradigms trickled down EU (and national) bureaucracies, they were bound up in the execution of security practices, thus producing policy change. This book also accounts for ideas that do not generate transformation when new norms fail to be associated with practices.

© The Author(s) 2017
G. Faleg, *The EU's Common Security and Defence Policy,*
DOI 10.1007/978-3-319-41306-8_1

Thus, the overall objective of this work is to test the "learning by doing" evolution of CSDP, revealing the conditions under which the doing triggers the learning process and, in turn, fosters change. The academic literature focusing on ideational factors as drivers of CSDP has highlighted the role of expertise-based or epistemic communities in shaping European security decisions (Cross 2011). This book engages this argument by explaining CSDP and the development of a specific set of non-military crisis management tools, from a communities of practice perspective.

Indeed, the empirical findings of this research demonstrate that learning has policy impact when the consensus on the lessons learned from the past is underpinned by a common set of normative and principled beliefs—which fits the definition of *episteme* in accordance with Haas' theory of institutional change; at the same time, it shows that policy impact turns into observable policy evolution and shapes broader socio-political processes (e.g. the design of CSDP as a "civilian" or "soft" provider of security) when the knowledge is embedded in communities of practice that structure experience and define the way actors socialise and learn.

In the case of the CSDP, common practices define the way EU actors learn. The nexus between new knowledge and practice is what makes CSDP learning by doing possible. The present contribution looks at the CSDP as an environment in which transnational learning, promoted by knowledge and practice-based communities, drives policy-making. Investigating the role of "learning communities" in CSDP also helps in detecting which one of the several communities discussed by the IR literature (Adler 2008: 199; Cohendet et al. 2001: 306) is more suitable to account for security cooperation within the EU framework. In fact, there is a strong need in IR theory "to clarify the main characteristics of diverse communities" (Créplet et al. 2003: 44), how they contribute to knowledge creation and what the implications in policy terms are. The CSDP includes sectors where learning by doing struggled to emerge, despite the evidence of knowledge-based policy innovation. Reappraising the concept of epistemic communities helps us in assessing the extent to which impactful learning depends on the overlap between knowledge and practice.

The conceptual bases of learning communities point out the notions of joint enterprise, shared beliefs (Haas 1990a) and repertoire (Wenger 1998). Learning communities are linked to the emergence of a dominant view of a social reality across different backgrounds, as in the case of epistemic communities (Haas 1992); or the existence of like-mindedness as the condition for the development, sharing and maintenance of common practices leading to collective learning (Adler and Pouliot 2011a; Bicchi 2011).

Dominance is power-based. The presence of interest-based constituencies (e.g. through the support by one or more member states) backing the formation of consensual views determines the ability of the communities to gain access to and influence politics. Accordingly, the creation of a policy consensus (McNamara 1998) on new forms of security cooperation leads to policy change when ideas are supported by interests and can rely on pre-existing practices.

These factors can largely account for the variation in impact of new norms or security prescriptions. Not all ideas, in fact, are equally successful in influencing policy-making. Some of them lead to the creation of new institutions, bureaucracies, or entail profound changes in actors' behaviour. Other may be diffused, but are discarded or do not manage to persist (Risse-Kappen 1994). Some norms have shaped the activities, perceptions and the institutional design of the CSDP. Others had a much more limited impact. Accounting for such variation is a main theoretical goal of this book.

1.1   THE ARGUMENT

Learning has obviously to do with change. What is less obvious is the definition of what type of change occurs as an international organisation learns, whether it is simple adaptation or more complex belief change (Zito 2009). Let us define learning as "the process by which consensual knowledge is used to specify causal relationships in new ways so that the results affect the content of public policy" (Haas 1990a: 23).

The Common Foreign and Security Policy (CFSP) of the EU has been marked by unprecedented developments in the field of security and defence. Prompted by the December 1998 Franco-British St Malo Declaration, the CSDP was officially launched at the Cologne European Council on June 1999. In the wake of the Yugoslav Wars, it was supposed to provide the European Union with the military *force de frappe* to support the critical mass of the, until then, inconclusive CFSP. It was also a response to major changes in the structure of the post-Cold War international system, which urged European states to enhance their power projection capability and decrease their reliance vis-à-vis the United States (Jones 2007; Howorth 2007).

The evolution "by doing" of the CSDP in the past fifteen years has involved three fundamental dimensions (Grevi et al. 2009). First, the building up of institutions and the consequent process of institutional reform, leading to the expansion of bureaucratic structures, and the creation of new ones, particularly since the entry into law of the Lisbon Treaty on December 2009. Second, the emergence of a European strategic debate resulting in the adoption of the 2003 European Security Strategy (updated in 2008). Third, the operational experience gained by CSDP missions from 2003 onward. In March 2003, in fact, the EU launched its first military operation (EUFOR Concordia, in the Former Yugoslav Republic of Macedonia) using NATO assets under the "Berlin Plus agreement", while the first autonomous CSDP military deployment came about only a few months later, in May 2003, with the launch of Operation Artemis in the Democratic Republic of the Congo (RDC). Since then, the EU has intervened as a crisis manager in many regions of the world (Western Balkans, Africa, Middle East, Caucasus and Asia). Such evolution of the CSDP by practice has led some analysts to qualify the evolutionary process as learning "by doing" (Juncos 2006: Grevi et al. 2009).

Institutionalists account for the CSDP as the product of endogenous institutional change, leading to unintended consequences (Menon and Sedelmeier 2010; Pierson 1996). As a matter of fact, whereas the nature of past errors (e.g. policy failure in the Balkans) and the lessons learned pointed to the absence of military means, the solution has rather gone in the opposite direction. In empirical, operational terms the CSDP has developed mostly on the civilian side of the crisis management spectrum (Drent 2011). The comprehensive approach (CA) and civil-military coordination have dominated the political, strategic and institutional dynamics. Although concrete guidelines for the Union's comprehensive approach were only laid out in the joint communication from the European Commission and the High Representative of December 2013, the concept has been extensively applied as a key organising principle for the EU's external action, including CSDP, since the mid-2000s, particularly in relation to conflict prevention and crisis resolution.[1] CA, as Chapter 3 will show, refers to the coherent and consistent deployment of all EU (internal as well as external) instruments and resources, including greater strategic coordination between the European Commission and member states, at any stage of the conflict cycle or external crises. Against this backdrop, CA denotes the EU's attempt to reach a coherent division of labour between the Brussels bureaucracy and member states, and link it to operational effectiveness in crisis-management missions launched under the CSDP framework. The concept emanates from a broader paradigmatic shift in the notion of security, by which international responses to crises and security threats start moving away from being strictly military and are increasingly understood to be linked with other dimensions such as development aid or governance, or that different types/methodologies of interventions are necessary alongside the use of force.

Concerned with clearing up why the EU started engaging in crisis management, where and with what implications on the Brussels-based bureaucratic machinery, the academic literature has failed to explain why something that was supposed to have a military outlook and outreach, ended up being overwhelmingly civilian or civil-military. Alternative explanations of the EU security architecture, as the next chapter will show, are undecided as to why actors learn and socialise in a specific manner, and how their common understanding of the CSDP as non-military is constructed.

The present analysis challenges institutionalism on two grounds: the processes and the outcomes of institutional change. Concerning processes, this approach reframes the study of socialisation within CSDP (Meyer 2006; Juncos and Pomorska 2006; Juncos and Reynolds 2007; Cross 2010) so as to focus on the conditions for persuasiveness defining how socialising forces matter. By doing so, it identifies learning communities as the carriers of change, mediating between structure and agency, as well as between interests and ideas, and leading to learning. The EU has become a comprehensive security provider because transnational expertise and practice-based communities have been pushing forward a new security thinking, changing the traditional—military—understanding of crisis management. Curiously enough, the academic literature has overlooked the nexus between the profound re-conceptualisation of security resulting from the changing nature of post-Cold War crises, on the one hand, and the new activities developed by international organisations, including the EU, on the other.

CSDP's adaptation to systemic pressures is characterised by an emerging consensus on the importance of non-military crisis management and on the value of civilian and integrated capabilities. These two ideas diffused and trickled down the EU decision-making by means of social interaction. Norm diffusion did not take place in a single institutional configuration, but *across* bureaucracies. For instance, in the initial formulation of the civilian crisis management policy, diffusion processes occurred both within member states ministries of defence and foreign affairs, and at the EU level (in the DG E IX of the General Secretariat of the Council), leading to the creation of new divisions, such as the CivMil Cell and the Committee for Civilian Aspects of Crisis Management (CIVCOM). The physical places where learning by doing and norm diffusion take place can then be conceived, not as separated or specific entities, but as a system characterised by networked governance: a set of bureaucracies within the European Commission, the Council Secretariat and national ministries (including diplomatic missions) where different types of networks interact, structuring relationship and balance of power among institutional actors. In this networked governance system, ideas affect the way states' preferences are shaped and gain salience in the CSDP setting, because the practice helps constructing and consolidating social interaction. Chapter 4 will outline in greater detail the main features of the EU security architecture and clarify the different levels where norm diffusion takes place: (1) governance level (supranational, intergovernmental and transgovernmental); (2) actors level (state and non-state actors); (3) field level (military, civilian, civ-mil, industrial and political).

This book shows how the practice of security enabled the EU to learn and evolve. It fills a lacuna in the institutionalist literature, which tends to focus on the creation or reshaping of institutions rather than their effect (Menon 2011a; Barnett and Finnemore 1999). A convergence on a comprehensive vision of the CSDP, in fact, does not automatically translate into the CSDP implementing comprehensive policies.

The following chapters describe the causal chain of events and reconstruct how specific concepts within the EU comprehensive approach framework turned into policies, and why specific ideas produced policy evolution by means of experiential learning while others did not. The framework develops four pathways of influence which describe the conditions under which ideas turn into policies. These include the presence of a power constituency supporting the diffusion and institutionalisation of the new ideas; the formation of cohesiveness and a "sense of belonging" among practitioners, facilitated by a common identity; a shared epistemic enterprise aimed at producing policy innovation; and the emulation of a successful model of cooperation or policy implementation.

1.2   Testing Learning by Doing

The hypotheses are tested on two case studies: security sector reform (SSR) and civilian crisis management (CCM). Both represent new or emerging policy fields in CSDP. They are also relevant for the EU comprehensive approach, in terms of civilian or holistic contributions to crisis management concepts/procedures. Each case has clearly defined policy frameworks with at least one CSDP operation carried out since 2003 (SSR and CCM missions).

Both SSR and CCM substantiate the presence of the communities of practice and/or experts promoting the diffusion of new norms that originate in the post-Cold War security environment. Both are examples of policy innovation, hence useful cases to explain how policy consensus emerges, diffuses, gets institutionalised and evolves. Because of the differences in policy outcomes—especially institutional developments and operational outreach—a comparative analysis between SSR and CCM is well suited to test the conditions under which some norms lead to policy evolution, while others do not. Hence, besides exploring the genesis of CA as a process of learning, the methodology used in this book is conceived to answer other important questions: Why did CCM have more impact in shaping the CSDP in terms of policy outcomes? Was a policy consensus on SSR more difficult to muster, or to turn into implementation, and if so, why? Starting from similar conditions of policy failure, followed by policy innovation, the relative success of CCM and poor evolution of SSR tell us that even if they are "grabbed" by policy-makers and enter the institutional arena, norms may still fail or struggle to survive in practice. Even the presence of national constituencies (e.g. backing from the United Kingdom, in the case of SSR) is not alone sufficient to cope with the intricacies of multilateral cooperation. The connection between ideas and interests needs to be complemented by the connection between knowledge and practice.

The comparison between SSR and CCM builds on Mill's method of difference and a qualitative, semi-structured interviews-based research. Research findings are presented according to three dimensions: (1) the types of learning communities, namely their composition and cohesiveness, which define the cognitive architecture of the policy area under study; (2) the diffusion process of ideas, according to an assessment of the pathways of influence and intervening factors; (3) the analysis of policy outcomes, and whether evolution as learning by doing has occurred or not.

1.3   SIGNIFICANCE

The CSDP's continuous process of institutional adaptation is addressed in this book. My theoretical framework seeks to overcome the realist emphasis on exogenous processes of change, but also engages the current inward looking analyses of institutional dynamics and social rules within the Brussels-based bureaucratic machinery (*aka* Brusselsisation) that has been gaining ground since the mid-2000s. The framework of analysis merges elements of sociological institutionalism (March and Olsen 1989; Christiansen et al. 1999; Checkel 2005), networked governance (Mérand et al. 2011) and epistemic/communitarian approaches to International Relations (Ruggie 1975; Haas 1990a; b; Verdun 1999; Cross 2011; Adler 2005), including the most recent "practice turn" (Adler 2008; Adler and Pouliot 2011a; Lachmann 2010). The sociological source of inspiration resides in the works of Foucault (1970) and Bourdieu (1990) and their conceptualisation of *epistemes* and background knowledge. The concept of learning communities (Adler 2008), brings ideas back into the debate on European security cooperation, while at the same time making clear that ideational forces and socialisation matter but do not operate independently from power.

There are two key and original contributions of this book. First, it visualises learning communities beyond formal institutional structures or committees, and pictures them as "islands of knowledge and practice", transcending states and international organisations' boundaries.

Second, it explores the extent to which previous experiences in a given policy field (e.g. civilian police) and the existence of networks of practitioners support the formation of new knowledge, and hence boosts learning. In terms of norm diffusion, the empirical case studies test the applicability of the policy evolution model (Adler and Haas 1992; McNamara 1998) to security policies. By going through the steps of failure, innovation and norm diffusion, important indications can be derived in order to understand how international organisations adapt their policy objectives and institutional setting to face changing circumstances.

Concerning the outcomes, CSDP learning by doing (Juncos 2006), previously looked at as an isolated concept, is now put into the broader context of institutional learning theories. According to my model, in fact, policy evolution should produce learning by doing, understood as the refinement of new policy tools out of the first waves of operational experiences leading to feedback loops. The absence of lessons learned may indicate that a convergence on the policy consensus has struggled to turn into convergence in outcomes and implementation.

1.4   The Structure of the Book

The remaining chapters identify the emerging consensus on non-military and civil-military approaches to crisis management as the foremost achievement of the CSDP since its creation in the late-1990s. The consensus came out as an adaptive response to changing international conditions leading states to no longer view purely military interventions as viable means to solve conflicts and to design security cooperation within the EU accordingly. This consensus, supported by key constituencies of member states, allowed the CSDP to find its niche in the European security landscape by investing in the comprehensive dimension of crisis management and hence differentiating itself from other international organisations dealing with security (e.g. NATO). The learning process, however, resulted in some norms being more influential than others and, as a consequence, in different patterns of policy evolutions across areas of cooperation.

Chapter 2 outlines the framework of analysis. It discusses how the concepts of epistemic communities and communities of practice are operationalised to explain the current shape of the CSDP. Policy evolution occurs if practice and knowledge overlap, through specific pathways of influence. The methodology section discusses how the learning process is assessed and expounds the qualitative methods used to trace learning communities. In particular, it specifies how the triangulation between semi-structured interviews, process-tracing and document analysis made it possible to detect the attributes and types of communities, the process of knowledge formation, its subsequent integration into the CSDP framework and the emergence of learning by doing.

Chapter 3 illustrates the origins of the EU comprehensive approach. It introduces the paradigmatic shift in security that occurred since the end of the Cold War, resulting from the new nature of crisis management to international responses—namely human security and peacebuilding. By doing so, it explains how the idea of "comprehensiveness" and its implementation through the EU comprehensive approach are rooted in a broader paradigmatic shift affecting the global security agenda. Therefore, the chapter seeks to link global norm generation to the rise of the EU's specificity in comprehensive crisis management. Special attention is placed on the culture of coordination and the institutional interface connecting military and civilian structures.

Chapter 4 describes the structures, actors and networks that combine to form the CSDP governance. The chapter seeks to provide an exhaustive explanation of the CSDP system by examining the interplay between the three dimensions. Conclusions show that CSDP networks are manifold and multi-level, thus extending beyond the formal institutional setting where intergovernmental negotiations occur: network's configurations vary depending on the sector analysed.

Chapter 5 introduces the two policy frameworks on civilian crisis management and security sector reform, particularly as regards their contribution to shaping an integrated or comprehensive vision of security cooperation. A state-of-the-art description of the scope, structures, procedures and practices related to the implementation of SSR and CCM is provided to help the reader to gett familiar with these policies.

Chapter 6 investigates the rise of SSR. It addresses the questions of why and how SSR principles were institutionalised by EU member states, what influenced EU policy-makers' choices and, finally, what are the outcomes of the policy consensus on the EU approach to SSR. Through a thorough investigation of the role of learning communities and by tracing back the dynamics of norm diffusion, it is concluded that convergence is driven by a confluence of ideational factors and state interests. Empirical evidence shows the role of national constituencies (the United Kingdom in particular) in supporting the diffusion of SSR's knowledge. At the same time, conclusions highlight the failure of SSR framework to turn into a real convergence in policy outcomes and evolution. As a result, SSR's overall impact on the shape and activities of CSDP has been limited.

Chapter 7 analyses the development of CCM in the EU through the lenses of conceptual evolution, and the resulting diffusion of ideas and practices across EU member states. By asking similar questions to the ones raised in the case of SSR, and with similar starting conditions (experience of policy failure and policy innovation), the chapter illustrates a different picture of learning. Knowledge is, in the CCM case, rooted in shared practices, born out of EU member states' previous experiences in civilian missions (e.g. police) with other international organisations. The genesis of a CCM policy framework and the EU's way to civilian crisis management (Nowak 2006) are hence practice-driven, and strongly supported by the constituency of Nordic EU member states—Sweden and Finland in particular. Conclusions to this chapter emphasise, in stark contrast with the previous case study, the much stronger impact of CCM in defining the CSDP, and the greater amount of policy evolution through learning by doing.

Chapter 8 summarises and compares the findings to explain variation, and uncover the causal link between learning communities and policy evolution. By linking the case studies to the broader argument of the book, this chapter answers the question of why some ideas turn into policy evolution while others do not. Policy recommendations and suggestions for future research agenda are included as final remarks.

NOTE

1. European Commission and HR/VP (2013: 3).

CHAPTER 2

The Framework of Analysis: Learning Communities in International Organisations

This book challenges the conventional wisdom that the soft or civilian focus of the CSDP results from the lack of a consensus among member states on the degree of military integration in the EU (Santopinto and Price 2013; Fiott 2015). Quite the contrary, the development of an overwhelmingly civilian CSDP is the end product of a growing transnational consensus on non-military approaches to crisis management. This explanation shows the limits of IR theories emphasising inter-state bargains and balancing/bandwagoning behaviour, and stresses the importance of ideational factors in shaping security policy-making. New ideas can affect security policies, but different channels for diffusion may lead to different outcomes in policy terms. The channels under study are transnational communities of experts and practitioners, who act as carriers of knowledge into policy-making structures. Understanding how ideas turn into policies through these channels may help in explaining the reason why some ideas produce change while others do not and, as a result, what type of cooperation stems from what ideational factors and under what conditions. Questions about how actors learn, what lessons they draw and how knowledge produces change in international organisations, have been salient in political science and IR debates over the past thirty years. These questions have also been relevant for the study of the European Union (Zito 2001, 2009; Zito and Schout 2009; Radaelli 1995, 2009). As with the other policy areas studied in the literature, learning also took place in EU security and defence, an area of cooperation that was created in the late-1990s and has grown substantially ever since.

© The Author(s) 2017
G. Faleg, *The EU's Common Security and Defence Policy*,
DOI 10.1007/978-3-319-41306-8_2

By way of introduction, let us briefly consider the historical and international context. Since the end of the Cold War, security has become a complex and multidimensional concept, owing to the decline of traditional inter-state wars and the rise of new challenges such as intra-state conflicts, asymmetric and unconventional warfare, terrorism, civil wars, or threats related to failing or failed states. The international provision of security and multilateral defence cooperation has evolved accordingly. Multilateral institutions have become increasingly absorbed in the management of security crises. Despite operational distress and budgetary constraints, crisis management has become a term of art in the post-1989 security discourse, and translated into a diffused international practice.

Collective security organisations started to engage in complex peace-keeping, crisis management or nation-building tasks, whose nature was not essentially military. Responding to momentous changes in polarity as well as to the nature of armed conflicts, comprehensive forms of intervention emerged, entailing profound changes in the way actors decide upon and implement their responses to crises. These new trajectories for crisis management involved the conceptualisation of different and longer phases of action, joining short-term combat responses with broad conflict prevention and post-conflict reconstruction involving long-term programmes.

The most immediate implication of these transformations for security and defence cooperation has been the increased value of civilians and civilian capabilities in what was previously considered a *domaine réservé* for the military. New scenarios opened up in the field of international security, with experts and practitioners gradually moving towards a consensus on the critical importance of civilian and civilian-military work to the success of crisis management operations (Chivvis 2010: 1).

From the mid-1990s onward, states and international organisations refined their crisis management goals, means and instruments according to new systemic priorities. However, the way these actors responded to structural stimuli varied from case to case. There is no universal doctrine or model for civil-military crisis management, since each actor developed different instruments, set out different goals, or used different terms according to contextual or historical considerations (Wendling 2010: 10). As a result, understanding "how" single actors responded to structural pressures is crucial in explaining "why" change took place in the international security environment.

The "how" question implies the presence of some intervening factors between agency and structure, which alters the way these two interact. These factors are social and ideational. Actors do not just adapt to structural constraints, such as changes in the distribution of natural resources or an alteration of the balance of power, in order to guarantee their self-preservation in an anarchic international system. States, and international organisations alike, learn by diffusing and assimilating new knowledge: Endogenous factors, such as ideas, identity, expertise or the social interaction with other actors, affect the way preferences are shaped.

What generates change in the CSDP is the overarching question addressed in this book, in order to account for the creation of new institutional structures; the operational outreach; the means at its disposal; the holistic procedures for crisis response. The determinant factors are framed as the combination between the practice, knowledge and power, which generally defines the process of learning and, in the case of the CSDP, was operationalised as learning by doing.[1]

The framework of analysis considers different pathways by which ideas turn into policy, which include communities of practice (Adler and Pouliot 2011a) as well as knowledge-based epistemic communities (Haas 1990a) as useful competing explanations. Hence the question arises as to whether practice-based communities, as opposed to other communities, played a determinant role in producing evolution.

This analysis shows that in European security, learning by doing has occurred in those sector areas in which practitioners endowed their joint enterprise with political validity, epistemic ground for action and intersubjective meaning. In other words, practices help constructing, or reconstructing from past experiences, the common knowledge as well as a common understanding of a political reality. By contrast, in other sector areas, common practices struggled to emerge.

In EU security cooperation, civilian crisis management expanded and prompted the launch of several CSDP missions. Security sector reform, on the contrary, failed to become a fully-fledged practice and now occupies a marginal role in the EU security framework. The presence of a community of practice in the case of CCM, and its absence in the epistemic-driven emergence of SSR, explain the failure of the latter, the successful evolution of the former and its impact on the overall strategic posture of the CSDP.

2.1   THE RISE AND EVOLUTION OF EUROPEAN SECURITY COOPERATION

2.1.1   CSDP Genesis

The CSDP originates in the EU's diplomatic *échec* in the Balkans (Pond 1999; Forster and Wallace 2000).[2] It pertains to the redefinition of the European security architecture according to the transformations in the post-1989 international system, namely vis-à-vis the US and NATO (Kupchan 2003). In this regard, the EU's inaction in the Yugoslav tragedy not only reflects a fundamental split in the interests of the three larger member states (France, Germany and the UK), but is also the logical consequence of the lack of a military underpinning, characterising a European diplomacy "without teeth" (Jopp and Diedrichs 2009: 100).

In his formulation of the "capabilities-expectations gap", Hill (1993) pioneers the conceptualisation of European foreign and security policy, based on the notions of actorness and presence (Hill 1993: 308), which shows the gap between what the EU is talked up to and what it is able to deliver (Hill 1993: 306). The first academic writings on the CSDP explain it as a reaction to exogenous stimuli affecting European security (Pond 2002; Duke 1999; Cornish and Edwards 2005). In particular, structural-realist perspectives emphasise the Europeans' attempt to reduce the involvement of the United States (Posen 2006). The main problem with this approach is that the "hard balancing" thesis—a robust military build up to rebalance the transatlantic relationship—has failed to materialise. Instead, the EU's crisis management machinery has been soft-security intensive. Variants of realism have sought to address this point. The idea of "soft balancing", developed by Pape (2005), contends that Europeans are instead more likely to balance the United States through "international institutions, economic statecraft, and strict interpretations of neutrality" (Pape 2005: 17).

Engaging realist scholars, Howorth (2007) argues that structural change is not the only factor that spurred European security cooperation. He identifies four underlying drivers behind CSDP: (*1*) exogenous forces deriving from the end of the Cold War, most notably the lessening strategic importance of Europe for the United States; (*2*) new tasks and concept entered the IR lexicon in the post-Westphalian new world order, such as crisis management, that meshed easily with the multilateral internationalism of most of the EU's activities; (*3*) the reappearance of military conflict in the European continent (Western Balkans); (4) the development of a European defence industry (Howorth 2007: 52).

Andrew Moravcsik (1998) also stresses the importance of endogenous sources such as the convergence of member states' interests and interstate bargains or the pressure from domestic groups having an interest in areas such as the production of weapons, economic sanctions and the creation of joint military forces. Without denying the primary role of power and interest in shaping interstate relations, Moravcsik's neoliberal theory of European cooperation maintains that the preferences of domestic actors and political processes in the domestic policy shape an institutional setting whose inner functioning abides by the rules of intergovernmentalism.

Gross and Juncos (2011) have studied the relationship between changes in the international security environment and EU operational approaches, focusing on the impact of EU crisis management capabilities on the EU's role and self-perception as a security actor.

2.1.2   CSDP Evolution

Works on CSDP implementation have been manifold and largely dominated the "second wave of CSDP theorising" (Kurowska and Breuer 2012: 2). As a result of the first of the operational experiences (2003–2009), studies on the evaluation of EU missions (Merlingen and Otrauskaite 2005; Emerson and Gross 2007; Grevi et al. 2009; Pirozzi and Sandawi 2009) and related institutional learning (Juncos and Pomorska 2006; Ioannides 2006; Adebahr 2009) have emerged in the literature. Academic writing has been particularly concerned with the functioning of Brussels-based institutions and the process of Brusselsisation (Duke 2005). Scholars belonging to this strand see CSDP as an institutional context within which "actors' identities and interests develop and change through interaction" (Checkel 1999: 550). Theories on socialisation and organisational learning have provided some additional insight on the process of identity construction and rearticulating of interests as significant change-inducing factors in an institutionalised and socialisation-prone setting (Juncos and Pomorska 2006; Adebahr 2009). However, the question remains open as to what extent CSDP has created dynamics of path-dependency (Kay 2005), constraining member states behaviour and letting security cooperation enter a path of unintended consequences.

CSDP's influence on states' behaviour has been looked at through the lenses of Europeanisation. Giegerich (2006) explores patterns of adaptation of national cultures to the emerging EU strategic culture. Meyer (2006) compares the evolution of public and élite opinion in selected countries to find areas of shared consensus and norm compatibility fostering the convergence of national interests. Gross (2009) analyses British, French and German policies with respect to CFSP/CSDP in two specific crises (FYROM and Afghanistan) in order to determine whether Europeanisation of national foreign security policies occurred or whether other considerations (such as the influence of the transatlantic alliance) are more pertinent to explain national preferences.

Several authors have also emphasised fierce tensions among member states as determinants of CSDP (Menon 2006; Howorth 2007, 2011). Cleavages can emerge across several dimensions (civilian *vs* military instruments; Atlanticists *vs* Europeanists; territorial defence *vs* force projection),[3] exert pressure on institutional structures and produce incremental institutional change.

The idea that the CSDP is about rescuing the waning power of European nation states is at the core of the classical realist framework proposed by Rynning (2011), which draws from Stanley Hoffman's thinking (Hoffmann 1966). Contrary to structural realists, Rynning sees the CSDP as a measure to "cope with Europe's inner weakness, not as an instrument to increase external power or balance the United States" (Rynning 2011: 25). Because the distribution of power can only be grasped "in relation to the power's purpose" (Rynning 2011: 37), a classical realist account depicts CSDP as an evolving institutionalisation of the inner weakness of European nation states. Evolution and foreign policy outcomes are largely driven by prudence, which prompts EU statesmen to minimise damage rather than pursue an ethical or ideological objective.

This brings us to consider the critical theoretical question as being not whether the CSDP evolves, but what its transformative potential towards policy change is. Such a question brings up the relationship between classical realism and constructivism. Seen through classical realist lenses, the transformative power of the CSDP—and the ability of political elites to manage change—is fundamentally limited by the fact that "nation-statehood defines and limits the purpose of the institution" (Rynning 2011: 37).

My reading of the CSDP is different and akin to that of constructivism. According to the constructivist theory, the CSDP is transformative because it builds on a process of transgovernmentalism, by which transnational networks of policy-makers can erode culturally and politically-rooted differences among states, hence acting as engines of change (Merand, et al. 2011). Transgovernmental networks hence anchor European security policies to a set of common frameworks, behaviours and ethics. Academic research has recently emphasised a collegial outlook over the social networks (Mérand et al. 2011) and the role of expertise as an "epistemic" shaper of policy change (Cross 2011). Mérand has looked at processes of socialisation within institutional settings. The CSDP is a "social field", comprised of policy-makers seeking to make sense of the world which in turn leaves them "open to new ways (rules, power structures, and symbolic representations) of structuring" the CSDP (Mérand 2008: 372). All in all, the analysis of networks and epistemic communities marks a rapprochement of sociological institutionalism to power, as it becomes clear that socialisation and ideational forces matter but could not float or operate freely (Risse-Kappen 1994).

2.2   Learning Communities and CSDP

The EU is an organisation involved in a kind of "lifelong institutional learning" (Jopp and Diedrichs 2009: 106), trying to incrementally improve its own set of procedures and instruments for better coping with external crises and problems (Ginsberg 2001: 43). This book looks at the CSDP as a social field, characterised by a multitude of learning communities. These communities produce change by mediating between structure and agency, and between exogenous and endogenous factors. Communities do not simply exchange knowledge, as networks do. They construct and diffuse cognitive content to achieve a specific policy enterprise.

New norms, ideas and shared beliefs, arising from policy failure and gradually turning into consensual knowledge, have activated CSDP learning towards non-military crisis management. This section defines the notion of learning in relation to the actors, or communities, performing it. It appraises the distinction between epistemic communities and communities of practice. While the former have been previously used by scholars to account for the role of expertise in shaping EU decisions (Cross 2011), the latter have gained ground to conceptualise the EU as a set of practices (Bicchi 2011) that constitute, and not result from, knowledge. Clarifying whether the carriers of learning are expertise or practice-based helps in determining who the agents of the learning process are.

2.2.1   What Does "An International Organisation Learns" Mean?

The notion of learning is, to use Jack Levy's famous expression, a "conceptual minefield (…) difficult to define, isolate, measure, and apply empirically" (Levy 1994: 280).[4]

A fundamental distinction is between individual (Stein 1994; Argyris and Schon 1978) and collective learning (Breslauer and Tetlock 1991; Haas 1990a; Nye 1987). Levy gives a basic definition of individual learning as "a change of beliefs (or the degree of confidence in one's beliefs) or the development of new beliefs, skills, or procedures as a result of the observation and interpretation of experience" (Levy 1994: 286). On the contrary, collective learning implies the possibility that a group of individuals (a government, an organisation, an institution) could learn in much the same way as single individuals do, thus having their distinctive (but shared) goals, beliefs and memories. Collective learning is commonly classified into two similar, but not identical categories: organisational learning and institutional learning.[5]

The literature also distinguishes between two levels of learning, determined by the degree of complexity and the effects of learning on the actors' behaviour. The distinction is between simple *adaptation*, involving simple instrumental change; and complex *learning*, involving belief changes (Zito 2009; Argyris and Schon 1978; Haas 1990a)—although the same notions have been given different labels by scholars.[6] Haas defines adaptation as the process by which "behaviour changes as actors add new activities (or drop old ones), thus altering the means of actions, but not the ends of the organisation". Instead, learning occurs when "the ultimate purpose of the organisation is redefined as means as well as ends are questioned and new ends are devised on the basis of consensual knowledge that has become available" (Haas 1990a: 3). As a result, true learning involves a reassessment of fundamental beliefs and values. It entails a reconsideration of how policy-makers approach a major problem and is fundamental in producing a situation in which the policy-makers' comprehension moves towards a more complex and integrated understanding of an issue accompanied by a new formulation of the problem-solving.

2.2.2   Learning Communities: Clearing the Conceptual Confusion

Learning communities are defined as those transnational communities within the IR literature that create the "social fabric of learning" (Adler

2008: 199): they are the social and epistemological enablers of institutional learning. The academic literature identifies the following types of learning communities: (1) communities of practice (Wenger 1998; Adler 2008); (2) epistemic communities (Haas 1992); (3) security communities (Deutsch et al. 1957; Adler, 2008); (4) critical communities (Rochon 1998).

Communities are a type of network, but differ from networks in terms of relationships among actors and the purpose of their interaction: while communities cluster around the construction and codification of a common/consensual knowledge, the rationale for the formation of networks is the exchange of knowledge or information among equal actors. Network analysis is used to depict sets of social interactions (Mérand et al. 2011: 126). The study of communities can locate the common causal models and set of political values within the ties (interactions) of the network, hence paying attention to what factors undergird the simple "representation of the social structure" (Knoke 1990: 8). Learning communities are cognitive: they rest on a common learning objective that determines the degree of members' involvement in the collective thrive of the community.[7]

From a practice perspective, all communities "can be seen as subsets of communities of practice, as long as the focus of the analysis is on the practices that undergird the communities" (Adler 2008: 199). Despite being subsumed under the practice paradigm, however, these concepts display some noteworthy differences. Critical communities, for instance, rest on ideas that are fundamentally critical. In that regard, they diverge from epistemic communities insofar as their perspectives are critical of the policy establishment rather than being oriented toward helping it to function better (Schurman and Munro 2010: 54). Security communities' inner features entail the process of peaceful change and shared identities and values within a region (Adler and Barnett 1998).

The units of analysis of this book are epistemic communities and communities of practice. In these two communities, knowledge creation occurs on a regular basis. Both communities influence political actors' decisions by developing, sharing and maintaining common causal beliefs through socialisation and persuasion. At the same time, they arise from two slightly different versions of institutional learning—one emphasising the epistemic and dominant constitution of consensual knowledge (Foucault 1970; Ruggie 1975; Haas 1990a), the other the evolution of background knowledge as a result of reiteration of shared practices (Wenger 1998; Adler 2008; Bourdieu 1990; Adler and Pouliot 2011a).

2.2.3   The Epistemic Communities Approach to Learning...

What is "expertise" and why should it matter in IR? Ruggie introduced the concept of epistemic communities in a special issue of *International Organization* (1975) co-edited with Ernst Haas (Ruggie 1975). According to Ruggie, processes of institutionalisation involve not only the grid through which behaviour is acted out, but also "the epistemes through which political relationships are visualised" (Ruggie 1975: 569). Ruggie borrowed the term epistemes from Foucault (1970), and defined epistemic communities as "a dominant way of looking at social reality, a set of shared symbols and references, mutual expectations and a mutual predictability of intention" (Ruggie 1975: 570). Haas later articulated the idea of epistemic communities as "professionals who share a commitment to a common causal model and a common set of political values" (Haas 1990a: 41). A more precise conceptualisation was finally given by Peter Haas as follows:

> An epistemic community is a network of professionals from a variety of disciplines and backgrounds. They have (1) a **shared set of normative and principled beliefs**, which provide a value-based rationale for the social action of community members; (2) **shared causal beliefs**, which are derived from their analysis of practices leading or contributing to a central set of problems in their domain and which the serve as the basis for elucidating the multiple linkages between possible policy actions and desired outcomes; (3) **shared notions of validity** – that is, inter-subjective, internally defined criteria for weighing and validating knowledge in the domain of their expertise; and (4) a **common policy enterprise** – that is, a set of common practices associated with a set of problems to which their professional competence is directed, presumably out of the conviction that human welfare will be enhanced as a consequence.[8] (Haas 1992: 3)

The emergence of epistemic communities is therefore related to the increasingly complex and technical natures, of the issues decision-makers need to address. Complexity and uncertainty push decision-makers to seek technical advice, which then contributes to the way interests are formulated and decisions are taken.

Epistemic communities have provided an important stimulus to research on transnational knowledge networks. In fact, they allowed researchers to identify the missing link between political objectives, technical knowledge and the formation of interests. This has profound consequences for the study of IR. In the current international society, characterised by globalisation and interdependence, knowledge and ideas must spread across state boundaries in order to be recognised by the wider international community. As a consequence, networks of experts cannot be conceived as belonging to single national community separated one from each other. Epistemic communities are transnational because their expertise and "vision" are carried over from the national levels into the international arena.

Rejecting simple notions of causality, in *When Knowledge is Power* (1990a) Ernst Haas maintains that international organisations (IOs) are created to solve problems that require collaborative action among states for solution; therefore, "the knowledge available about the problem at issue influences the way decision-makers define the interests at stake in the solution to the problem; (...) when knowledge become consensual, we ought to expect politicians to use it in helping them to define their interests" (Haas 1990a: 9–12).

Consensual knowledge refers to "generally accepted understandings about cause-and-effect linkages about any set of phenomena considered important by society" (Haas 1990a: 21). An important characteristic of the Haas definition is that consensual knowledge is socially constructed and is constantly tested and examined through adversary procedures. For instance, as Haas himself put it, consensual knowledge differs from ideology because it must constantly prove itself against rival formulas claiming to solve problems better (Haas 1990a: 21).

2.2.4   ...and Communities of Practice (CoPs)

The understanding of how knowledge is formed and affects learning has been revisited by the agenda on international practices, which has gained momentum in social theory (Schatzki et al. 2001) and IR theory in the mid-2000s (Adler 2005, 2008; Adler and Pouliot 2011a, b; Pouliot 2008, 2010; Bicchi 2011). This agenda comprises a vast array of analytical frameworks that see practices as the key entry point to the study of world politics. Practices are competent performances, that is, socially meaningful patterns of action, which "embody, act out, and possibly reify background knowledge in and on the material world" (Adler and Pouliot 2011b: 4). Here, knowledge is therefore understood as practical, since intersubjectivity is bound up in performance and can only be expressed as such (Adler and Pouliot 2011a: 8). In other words, social activities embedded in communities, routines and organizations, structure experience which in turn constitutes knowledge.

Against this backdrop, the notion of communities of practice defines the transnational, like-minded groups of practitioners who are informally as well as contextually bound by a shared interest in learning and applying a common practice (Adler 2008: 196).[9] As in the case of epistemic communities, CoPs develop, share and maintain new cognitive content (originating in new causal beliefs), agree on a joint enterprise and have mutual expectations and predictability of intention. Therefore, as in the case of technical expertise carried through by epicoms, CoPs generate transformation, via what literature describes as the "practice's lifecycle" (Adler and Pouliot 2011a; Finnemore and Sikkink 1998) involving the generation, diffusion, institutionalisation and fading of a specific practice. Practices can also interact with one another or overlap, through constellations (assemblages) of practices (Wenger 1998), or communities operating at different levels (Hansen 2011).

CoPs expand inter-subjective knowledge and establish it as social structures by means of institutionalisation processes.

2.2.5   Epicoms and CoPs: Competing or Compatible?

It is important to clarify the differences between epistemic communities and communities of practice. Professionalism or like-mindedness is a first key difference. Individuals belonging to a given community hold culture, values and interests, and therefore identities, which are intrinsic to their practice. CoPs are, in this sense, professional networks of people sharing the same background, whereas epicoms are networks of professionals who do share a practice, but come from a variety of backgrounds. It follows that what brings a CoP together is the set of shared expectations, routines and intentions rooted in professionalism (but not in uniformity[10]): self-consciousness develops around the activities commonly understood and continually renegotiated by its members, by a process taking the shape of "war stories" (Brown and Duguid 1998) which includes a common jargon (Cohendet et al. 2001).

Epicoms, instead, cluster around a common causal model or epistemic interpretation of reality. Identity is weaker: what holds an epistemic community together is a procedural authority to attain progress towards a cognitive goal set by the community. Individuals are creative; they gather knowledge not just as a result of the reiteration of know-how, or by interaction with other members resulting from common experiences, but also as a function of their own experience outside the community. Agency is heterogeneous. Last, but not least, epistemic communities emerge in an uncertain context calling for the creation of a new paradigm, which is not necessarily the case for communities of practice (Whiteneck 1996).

Another difference has to do with the distinction between consensual/causal knowledge (*episteme*) and background knowledge (*habitus*), which can be simplistically redirected to the sociological divide between Michel Foucault and Pierre Bourdieu. Background knowledge originates in *habitus*, defined by Bourdieu as "systems of durable, transposable dispositions that constitute people's thoughts and practices" (Bourdieu 1990: 53). From a CoP perspective, learning entails the evolution of background knowledge (Adler 2005: 20), a change of *habitus*. Consensual knowledge has a slightly different rationale. Ernst Haas then defines learning as the process by which "consensual knowledge is used to specify causal relationships in new ways so that the result affects the content of public policy" (Haas 1990a: 23). Consensual knowledge refers to "cause-and-effect linkages about any set of phenomena considered important by society, provided only that the finality of the accepted chain of causation is subject to continuous testing and examination". (Haas 1990a: 21) (Table 2.1).

2.3   THE CSDP HAS LEARNED: BY DOING?

Communities of practice expand because like-minded groups of practitioners are bound by a shared interest in learning and the application of a common practice. Does this explanation fully account for the evolution of CSDP as a civilian security provider? Are there counterexamples of policies in which a common practice (and the relevant communities) did not exist?

Generative relationships (Adler and Pouliot 2011b: 24–25), meaning those episodes of formative interactions that facilitate the emergence of a new practice, have not been sufficiently investigated by the academic literature. Nor were the dynamics of formation linked to the expansion and diffusion of practices, whereby intersubjective knowledge becomes established as social structures. Similarly, cases of "non-practice" in which practices fail to emerge and to meet the last phase of a practice's lifecycle have been overlooked by the literature, hence missing an important step in the genealogy of practice development.[11] This leads to three considerations.

First, an international policy consensus facilitates the formation of transnational communities. EU policy-makers learned the importance of civilian security thanks to the progressive diffusion of new ideas globally. This claim challenges alternative explanations for the rise of civilian

Table 2.1 Differences between knowledge-based networks, epistemic communities and communities of practice[a]

Group	Membership	Practice	Objective	Selection	Identity	Function
K-B Networks	Heterogeneous	Coordination (no common practice)	Knowledge exchange	Members have equal rights	No common identity	Access to knowledge
Epicoms	Heterogeneous	Common practice	Construction/codification of consensual knowledge	Authority and reputation: Members are self-selected	Linked to the objective, but no strong sense of belonging as agents come from different background	External Advancement of a set of knowledge, "change the world"
CoPs	Homogeneous	Common practice	Accumulation of background knowledge	Professionalism ("by peers")	Strong	Achievement of internal shared learning

[a]The categorisation draws from Cohendet et al. (2001: 309–310)

and civil-military crisis management. Dwan (2002) emphasises the convergence of interest between small, neutral and anti-federalist EU member states, willing to counterbalance the attempt to create a military CSDP. Other authors (Quille et al. 2006; Chivvis 2010) account for the CSDP "soft" identity as the result of an ongoing struggle between Atlanticists and Integrationists and the troublesome relationship between NATO and the CSDP. Gross (2008) and Tardy (2011) focus instead on the reshuffle of the security architecture after the end of the Cold War, and the EU's efforts to put into practice the comprehensive approach to meet the growing demand for civil-military planning. According to Santopinto and Price (2013), this shows the lack of strategic coherence and divergence among EU member states' interests (Kagan 2004; Menon et al. 2004). Finally, Dijkstra (2013) stresses endogenous-driven institutionalisation, and the influence of the Brussels-based bureaucracy on the creation of CSDP institutions.

Second, the EU has not only learned. It has learned by doing. Innovation has a better chance to shape policies if a community of practitioners are already in existence and actors already share a common set of experiences. Fig. 2.1 elucidates the expansion of a practice.

Cognitive evolution is not just mediated by practice (Adler 2008: 202). Cognitive evolution has more chance to succeed if it is generated into a pre-existing practice, which facilitates social learning (Checkel 1999: 549). This hypothesis switches the analytical focus from governance and network analyses (Mérand et al. 2011) to the investigation of the formative actions that explain the genealogy of ideas by mapping the communities committed to its institutionalisation. It also engages the debate on European strategic cultures (Biehl et al. 2013; Meyer 2006; Giegerich 2006) by stressing the practice-based strategic interactions and learning by experience affecting the development of the CSDP.

Third, when learning is knowledge-based, but does not emanate from a shared practice, influence on policy evolution is slower and change is more difficult to achieve. Despite favourable conditions and supportive agencies facilitating innovation and diffusion, some ideas may struggle to have a policy impact and produce change. This third claim challenges arguments that epistemic communities and networks have shaped European security and defence (Cross 2011; Howorth 2004), and hence that the simple intersection between power and ideas (Risse-Kappen 1994) can lead to change.

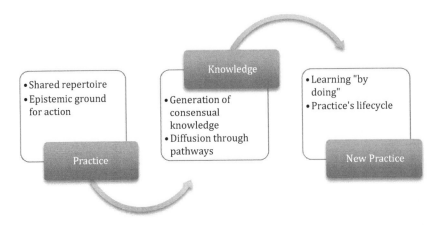

Fig. 2.1   Practice-based learning

Fig. 2.2   Policy evolution (Adler and Haas 1992)

2.4   PATHWAYS OF INFLUENCE AND IMPACT OF LEARNING

How does a norm become practice? Adler and Haas elaborated a model explaining the role of epistemic communities in a five-step process involving policy innovation, diffusion, selection, persistence and evolution[12] (Adler and Haas 1992: 375–387). Between generation and diffusion there is a tipping point, at which a critical mass of relevant state actors adopt the norm (Finnemore and Sikkink 1998) (Fig. 2.2).

The learning dynamic leading to policy evolution can take essentially two forms: (1) intentional, when the policy outcomes reflect the new ideas diffused throughout the learning process; (2) unintentional, when the policy outcomes are different from the ideas diffused throughout the learning process.

Unintentional learning does not necessarily mean that an institution has failed to learn. It can mean, however, that policy evolution through learning by doing has not led to the desired policy outcomes;

hence resulting in an incomplete learning process (this may include a "non-practice" scenario).

Based on this typology and drawing from previous works on ideas and norm diffusion by McNamara (1998), Adler and Haas (1992), Finnemore and Sikkink (1998) and Risse-Kappen (1994), Table 2.2 maps out the possible interactions related to the pathways of influence through which learning communities turn ideas into policy. The table identifies four main pathways. For each one of them, it outlines the underlying logic of action, the processes and actors involved, the impact on the learning process and ultimately, the way it affects policy outcomes.

Ideas turn into policy outcomes if the following four conditions are met:

1. the presence of a power constituency supporting the diffusion and institutionalisation of the new ideas;
2. the formation of cohesiveness and a sense of belonging among practitioners, facilitated by a common identity;
3. a shared epistemic enterprise aimed at producing policy innovation;
4. the emulation of a successful model of cooperation or policy implementation.

The cohesiveness of a community is a key parameter in measuring its persuasiveness. Cohesiveness depends on the creation of a sense of belonging and a common rationale for action through socialisation, which defines the identity of a learning community. Whether the result of organisational routines and experiences (CoPs) or the agreement on a common causal belief and joint policy enterprise (epicoms) identity formation is a main element of the set of generative interactions that allow a community to form.

Constituencies, whether domestic coalitions or government networks, advocate and support the diffusion of ideas by means of resources or political action. Constituencies can be individual member states, an institution (i.e., the European Council) or even an external organisation, provided that it is able and capable of exerting an influence on the target institution through advocacy. Constituencies are often related to policy networks. To achieve institutional learning, experts and practitioners need channels into the institutional system and institutional partners (decision-makers) to build up winning coalitions (Risse-Kappen 1994). Policy networks are therefore all important to ensure that ideas are injected into the institutional arena.

Table 2.2 Pathways of influence: how ideas turn into policy outcomes

Logics of action	Pathways	Ideational processes and actors	Intervening factors	Impact on learning	Expected policy outcomes (cf. Legro's criteria)
Interest-based	**Sponsorship**	Political and financial capital provided by key constituencies or "winning coalitions" in support of ideas	Timing, domestic structures	Relevance and dominance of new ideas as a result of the link with key political stakeholders	Durability
Identity-based	**Socialization**	Interactive process of identity formation through socialization and cross-fertilization among actors, which creates a sense of "belonging"	Institutional-bureaucratic	Cohesiveness of the learning actors and development of a logic of appropriateness forging shared learning	Concordance
Epistemic	**Innovation**	Shared understanding of the link between policy failure and policy innovation that creates the rationale for action	Institutional and cultural	Authority and cohesiveness of the learning process as learning actors agree on a joint enterprise	Concordance, specificity
Isomorphic	**Emulation**	Presence of successful models that provides ground for action via their imitation	Cultural	Transnational diffusion of ideas. Outside-in process of diffusion	Durability, specificity

Learning is also a process of acquisition of new cognitive content, or paradigm innovation. An experience of policy failure is a necessary condition for shared beliefs to be developed and diffused. Widespread perception and common interpretation among stakeholders of an unsuccessful policy experience is the key factor that paves the way for the rise of an alternative paradigm. This creates both the "cognitive authority" (Adler 2008: 203) or symbolic power (Bourdieu 1990) to offer previously unavailable understanding of a cause-effect linkage.

Policy failure concurs to define the boundaries of a learning community. The fiascos of the UN-led peacekeeping operations in the 1990s, as well as the failure of EU member states to effectively tackle conflict in the Western Balkans, pushed EU decision-makers and security experts, particularly in neutral and Nordic member states, to reconsider security policies. Similarly, the growing scepticism surrounding development aid in eradicating poverty convinced major aid donors (such as the UK, The Netherlands or the Nordic countries) to reframe the link between development, security and good governance, in order to ensure a more effective allocation of funds. In the case of security sector reform, the need for a transparent and democratically accountable security sector gained salience in the wake of the EU and NATO enlargement to Eastern Europe. Public awareness in the UK, a country whose contribution was all-important to make SSR politically salient, was raised out of policy failure in Sierra Leone.

Emulation results from the information gathered about the experiences of other international actors. It includes processes of institutional isomorphism[13] (Dolowitz and Marsh 2000: 5) as well as the exchange of best practices both at the operational and decision-making levels. Sociological institutionalism and the English school approach associate policy emulation to the expansion of Western cultural values shaping the formation of the international society.[14] The concept stems from a "common perspective or international policy culture" (Ikenberry 1990: 89), embedding rules and values that shape agency and behaviour and constituting a precondition for emulation to occur.

What allows international actors to reproduce institutions by imitation is then a common social structure, making participation in a growing multilateral network culturally "necessary and appropriate" (Finnemore 1996; March and Olsen 1989). Social structures construct what actors want— think about member states participation in the EU or the EU relations with NATO and the UN—but the relation between structure and agency

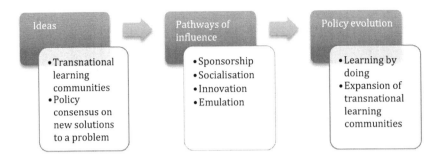

Fig. 2.3   The core argument of the book

is mutually constitutive. Therefore, inter-subjective learning dynamics and socialisation occurring at the micro-level between agents, also affect social structures.

This co-constitutive relationship between structure and agency creates the room for learning communities to influence policy by an emulation path. A successful model can provide learning communities with ground for action via imitation. An example to be replicated facilitates the impact of new ideas into policy (Fig. 2.3).

2.4.1   Learning Environment

Learning interactions are linked to the environment in which they operate. This includes domestic, institutional and cultural factors as well as time.

Cultures shape organisations' (or units therein) self-perception, hence their behaviours and calculations. When different cultures coexist in the same institutional space, it is likely that each of them will try to defend its autonomy, protect its environment and possibly dominate the other, especially in those situations where cooperation and close coordination is required. As a result, if the institution is not able to manage conflict between different cultures, competition across overlapping communities may occur, leading to confrontation, miscommunication and competing compartmentalised processes. This outcome is the opposite process of learning: instead of producing shared solutions to complex problems, it encourages separate habit-driven behaviours.

Institutional factors also affect learning. Homogeneous or multi-level structures of governance can facilitate or hamper information sharing and

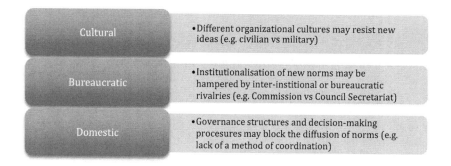

Fig. 2.4 Intervening factors

the institutionalisation of new knowledge into the decision-making. They also affect the persistence—duration of lessons learned.

Domestic conditions refer to the degree of openness of a political culture to the diffusion of ideas and, as a result, to their institutionalisation. Some political élites are more prone than others to seek the advice of formal or informal epistemic communities, or to facilitate the expansion of a practice (Fig. 2.4).

Finally timing matters, defined as a point in time when a problem gets political salience and as a result becomes problematised. According to Rose and Miller (1992), problems involving public policy choice can first arise through a process of problematisation which can begin when existing practices are criticised as not "ideal". These practices may, as a result, be made to appear deficient in some way or ways, leading to the identification of a problem for which an appropriate solution is required. Timing, as problematisation, is an important intervening factor creating the awareness of policy failure that helps new ideas move towards the tipping point.

2.5 METHODOLOGY

CSDP institutional change, the independent variable of this study, is measured in terms of policy outcomes, involving goals, means or instruments-related change. Goals refer to the ultimate purpose of the institution, its ends, values or strategic prescriptions underlying the institution's means of action. Means refer to the organisational structures, programmes and policies that are set out to achieve the institution's goals. Finally, instruments are material and non-material resources (capabilities) available to achieve the institution's goals through its means.

As for the independent variable, this analysis adopts a constructivist approach. It focuses on the role of ideas and knowledge in politics, stressing the role of collectively held or intersubjective understandings of social life. Ideational factors are shared, and construct the interests and identities of actors. Understanding how those social facts construct reality is the primary objective of this work. Accordingly, the framework is not elaborated along causal "Big-T" claims (Price and Reus-Smit 1998), but in such a way as to emphasise constitutive explanations with some limited causal properties (Finnemore and Sikkink 2001). Learning communities, in this regards, are neither a proper independent variable, nor simple transmissions belts: they are part of the constitution process.

The methodology used is hence designed to capture the intersubjectivity at the core of this approach. To assess the relationship between ideas and policy outcomes, it is useful to refer to Legro's definition of the "robustness" of a norm. Legro defines norms as "collective understandings of the proper behaviour of actors" (Legro 1997: 33). Their robustness, defined as the influence on actors regardless of their identities, interests and individual behaviour, is determined by three criteria: specificity, durability and concordance. Specificity refers to how well the guidelines embedded in the norm are understood by actors. Durability is about how long the rules have been legitimately in effect and what factors questioned such legitimacy. Finally, concordance concerns the acceptance of the rules across formal and informal settings; that is the degree of inter-subjective agreement among actors (Legro 1997: 34–35).[15]

The selection of case studies reflects the concern of accounting for variation in the way ideas influence policies. Civilian Crisis Management (CCM) and Security Sector Reform (SSR) are part of the CSDP toolbox for crisis management. They can be defined as two concepts or new forms of activity in international security[16] that have been incorporated into the European Union's functions in the late 1990s and early-2000s, that became fully integrated in the CSDP through policy frameworks and started being implemented as part of the EU's operational efforts to prevent conflicts and maintain peace and stability. As such, they lie at the same level of analysis. EU documents present them as CSDP tools in support of international peace and security.[17] Although some degree of overlap between SSR and CCM missions occurs in the field, the borders between the two concepts are clear in terms of the activities covered, instruments,[18] training and personnel.[19]

Both cases have concurred to the definition of the framework for the EU comprehensive approach, which the European Commission defines as the "strategically coherent use of the EU tools and instruments for external action".[20] Both can be also understood as emerging practices in EU security. However, despite having a similar genesis, CCM and SSR resulted in very different evolutionary patterns. Civilian crisis management has undergone a learning curve, with lessons learned growing exponentially with experience and leading to evolution and the impact of the concept on the activities and institutional design of the CSDP. SSR implementation has been poor and learning by doing almost absent.

To account for such variation, the two cases are compared following Mill's method of difference, according to which everything between the two cases is constant except for the explanation (dependent variable) and the outcome (policy and institutional evolution). A combination of semi-structured experts and élites interviews, process tracing and document analysis was used to identify and find evidence of consensual knowledge formation, diffusion and impact on security policies. Interviews were structured in a survey inspired by social network analysis (SNA). The resulting map of learning communities frames and describes the distinct structure of epicoms and CoPs in each of the two case studies: their composition, individual and institutional members, selection and socialisation processes and evolution over time.

The survey was designed to spot social relations among policy actors and experts. It allowed the identification of the type, membership and boundaries of the learning communities in the two case study areas. In particular, it has been used to detect the presence of a common practice binding the actors involved in those communities during the formative interaction and diffusion processes.

Network analysis offers "a method for measuring the sources of socialisation and diffusion of norms based on the strength of ties between states, collective state identities such as security communities, and the importance of individual states" (Hafner-Burton 2009: 569). Material and social relationships create structures among actors through dynamic processes, which define, enable or constrain agency, therefore affecting collective action (i.e. international cooperation and governance). Network analysis concerns relations (ties) between nodes (or agents). Methodologically, networks are defined as any set or sets of ties between any set or sets of nodes, grounded in three principles:

(a) nodes and their behaviours are mutually dependent, not autonomous;
(b) ties between nodes can be channels for transmission of both material and non-material products (i.e., information, beliefs and norms);
(c) persistent patterns of association among nodes create structures that can define, enable or restrict the behaviour of nodes. (Hafner-Burton et al. 2009: 560–561)

The population of CSDP networks was defined by using Kriesi and Jegen's (2001) criteria for delineating the boundaries of the network:

1. *positional criterion*: scanning and identification of all actors interested in security policy in a given area of analysis (i.e. Europe);
2. *participative criterion*: in-depth study of conferences, seminars and summits in order to extract actors who took a stand on the issue at stake, independently or on behalf of their organisation;
3. *reputational criterion*: submission of the list drafted on the basis of the previous two criteria to a small group of experts who would add the names of other experts that were mission or would subtract those who they would consider as playing a marginal role in the debate.

These three criteria represented a fairly good starting point to draw a list of the actors involved in one learning community, as they show that members are:

1. actively involved in the network-building phase, either by attending meetings and conferences or by publishing papers or getting involved in projects related to the issue;
2. recognised as members of the community by other individuals or organisations; or that they hold as many shared contacts as possible and as less grades of separation as possible with other members, hence corroborating their affiliation with the community.

More than 25 semi-structured élites and expert interviews were arranged for each of the two case studies, for a total of 50+ interviews. From each interviewee's transcripts, the main relationships the individuals had with colleagues and acquaintances were extracted to draw the overall network of communications and interactions. Drawing from Créplet et al. (2003: 49), two types of relationships could be distinguished (cf. Table 2.3): groups whose members develop close working relationship,

Table 2.3 Attributes of CoPs and epicoms

	Community of practice	*Epistemic community*
Relationship with other agents	*Close working experience, similar or complementary practice*	*Advancement of specific knowledge or new thinking*
Expectation—case study	*CCM*	*SSR*

with similar or complementary practices (a CoP); and groups whose aim is the advancement of specific knowledge, for instance by promoting a new thinking (an epistemic community).

Finally, to ensure rigorous data collection and analysis, different sources of observation were triangulated. The mapping methodology was complemented by process tracing and content analysis, to assess the impact of the communities in shaping decisions at key points in time and finding a correspondence of their ideas in the new policy frameworks created.

Process tracing was used to identify the critical junctures and reconstruct the events leading to policy evolution in the selected case studies. Qualitative document analysis was used to assess whether the ideas and knowledge diffused by the communities reflect in the content of EU official documents; what conceptualisation emerged as a result of the process of learning; or whether emulation patterns were detected by the comparison with official documents of other international actors.

2.6 Notes

1. In the words of the EU Institute for Security Studies' former Director Alvaro de Vasconcelos, who quoted the Spanish poet Antonio Machado, "walking is how you learn to walk" (Grevi et al., 2009: 12).
2. As Fraser Cameron put it, "the lessons of the Yugoslav conflict were never far from the minds of the negotiators at the 1996 IGC preparing improvements in the CFSP" (Cameron, 1999: 32).
3. See also Giegerich (2006).
4. Each one of the major paradigms in IR Theory has coped with the problem posed by learning lessons to achieve change. While for neorealist scholars learning takes a "deceptively simple meaning" (Breslauer and Tetlock, 1991: 24) as mechanical adaptation to structural pressures (Waltz, 1979), neoliberals maintain that regimes may foster organisational learning by creating or reinforcing institutional memory (Nye, 1987). Social constructivism found a particular interest

in collective, shared learning and socialisation (Checkel, 2001; Finnemore, 1996).

5. Organisational learning is commonly used in sociology, whereas political scientists give preference to the term "institutional learning" so as to encompass the broader definition of "institutions" covering organisations, rules, norms and regimes. That being said, the two terms have been often used interchangeably.

6. *Adaptation* is also known as single-loop (Argyris and Schon, 1978) structural adjustment (Levy, 1994) or simple learning. *Learning* is also labelled double-loop learning (Argyris and Schon, 1978) or complex learning.

7. The value of communities on networks is that a community is not just a set of relationships; it is "about something" (Wenger et al., 2002: 43).

8. Bold added for emphasis.

9. Cf. Also Wenger (1998).

10. Cf. Adler and Bernstein (2005: 296). As Adler noted, "boundaries of CoPs are determined by people's knowledge and identity and by the discourse associated with a specific practice" and hence are not necessarily "congruent with the reified structures or institutional affiliations, divisions and boundaries. (...) boundaries form in and around practice" (Adler, 2008: 200).

11. On the genealogy of practice development, and its more general role in explaining strategic interaction from a practice perspective, cf. Adler and Pouliot (2011a: 24).

12. According to the model, communities act first as policy innovators, by identifying the nature of the issue-area and framing the context in which new ideas are interpreted. Second, communities diffuse their policy recommendations transnationally, through communication and socialisation processes. New knowledge is shared and exchanged across research groups, national governments and international organisations through different channels (conferences, meetings, research networks), so that innovation becomes consensual. Policy selection mechanisms intervene to select certain advices and discard others. Policy persistence refers to the continuation of consensual and background knowledge about an issue within the members of an epistemic community, to determine how long it will remain influential. Finally, learning communities stimulate policy evolution as learning. Cf. Adler and Haas (1992: 375–387).

13. Dolowitz and Marsh define policy transfer, emulation and lesson drawing as the processes by which "knowledge about policies, administrative arrangements, institutions and ideas in one political system (past or present) is used in the development of policies, administrative arrangements, institutions and ideas in another political system" (Dolowitz and Marsh, 1996: 344).

14. On the English School approach, see Bull (1977); Bull and Watson (1984); Gong (1984); Buzan, (1993).

15. See also Keohane (1989) and Young (1989).

16. Cf. Finnish Government (2008: 5) and Meharg et al. (2010: 1, 14).

17. Cf. ENTRi (2013: 81) and European Union (2008: 2).

18. The activities (and instruments) covered by CCM correspond to the four priority areas of civilian action defined by the Feira European Council in June 2000: police, rule of law, civilian administration and civil protection. The activities (and instruments) covered by SSR are defined in line with the 2004 OECD guidelines for the implementation SSR. For a detailed list, see Chapter 5. For a discussion on the fuzziness of the SSR concept, and the confusion among EU policy-makers, see Chapter 6.

19. For instance, as Bloching notes, Civilian Response Teams (CRT) for CCM and the SSR Pool of experts belong to separate domains and do not relate to the same expertise or mode of deployment, although they operate within the framework of EU crisis management (Bloching, 2011: 23).

20. Cf. European Commission and HR/VP (2013: 1).

CHAPTER 3

A Comprehensive Approach to EU Security

The EU defines the comprehensive approach (CA) as the "strategically coherent use of EU tools and instruments" (European Commission 2013: 1) for external action in crisis or conflict situations.[1] The need for comprehensive responses to crises, in order to consolidate sustainable development, peace and security in fragile situations has dominated EU policy debates over the last decade, out of the realisation that security and development challenges are inter-twined. The EU's external action involves a multitude of civilian and military actors, 28 member states and bureaucratic entities. Those actors have sometimes conflicting objectives and political priorities, distinct mandates and ways of operating, financial instruments and timeframes of intervention (Faria 2014: 2). Providing coherent, coordinated and context-driven responses to fragile and crises situations has been a daunting task for EU policy-making and constitutes the rationale for establishing clearer guidelines under the CA framework. Since its adoption as the guiding principle of EU foreign policy through the European Commission and High Representative's joint communication of December 2013 (European Commission and HR/VP 2013), the EU Comprehensive Approach has moved closer to the Integrated Approach of the United Nations, covering not just internal EU coordination but also implementing external cross-sector activities linking security, stabilisation, reconstruction, governance and development. Thanks to the CA framework, the EU has started implementing economic, political and military

© The Author(s) 2017
G. Faleg, *The EU's Common Security and Defence Policy*,
DOI 10.1007/978-3-319-41306-8_3

instruments in a coordinated and inter-operable way, namely in the Horn of Africa and the Sahel region and, most recently in the Mediterranean, in response to the 2015 migrant crisis. In the Horn of Africa, the EU has intervened alongside the UN, the African Union and NATO, with complementary civilian (EUCAP Nestor) and military (EUNAVFOR Atalanta) missions. The EU Horn of Africa Strategic Framework, adopted in 2011, and the Horn of Africa Action Plan 2015–2020, adopted in October 2015, assert the importance of the CA for political dialogue and CSDP engagement in the region (Council of the European Union 2011, 2015). The EU's interventions in the Sahel are based on the coordination of security and development instruments outlined in the EEAS Strategy for Security and Development in the Sahel (EEAS 2012), which paves the way for integrated CSDP civilian and capacity building missions in Niger (EUCAP, launched in 2012) and Mali (EUTM, launched in 2013, and EUCAP, launched in 2015).

Security sector reform and civilian crisis management are part of the EU's CA at the conceptual, institutional and operational level. Conceptually, coordinated cooperation and coherent measures resulting from the comprehensive approach are essential preconditions for an effective implementation of SSR and CCM policies. Institutionally, CA offers the organisational basis for cooperation, encouraging the creation of structures and the division of labour/distribution of resources for SSR and CCM. Finally, at the planning and operational level, the coordination between actors enables the definition of the common objectives, of the instruments to be used as well as the criteria for appropriate and timely action (SWP/ZIF 2012: 25). Therefore, CA provides the basis for SSR and CCM tools to be effectively operated within the CSDP.

This chapter illustrates the conceptual origins of the EU's comprehensive approach and the new global security agenda since the end of the Cold War. The EU has in fact developed its crisis management structures and capabilities at a time of profound change and re-conceptualisation of the definition of security. The changing nature of security threats compelled international actors to adapt their responses, therefore altering the character of crisis management. Chapter 4 will outline the impact of this new multi-dimensional understanding of security provision on the actors, structures and networks involved in European security cooperation.

The chapter is also a starting point to explain the civilianisation of CSDP (Drent 2011). It addresses the normative transformations that underpin the rise of "comprehensiveness", which, combined with experiences of policy failure (e.g. the Balkan crises in the 1990s), drove the evolution of the CSDP. Comprehensiveness refers to the need for multi-faceted, rapid response capabilities, and a complementary long-term strategy, to address all possible aspects of a particular crisis in a coherent manner (Barry 2012: 2). It embraces a holistic approach in resolving crisis situations and moves away from purely military responses that dominated the security discourse during the Cold War.

There is no single or common definition of comprehensive approach in the international community. States and international organisations understand and implement comprehensiveness in slightly different ways, in most cases using different models, strategies and terminology (Wendling 2010: 10). The European Union translated the idea of comprehensiveness into a framework for coordination among the different EU actors. Accordingly CA acquires a very specific meaning in EU jargon, although the same term may be present in member states' national doctrines or other international organisations' policies.[2]

Building on the available literature and on interviews with security experts and practitioners, this chapter identifies human security and peacebuilding as the intellectual and paradigmatic ground underpinning the notion of comprehensiveness. The following sections will explore the conceptualisation of these two paradigms, in order to explain how the EU has responded to the need for a more integrated understanding of crisis management by developing its own concept of CA.

Contemporary crisis management has essentially changed in three dimensions: (1) an expansion of the spectrum of tasks beyond traditional military peacekeeping; (2) a dilation of the timeline of intervention (from short to long-term conflict prevention interventions); (3) as a result of the previous two, the rise and diversification of the actors involved (Major and Molling 2009: 21). These changes created the international awareness for new appropriate responses on three levels: a broader level where new global norms are generated, leading to the peacebuilding international agenda; a theoretical one, prompting the human security approach; and the narrower, implementation level of the CA.

3.1   CONCEPTS AND PRACTICES OF PEACEBUILDING IN INTERNATIONAL POLITICS

The term "peacebuilding" (PB) officially entered the international politics lexicon in 1992, with the report *An Agenda for Peace* released by UN Secretary-General Boutros Boutros-Ghali (United Nations 1992). However, it is widely recognised that the conceptual origins of the term date back to the mid-1970s, thanks to the work by Johan Galtung *Three Approaches to Peace: Peacekeeping, Peacemaking, and Peacebuilding* (Galtung 1976). Galtung posited that "structures must be found that remove causes of wars and offer alternatives to war in situations where wars may occur" (Galtung 1976: 298). His observations provided the intellectual cradle for the subsequent evolution of the peacebuilding concept during the 1980s/1990s and its integration into the peace studies academic debate. Along with a social and holistic vision of the resolution of conflict, a consensus progressively developed within the academic and intellectual community on peacebuilding as a tool for conflict transformation (Lederach 1997): a comprehensive concept encompassing "the full array of processes, approaches, and stages needed to transform conflict toward more sustainable, peaceful relationships" (Lederach 1997: 20).

As it is often the case, major structural transformations—the end of the Cold War—and subsequent changes in the morphology of conflicts created a window of opportunity for new principles to be officially adopted by international actors. The window of opportunity was further opened by a sharp increase in unsolved, protracted and complex conflicts across the globe—Sudan, Somalia, Rwanda, Mozambique, Afghanistan—and relevant dramatic episodes such as the Rwandan genocide—that highlighted the fiasco of international responses and the need for more appropriate instruments for intervention. Both in global (e.g. the UN's failure to deal with fragility in Sub-Saharan Africa) and regional policy arenas (e.g. Western European states facing instability in their immediate neighbourhood); all conditions were met for peacebuilding principles to become mainstream, and for conflict prevention and development assistance tools to be integrated. Institutional change occurred through the creation of new policy and planning methodologies (Gaigals and Leonhardt 2001: 8). In many cases, these processes overcame bureaucratic resistance to maintain conventional aid and post-conflict assistance (Menkhaus 2004). The new approaches also coped with the general reluctance of international agencies to intensify mutual dialogue and to deepen coordination as required by the integrated approach.

UN Secretary General Boutros Boutros-Ghali outlined the principles of post-conflict peacebuilding as regrouping "comprehensive efforts to identify and support structures which will tend to consolidate peace and advance a sense of confidence and well-being among people", and based on the belief that "only sustained, cooperative work to deal with underlying economic, social, cultural and humanitarian problems can place an achieved peace on a durable foundation" (United Nations 1992: VI). Initially linked to preventive diplomacy, peacemaking and peacekeeping, the UN's work on peacebuilding continued steadily throughout the 1990s, nailing down the conceptual links between previously disconnected fields of interventions (security, development, governance). Table 3.1 lists the different initiatives and publications contributing to a deepened

Table 3.1   Institutionalisation of peacebuilding (UN)

UN Document	Year	Contribution to PB
An agenda for peace	1992	*PB officially enters the UN language. Definition of PB*
An agenda for development; UNDP report on human security; An agenda for democratization	1994 1994 1996	*Conceptual work on the links between security, development, democratization and human rights feeding the debate on PB*
Supplement to an agenda for peace	1995	*Expansion of the PB concept to address all conflict phases. PB aim: institutionalization of peace*
An inventory of post-conflict peace-building activities	1996	*Identification of PB activities to be undertaken by UN agencies*
Brahimi report	2000	*Re-definition of PB: "activities undertaken on the far side of conflict to reassemble the foundations of peace and provide the tools for building on those foundations something that is more than just the absence of war"*
Review of technical cooperation in the United Nations	2003	*Call for an action plan to identify ways in which different actors within the UN system may devise joint, country specific PB strategies*
A more secure world	2004	*Recommendation for the establishment of a PB Commission and Support Office*
In larger freedom	2005	*Further elaboration of PB Commission plan*
Establishment of the Peacebuilding Commission, the Peacebuilding Fund and the Peacebuilding Support Office (UNSC and UNGA)	2005	*Creation of permanent institutional structures to address PB needs*

shared understanding and implementation of peacebuilding within the UN system.

In the UN context, the new PB structures became operational by mid-2006. They succeeded in breaking new ground in the organisation's security agenda, although in stark contrast with poor operational achievements in theatres such as East Timor, Democratic Republic of Congo and Kosovo. Criticism over PB practices was also expressed by some analysts and scholars (Betts 1996; Rieff 2002; Le Sage 1998), who highlight the gap between the neoliberal international consensus[3] on PB and the inadequacy of interventionary commitment (Richmond 2004).

Despite such growing criticism of the effectiveness of UN peace operations, the institutionalisation of peacebuilding within the UN system contributed to raise international awareness concerning the need for multi-dimensional and comprehensive missions to consolidate peace and prevent the recurrence of conflicts. States, international organisations and non-state actors (NGOs and civil society organisations in particular) jumped on the bandwagon (Barnett et al. 2007). It is not just a consequence of the UN's legitimising power in the international arena, nor a mechanical cascade effect originating in structural changes affecting conflicts. According to Menkhaus (2004), think-tanks and advocacy groups on conflict prevention and peacebuilding appeared in the mid-1990s, producing fieldwork-based research and lobbying to persuade donors and multilateral agencies that narrow sectoral strategies were ineffective in complex post-conflict environments (Menkhaus 2004: 3). This advocacy strategy eventually paid off in mainstreaming PB. Certainly, the UN cover was essential to give credibility and legitimacy to those voices, and so was the adherence to a specific epistemic—Western, liberal—vision of PB (Paris 2002). Tschirgi describes a "gradual elaboration of an expanded normative framework" (Tschirgi 2003: 3) for international affairs under the UN umbrella, with a series of international conferences in the early part of the 1990s seeking to generate an agenda with the concept of peacebuilding at its core.

Swift normative diffusion through bandwagoning produced a general overhaul of structures and policies to respond to the security challenges under the new paradigm. Institutional revisions affected individual governments and IOs alike, through the establishment of conflict prevention and/or peacebuilding units (e.g. CHAD in DFID, the Post-Conflict Unit at the World Bank) or networks (the OECD's CPDC, now INCAF). Many governments aligned their programs in the foreign, security and development policy fields (Tschirgi 2003). However, these efforts did not produce substantial results in terms of overall coherence of peacebuilding objectives. A major side effect was the proliferation of definitions and approaches to PB, many of which went far beyond the principles established at the UN level in an uncoordinated manner.

Terminological confusion and inconsistency between different PB objectives undermined multilateral cooperation, implementation and impact assessment, with obvious implications on learning infrastructures.[4] Actors "comply with notions of peacebuilding that are consistent with their own mandates, worldviews, and organisational interests" (Barnett et al. 2007: 53); consequently, the idea of building peace was operationalised with considerable differences.

Table 3.2 provides an overview of the different international actors involved in PB, and the different concepts and practices developed within each one of them.

Against this backdrop, the EU has been a distinctive actor in peacebuilding, which was conceived at its origin as a peace project. Many concepts related to peacebuilding (sustainable peace, conflict prevention, post-conflict reconstruction, effective multilateralism, democracy promotion and human rights) are part of the EU's DNA. Politically, the EU is also the world's biggest donor and a key provider of security in its neighbourhood. Finally, the EU can be seen as the incubator of evolving, peacebuilding practices, built on a *habitus* that has pioneered new forms of internal post-sovereign politics (Björkdahl et al. 2009) together with an integrationist, humanitarian and multilateral outward focus.

Because of these features, the EU has been described as a PB actor distinct from the others. This peculiarity is also due to the way the Union has internalised PB. On the one hand, the EU consensus on PB emanates from the international consensus on liberal PB and follows closely on the UN PB agenda, adding the focus on regional frameworks of integration and association (Björkdahl et al. 2009: 8); on the other hand, however, EU institutions and member states have developed different strategies and methodologies, thus generating additional confusion.

The institutional reform launched by the Lisbon Treaty failed to introduce a coherent model. Despite the creation of a specifically dedicated division on "Conflict prevention, peacebuilding and mediation instruments" within the EEAS, fragmentation persists,[5] exacerbated by a conflict of responsibilities among institutions. PB areas are manifold[6] and the distinction between Commission's long-term or CFSP's short-term interventions tends to be fuzzy.

Table 3.2   Definitions of peacebuilding

Agency	Concept	Definition
UN DPA	Post-conflict peacebuilding	*All external efforts to assist countries and regions in their transitions from war to peace, including all activities and programs designed to support and strengthen these transitions*
UNDP	Conflict prevention and peacebuilding	*Activities undertaken on the far side of conflict to reassemble the foundations of peace and provide the tools for building on those foundations*
World Bank	Post-conflict reconstruction	*Activities that support the transition from conflict to peace in an affected country through the rebuilding of the socioeconomic framework of the society*
European Commission	Conflict prevention and crisis management	*Activities aiming not only at easing a situation where an outbreak of violence is imminent (conflict prevention in a narrow sense) but also at preventing the occurrence of such a situation (conflict prevention in a wider sense)*
US Department of state	Post-conflict reconstruction and stabilization	*Activities to help post- conflict states lay a foundation for lasting peace, good governance and sustainable development*
UK Foreign and Commonwealth Office	Post-conflict reconstruction	*An umbrella term covering a range of activities required in the immediate aftermath of a conflict*
UK Ministry of Defence	Peacebuilding	*Activities relating to the underlying causes of conflict and the longer-term needs of the people require a commitment to a long-term process*
UK Department for International Development	Conflict reduction and post-conflict peacebuilding	*Conflict reduction includes conflict management (activities to prevent the spread of existing conflict); conflict prevention (short term activities to prevent the outbreak or recurrence of violent conflict); conflict resolution (short term activities to end violent conflict); and peacebuilding (medium and long term actions to address the factors underlying violent conflicts). Essential post-conflict peacebuilding measures include disarmament, demobilisation and reintegration programs, and building the public institutions that provide security, transitional justice and reconciliation and basic social services*

Table 3.2   (continued)

Agency	Concept	Definition
German Federal Foreign Office	Civilian crisis prevention	*The concept of civilian crisis prevention encompasses conflict resolution and post-conflict peacebuilding and is understood through a number of strategic leverage points, such as the establishment of stable state structures (rule of law, democracy, human rights and security) and the creation of the potential for peace within civil society, the media, cultural affairs and education*
German Federal Ministry for Economic Cooperation and Development	Peacebuilding	*Peacebuilding attempts to encourage the development of the structural conditions, attitudes, and modes for political behaviour that may permit peaceful, stable and ultimately prosperous social and economic development. As conceptualised in the joint Utstein study, peacebuilding activities fall under four main headings: security, socio-economic foundations, political framework for long term peace, and reconciliation*
French Ministry of Defence	Peace consolidation	*Activities in support of peace consolidation include monitoring compliance with arms embargoes, deployment of peacekeeping troops, DDR and deployment of police and gendarmerie in support of the rule of law*
French Ministry of Foreign Affairs	Crisis management	*Policy primarily pursued through multilateral organizations: peacekeeping, political and constitutional processes, democratization, administrative state capacity, technical assistance for public finance and tax policy, and support for independent media*
Canadian International Development Agency	Peacebuilding	*Efforts to strengthen the prospects for internal peace and decrease the likelihood of violent conflict in order to enhance the indigenous capacity of a society to manage conflict without violence*
Department of National Defence and Canadian Forces	Peacebuilding	*Actions to support political, economic, social and military measures aimed at strengthening political stability, which include mechanisms to identify and support structures that promote peaceful conditions, reconciliation, a sense of confidence and well-being, and support for economic growth*

3.2   HUMAN SECURITY: THEORY, NARRATIVE
AND *PRAXIS*

Peacebuilding and human security (HS) are two interrelated concepts. Both have dominated the post-Cold War conflict transformation, and challenge the traditional security paradigm based on state power and military force, which no longer seemed well-equipped to meet challenges facing weak and fragile states: intra-state conflicts outnumbering interstate ones, underdevelopment as a source of increased violent upheavals, or the relationship between conflicts and social development.

The fundamental difference between the two concepts is epistemological. PB is an international, multidimensional agenda redefining actors' engagement in promoting sustainable peace and providing the practical guidelines for the achievement of such a goal. HS is a new paradigm that ensues from a profound change in the basic models of thinking that explain a social reality: it changed the way academics and professionals view and talk about security.

A debate opened up in the early-mid 1990s on the subjective nature of security, leading to the fundamental question: "whose view of security should count?" (United Nations 2009: 6). Proponents of HS demanded a deepening and widening of the notion of security, traditionally understood as defence of a sovereign state or territory from a military threat. Human security refers to the welfare of individuals and communities, expressed in its security and development dimensions as "freedom from fear" and "freedom from want" respectively (Kaldor et al. 2007: 273). Officially launched through the UNDP report in 1994, HS was endorsed by a group of states and NGOs led by the governments of Canada and Norway, which took the organisational shape of the Human Security Network[7] (Paris 2002: 87). HS principles had already entered the security discourse during the 1970s–1980s, although at that time they were not part of a compact theoretical framework, and not labelled as "human security": for instance, the pioneering 1982 Report of the Palm Commission uses the term "Common Security".[8]

Progressively, from the late-1990s onward, the paradigm made its way through academia (Richmond 2001; Stoett 1999; Suhrke 1999), while actors begun to adopt more or less similar conceptual templates to institutionalise the concept.[9] Degree and research programmes on human security proliferated in the early-2000s and a new body of literature emerged to engage, expand or even attack the paradigm (Fukuda-Parr and Messineo

2012). Since the HS suffered from lack of consensus, disagreement over common parameters, purposes and contexts, international debates on broad/narrow formulation and institutionalisation across different organisations, blossomed (Tadjbakhsh and Chenoy 2007). As in the case of PB, actors and authors offered competing definitions, according to different visions of HS (Liotta and Owen 2006; MacFarlane and Khong 2006; King and Murray 2001).

The 1994 UNDP's Human Development Report is generally considered as the standard and most diffused reference for HS, although detractors point out that such a definition fails to introduce criteria facilitating implementation. The key dimensions identified by the UNDP report are economic, food, health, environmental, personal, community and political security (UNDP 1994: 24–25). Table 3.3 displays the main definitions of human security.

As the dimensions of human security encompass a complex net of tasks and categories, their practical use for policy-makers and analytical feasibility for scholars has been questioned (Paris 2002).

An interesting illustration of this problem has to do with the linkage between the theoretical precepts of HS and the operationalisation of peacebuilding missions in fragile contexts. Conducting peacebuilding following a human security approach implies the selection of four basic parameters: focus on root causes of conflict, attention to differences in local conditions when launching new operations, target of sustainable and durable results and mobilisation of local actors and resources in support of peace. This narrows down the applicability of HS to a necessary arbitrary understanding of its prescriptions. Since HS means practically anything, then it effectively means nothing (Paris 2002: 93) unless actors single out a specific operational orientation to avoid problems of conceptual stretching. To what extent has this confusion affected the EU's approach to human security?

Studying the importance of HS as a new strategic narrative for the EU, Kaldor et al. distinguish between *lexis*—what is written about HS—and *praxis*—HS-based actions, policies and tactics on the ground (Kaldor et al. 2007: 273). They argue that HS is in essence European. It is deep rooted in the EU security discourse. What the CSDP does in three areas—crisis management, civil-military co-ordination and conflict prevention—already is a HS approach, only it is not called that way (Kaldor et al. 2007: 274). The main contribution of HS to European security is to bring greater coherence to the formulation of EU policies by offering a set of principles applying to the ends and means of CSDP, namely (1) the respect for human

Table 3.3   Definitions of human security

International Actors (Organisations/ States/Individuals)	Definition/Components of HS[a]
UNDP	*Human security can be said to have two main aspects. It means, first, safety from such chronic threats as hunger, disease and repression. And second, it means protection from sudden and hurtful disruptions in the patterns of daily life—whether in homes, in jobs or in communities. Such threats can exist at all levels of national income and development* (UNDP 1994: 23)
Human Security Network	*A humane world where people can live in security and dignity, free from poverty and despair, is still a dream for many and should be enjoyed by all. In such a world, every individual would be guaranteed freedom from fear and freedom from want, with an equal opportunity to fully develop their human potential. Building human security is essential to achieving this goal. In essence, human security means freedom from pervasive threats to people's rights, their safety or even their lives* (Human Security Network's official website)
Japan	*Japan emphasises "Human Security" from the perspective of strengthening efforts to cope with threats to human lives, livelihoods and dignity as poverty, environmental degradation, illicit drugs, transnational organized crime, infectious diseases such as HIV/AIDS, the outflow of refugees and anti-personnel land mines and has taken various initiatives in this context. To ensure "Human freedom and potential," a range of issues needs to be addressed from the perspective of "Human Security" focused on the individual, requiring cooperation among the various actors in the international community, including governments, international organizations and civil society* (Government of Japan, Ministry of Foreign Affairs. Diplomatic Bluebook 1999, Chapter 2, Section 3)

Table 3.3 (continued)

International Actors (Organisations/States/Individuals)	Definition/Components of HS[a]
Canada	For Canada, human security means "freedom from pervasive threats to people's rights, safety or lives." Canada has identified five foreign policy priorities for advancing human security: 1. Protection of civilians, concerned with building international will and strengthening norms and capacity to reduce the human costs of armed conflict 2. Peace support operations, concerned with building UN capacities and addressing the demanding and increasingly complex requirements for deployment of skilled personnel, including Canadians, to these missions 3. Conflict prevention, with strengthening the capacity of the international community to prevent or resolve conflict, and building local indigenous capacity to manage conflict without violence 4. Governance and accountability, concerned with fostering improved accountability of public and private sector institutions in terms of established norms of democracy and human rights 5. Public safety, concerned with building international expertise, capacities and instruments to counter the growing threats posed by the rise of transnational organized crime (Foreign Ministry's official website)
Kofi Annan	In the wake of these conflicts, a new understanding of the concept of security is evolving. Once synonymous with the defence of territory from external attack, the requirements of security today have come to embrace the protection of communities and individuals from internal violence. The need for a more human-centred approach to security is reinforced by the continuing dangers that weapons of mass destruction, most notably nuclear weapons, pose to humanity: their very name reveals their scope and their intended objective, if they were ever used (United Nations Secretary-General Kofi Annan. Millenium Report, Chapter 3, pp. 43–44)

(continued)

Table 3.3 (continued)

International Actors (Organisations/States/Individuals)	Definition/Components of HS[a]

Astri Suhrke	*Whether the threat is economic or physical violence, immediate protective measures are necessary if longer-term investments to improve conditions can be relevant at all. It follows that the core of human insecurity can be seen as extreme vulnerability. The central task of a policy inspired by human security concerns would therefore be to protect those who are most vulnerable. …The philosophers do not tell us precisely who the vulnerable are, but it is self-evident that those exposed to immediate physical threats to life or deprivation of life-sustaining resources are extremely vulnerable. …Other persons can be place in equally life-threatening positions for reasons of deep poverty or natural disasters. This gives us three categories of extremely vulnerable persons:*
	   victims of war and internal conflict;
	   those who live close to the subsistence level and thus are structurally positioned at the edge of socio-economic disaster; and
	   victims of natural disasters.
	   In this schema, the condition of abject poverty or powerlessness is not qualitatively different from vulnerability to physical violence during conflict. Indeed, it recalls the concept of 'structural violence' developed in the 1970s by Johan Galtung. (Suhrke 1999)

Gary King and Christopher Murray	*"…the number of years of future life spend outside a state of generalized poverty"* *"…our suggestion for a parsimonious set of domains for measuring human security would be income, health, education and political freedom and democracy"* (King and Murray 2001)

Table 3.3   (continued)

International Actors (Organisations/ States/Individuals)	Definition/Components of HS[a]
David T. Graham and Nana K. Poku	*Rather than viewing security as being concerned with 'individuals qua citizens' (that is, toward their states), our approach view security as being concerned with 'individuals qua persons' (Krause and Williams 1997). Implicit then, in this conjunction of issues with ideas of human security and liberation is the notion of the ethical and moral. As an approach that focuses upon the importance of the insecurities facing people rather than governments or institutional agencies, human security is concerned with transcending the dominant paradigmatic orthodoxy that views critical concerns of migration—recognitions (i.e. citizenship), basic needs (i.e. sustenance, protection (i.e. refugee status), or human rights (i.e. legal standing)—as problems of interstate politics and consequently beyond the realm of the ethical and moral. (Graham and Pok 2000: 17)*

[a]*Source*: Global Development Research Center (GDRC) website, "Definitions of Human Security" (Available from: http://www.gdrc.org/sustdev/husec/Definitions.pdf)

rights, (2) the establishment of legitimate political authority through limitations in the use of military force and (3) effective multilateralism.

According to Glasius and Kaldor (2005) the EU's motivation to adopt human security is threefold: morality (e.g. moral commitment to provide security where this is lacking), legality (e.g. obligations coming from the EU legal framework) and self-interest (e.g. Europeans cannot be safe as long as other states and people live in insecurity), underpinned by the outcomes of globalisation impacting on traditional state security (Sira and Grans 2010).

3.3   The EU's Comprehensive Approach to Security

3.3.1   Genesis of the EU's CA

The difference between peacebuilding and human security can be framed in these terms: HS has to do with a shared understanding of *the why*, whereas PB relates to *the how* comprehensiveness in security is implemented through integrated policies.[10] Against this backdrop, it is important to note that comprehensiveness and the EU's comprehensive approach are not the same thing. Comprehensiveness denotes a general understanding in the international community that responses to security threats cannot be strictly military and, therefore, links with other dimensions or different types/methodologies of interventions are necessary alongside the use of force. Governments and international organisations have gradually adapted their strategic doctrines and procedures so as to take into account greater comprehensiveness, with many overlapping terms such as "whole of government" (used by the British government), "multi-dimensionality" or "integrated mission" (United Nations) and 3D approach (Defence, Development and Diplomacy, in Canada and the Netherlands).[11]

The EU's comprehensive approach is the process of institutional change within the Union aimed at instilling a culture of co-ordination among the different actors involved in crisis management and as part of a broader holistic framework for intervention by means of the Petersberg tasks. Accordingly, CA can be described as the operationalisation of "the why" and "the how" within the EU institutional setting.

CA essentially relies on two components: civil-military cooperation (CIMIC)[12] at the tactical level and civil-military coordination (CMCO)[13] at the political/strategic/institutional levels. The CIMIC doctrine is a military development, introduced in NATO member states since the mid-1990s as a result of a set of lessons learned on the ground, namely in the Western Balkans. The EU officially adopted the CIMIC concept in 2002, upon recommendation of the EU Military Committee and based on a Council's decision (Council of the European Union 2002a).[14]

CMCO serves a more internal function of coordination of the planning and implementation phases of the EU's crisis response, therefore addressing "the need for effective coordination of the actions of all relevant EU actors involved in the planning and subsequent implementation of EU's response to the crisis" (Council of the European Union 2003).

The CMCO concept was developed by the EU context only, given the *sui generis* nature of decision-making. Understanding the genesis of CMCO implies grasping the EU multi-level governance and the divide between the European Commission, the Council and member states in handling the security agenda. CMCO came at a crucial point in time, when debates over the future trajectories of the CSDP were intensifying and a growing consensus was arising on the need to equip crisis management policies with non-military, conflict prevention and integrated civil-military means. In particular, this resulted in the European Commission (namely through Development Cooperation and Humanitarian aid) exerting influence in the security dimension of European integration and, as a result, in the urgency to establish mechanisms for effective coordination to avoid a deadlock. Accordingly, while CIMIC is the integration of a doctrine within the EU crisis response machinery to satisfy operational needs, CMCO has both an external (building up a more holistic crisis response capacity) and an internal (avoid turf wars between new and previously existent institutions dealing with overlapping agendas rooted in PB and HS) rationale.

The establishment of a culture of coordination can be seen as one of the most important examples of institutional learning in EU security. From the beginning in 2001, the implementation of CMCO built on the awareness of previous policy failures to create and revise CSDP institutions. Specifically, it concentrated on the following aspects: the sharing of knowledge and experiences between relevant actors (e.g. the European Commission and the Council Secretariat)[15] to create synergies and enforce coordination, especially during the routine phases of crisis management planning (Mostl 2011: 32; Khol 2006); the accumulation of experiences through EU missions, leading to the implementation of a structured operational evaluation process and drawing from shared comprehensive assessments of CMCO operationalisation[16] (Perruche 2006; Erhart 2007; Khol 2006).

All this was complemented by a strong national backing, as three consecutive presidencies of the EU (the United Kingdom, Austria and Finland)[17] made CA and CMCO the centrepiece of their agendas (Drent 2011: 8). In sum, the creation of a culture of coordination can be described as getting practices closer to each other, sharing previously existing knowledge and gathering new experiences under the same roof.

Through the institutionalisation of CIMIC and CMCO, the EU has fully taken on board the concept of CA. A shared understanding developed among member states and institutions on the use of comprehensive tools and procedures for all phases (planning, conduct, as well as routine procedures) leading to concrete operations. Institutional, structural and tactical problems remain, notwithstanding the entry into force of the Lisbon Treaty and the consequent reform of the pillar structure: do coordination problems really lie in practice, as it has been argued (Ehrhart 2007: 10)?

3.3.2   The Implementation of the Comprehensive Approach

The European Union's CA applies to all phases of the conflict cycle, including prevention, early warning, crisis management, stabilisation, state-building and longer-term peace building (Council of the European Union 2014: 3). The integration of civilian and military instruments of crisis management is considered vital for the operational success of CSDP, due to the emphasis put by European policy-makers and by all the three High Representatives so far (Javier Solana, Catherine Ashton, Federica Mogherini) on the capacity of the EU to effectively apply a comprehensive approach to crisis management.[18]

The academic literature has covered the creation of the EU's comprehensive actorness in the field of crisis management, including the operational developments. Pirozzi and Sandawi (2009) identify the following main features: (1) the progressive expansion of the operational area and spectrum, that is the operative readiness to intervene in traditional (i.e. Balkans) and new (i.e. Central Asia) scenarios and the broadening of the security-related range of tasks; (2) the low-escalation spectrum of military operations, which eventually casts doubts about the capacity of the EU to act autonomously and efficiently in high-intensity conflicts; (3) an increasing integration of civilian-military components of crisis management and the inclination towards a comprehensive approach to crisis management, which however has not led (yet) to a genuine civil-military coordination at the planning level; (4) a growing intertwining of the first (Commission) and second (Council) pillars; (5) an increasing importance of the EU Special Representatives, considered as playing a big role in the field in terms of managing coordination between the different parts involved in the theatre of operations; (6) a truly multinational character and a high degree of participation by non EU states; (7) an increase of financial requirements for CSDP operations[19] (Pirozzi and Sandawi 2009: 9–12).

The academic debate has also highlighted the initial problems for CSDP missions in assuring an effective coordination of its military and civilian operations and instruments.[20] Ladzik (2009) and Juncos (2006) point out the example of Bosnia, where the military operation (EUFOR Althea) clashed in many areas with the work of the police mission (EUPM). As a result, the police mission (whose mandate was too weak to deal with a precarious situation in the theatre) suffered in terms of reputation and motivation for not having the power to fulfil those tasks for which the mission was deployed. The military, instead, were entrusted with the police tasks, thus leading to a general confusion about commitments (Gross 2008).

The real challenge for the implementation of the CA in the post-Lisbon era has therefore been ensuring a sequenced transition between different instruments and methodologies, within the EU, with member states as well as with all other organisations that operate in crisis zone (Pirozzi 2013: 13). Notwithstanding those difficulties, in recent CSDP operations (Aceh Monitoring Mission, EUFOR RD Congo and EUPOL Kinshasa) and since the creation of the Civil-Military Cell within the EU Military Staff in 2005, the EU has succeeded in improving civil-military coordination (Ladzik 2009; Pullinger 2006).

In December 2013, the European Council approved a common strategic document, jointly issued by the High Representative and the European Commission to improve the efficiency and effectiveness of the CA (European Commission and HR/VP 2013). The EU has since then put the CA into practice mainly in the Horn of Africa and the Sahel. In the Horn of Africa, the strategic framework approved by the Council of the European Union on November 14, 2011, and subsequently the EU Horn of Africa Regional Action Plan 2015–2020, approved on 26 October 2015, outline the condition for effective cooperation among all different actors involved in ground operations (Council of the European Union 2011, 2015). Greater convergence of mandates and synergy between regional CSDP missions was achieved as a result. EUCAP Nestor (for regional capacity-building), EUNAVFOR Atalanta and EUTM Somalia coordinate with three large EU projects in the region, managed by the European Commission and funded through the European Development Fund and the Instrument for Stability: the Regional Maritime Security Programme (MASE), the Pilot project on Piracy, Maritime Awareness and Risks, the Critical Maritime Routes Programme and the project Enhancing Maritime Security and Safety Through Information Sharing and Capacity Building (MARSIC).

In the Sahel region, the EU Strategy for Security and Development in the Sahel was delivered by the EEAS in 2012. It articulated the CA by assessing that problems in the Sahel are cross-border and intertwined, and that inter-dependence on security and development is needed (EEAS 2012). The strategic framework was implemented in Mali and Niger through CSDP missions (EUCAP Nestor Sahel, EUTM Mali) and a number of other projects launched by the European Commission and members states to support the justice sector, reinforce the criminal justice system, funded through the EDF, the IfS as well as member states' ministries.

Despite the delivery of new policy guidelines, the operational practice shows problems arising from consistency and coordination among EU institutions, particularly between the European Commission and the Council. Police missions, for instance, fall within the category of CCM, but rely on the CA as they involve a highly complex cross-pillar coordination, which may also include instruments from the III pillar for the combat against crime and border management (Gross 2008).[21] The literature has stressed, in particular, the inter-institutional problems encountered by EU missions in Bosnia (EUPM), RDC (EUPOL Kinshasa, EUFOR, EUSEC) and Macedonia (PROXIMA). In the latter case, fierce battles take place over competence between the Head of the Mission, the Special Representative and the European Commission delegation, with no effective division of labour between existing development efforts and CSDP activities (Ladzik 2009; Ioannides 2006).

Ursula Schroeder has analysed the inter-institutional issues by using the theoretical framework of "negative coordination", according to which institutions act on the basis that any new initiative from another conflicting body will not undermine its status or interests. Schroeder's findings show an expansionary strategy of the Council, giving itself mandates to enter fields such as rule of law and civil protection, and a defensive reaction by the Commission, which result in the emergence of a large grey area of competences and an enduring institutional tension in the field of peacekeeping and crisis management (Schroeder 2007). Gross points out that lately the two institutions have "learned" to work more smoothly (Gross 2008): the creation of the Civil-Military Cell is a good example of how a certain degree of inter-institutional coordination was achieved, since in this body experts of the European Commission are associated to the Council staff.

In line with these conclusions, and resulting from a process of learning by doing, namely in Bosnia and Herzegovina (EUPM and EUFOR Althea), new institutional arrangements (such as the Civil-Military Cell and the CMCO) have been established both at the decision-making level and on the ground to guarantee a better coordination of military and civilian crisis management instruments (Juncos 2006). The Lisbon Treaty has marked some progress increasing the degree of convergence by different actors towards the elaboration of the CA, for instance through common strategic documents for regional engagement in the Sahel and the Horn of Africa

(Pirozzi 2013: 19). The implications and limits of experiential learning in the sub-fields of SSR and CCM will be discussed in Chapters 6 and 7.

3.4 Conclusion

The comprehensive approach is the attempt to reach a coherent division of labour between the Brussels bureaucracy and member states, and link it to operational effectiveness in crisis management. SSR and CCM activities are not separated from the CA: they are embedded in it.

This chapter accounted for the link between global norm generation in response to structural changes and the rise of the comprehensive approach to crisis management within the European Union. It explored the way a new, multi-dimensional understanding of security translated into a paradigmatic shift, which in turn impacted on the way international actors defined their commitment to security provision through peacebuilding and human security. The EU internalised and operationalised these norms within the CSDP through the integration of civilian and military tools and the creation of an internal culture of coordination.

Conclusions point to several directions. First, in the origins of the EU, CA are located in the wider debate on human security and peacebuilding. Addressing a veritable conceptual labyrinth, the chapter clarified the relationship between "the why" (HS), "the how" (PB) and the operational (CA) aspects of the complex paradigm innovation process aimed at introducing comprehensiveness and holism in peace and conflict studies and practices.

Second, as the three cases of PB, HS and CA have shown, knowledge exchange and the creation of communities in support of the new agendas contributed to mainstreaming new norms by bandwagoning, lobbying and advocacy, complemented by states support and under the legitimacy of key international bodies, such as the UN. At the same time, a high degree of fragmentation over the definitions and the scope of human security and peacebuilding existed, hampering the effective use of multilateral instruments when translating policies into practices. Shared beliefs produced only limited international policy consensus, mostly tied to a liberal or Western conception of interventionism. It therefore failed to translate into a global networked governance in the field of security.

To sum up, this chapter showed the importance of understanding the causes and effects of the paradigmatic shift in security in order to explain how consensual and influential knowledge shaped the current institutional design and policy objectives of the CSDP, as they go beyond military peacekeeping.

NOTES

1. This is the definition used in the Joint Communication by the High Representative and the European Commission, released in December 2013. Cf. European Commission and HR/VP (2013).
2. For instance, NATO's Strategic Concept adopted at the Lisbon Summit in November 2010 calls for a comprehensive approach involving political, civilian and military instruments. Cf. the definition of the comprehensive approach on NATO's website: http://www.nato.int/cps/en/natolive/topics_51633.htm.
3. On the "liberal bias" of peacebuilding, see Paris (2002).
4. On organisational learning and peacebuilding, see Benner et al. (2007).
5. For a detailed description of the roles of the EU institutions in peace-building following the entry into force of the Lisbon Treaty, see EPLO (2011).
6. For a list of PB areas and activities, and their definitions, cf. Appendix 1 in Barnett et al. (2007: 56–57).
7. The network originally included also Austria, Chile, Greece, Ireland, Jordan, Mali, the Netherlands, Slovenia, Switzerland and Thailand (Paris 2001: 87).
8. The *Independent Commission on Disarmament and Security Issues* (aka the "Palm Commision") was formed to examine international security problems. Available from http://www.foreignaffairs.com/articles/36555/andrew-j-pierre/common-security-a-blueprint-for-survival.
9. Criticism has been raised, however, about how states have customised their definition of human security to suit their own foreign policy or strategic needs. Cf. Paris (2001: 90).
10. This differentiation takes inspiration from Drent (2011): "Key to comprehensive approaches to security is the shared understanding of *the why* (human security), but also of *the how* (with integrated policies)" (Drent 2011: 4).
11. Cf. Drent (2011: 4).
12. Cf. Council of the European Union (2009a).
13. Cf. Council of the European Union (2003, 2006a).

14. On the origins of CIMIC in the EU and on the distinction between CIMIC and CMCO, cf. Khol (2006: 122).
15. As Mostl notes, "the first conceptual work on CMCO took up the issue of inter-institutional coordination in 2001, when the European Commission and the Council of the EU shared their relevant experiences" (Mostl 2011: 32).
16. For instance through the *EU Concept for Comprehensive Planning* (GAERC 2005). Cf. also Juncos (2006).
17. See, for instance, the non-paper on CMCO produced by the three member states in 2005, addressing the issue in terms of five parameters: analysis, planning, management of operations, methodology of measuring progress, and management of capabilities (Perruche 2006). Cf. Non-paper by the United Kingdom, Austria and Finland (2005).
18. The literature on the civil-military co-operation and integration is abundant. For a good introduction into the topic, see Weiss (1999).
19. On this point, see Scannell (2004) and Menon (2009: 238–239).
20. For an introduction of decision-making procedures and the resources of crisis management operations, see Gourlay (2004).
21. On the governance aspects of EU crisis management and inter-institutional coordination, see Ursula Schroeder, *Governance of EU Crisis Management*, 2007 (in Emerson and Gross); For a more detailed account of civilian crisis management, cf. Nowak (2006).

CHAPTER 4

The EU Security Architecture and Networked Governance

The EU security architecture can be best depicted as a system of networked governance. Different types of networks and communities interact and, in some cases, overlap. By structuring the relationships and balance of power among actors, this system of interactions determines the institutional configurations and the policy outcomes of the CSDP.

This chapter analyses the attempt to improve EU institutional coordination between the civilian and military instruments of crisis management. The analytical focus of this chapter is on the CSDP's bureaucracy, on the actors that are part of those structures and on the networks that connect and foster coordination between the two. Each one of these dimensions contains, in turn, three levels of analysis: (1) governance processes (supranational, intergovernmental and transgovernmental); (2) actorness (state and non-state actors); (3) field (military, civilian, civ-mil, industrial and political). The CSDP system results from the interplay between dimensions within the three levels of analysis.

The European Union is often depicted as the institution with the greatest ability and experience to operationalise the CA (Major and Molling 2009), and also one that has made significant efforts to adapt its institutions in accordance with the demand for greater internal coordination. Broadly speaking, the CA "enhances the likelihood of favourable and enduring outcomes in the political, diplomatic, security, economic, development, rule of law and human rights dimensions of international

© The Author(s) 2017
G. Faleg, *The EU's Common Security and Defence Policy*,
DOI 10.1007/978-3-319-41306-8_4

engagements in pursuit of a common goal both within and beyond the EU" (Wendling 2010: 27). In a narrower sense, it refers to the "effective co-ordination of the actions of all relevant EU actors involved in the planning and subsequent implementation of EU's response to the crisis" (Council of the European Union 2003). This chapter focuses mostly on the latter. The next three sections analyse respectively, structures, actors and networks that compose the CSDP system and their evolution.

4.1   An Overview of CSDP Structures:
The Institutionalisation of Comprehensiveness

CSDP falls under the authority of the European Council and the Foreign Affairs Council. Its key feature, in terms of decision-making and compared to other fields or policies of the EU, is the requirement for unanimity, which makes the CSDP governance fully intergovernmental.[1] Overlaying that, bureaucratic structures also reveal a mix of supranational (e.g. the Council Secretariat's structures), intergovernmental (e.g. the PSC) and national (e.g. Foreign or Defence Ministries) bureaucratic actors.

The creation of Brussels-based bureaucracies characterised much of the initial efforts by EU member states in the wake of St Malo (1998) and Cologne (1999). Permanent structures were established since the Helsinki Council (1999) to run the CSDP according to the objectives outlined in Council documents and, subsequent to (2003), to the strategic guidelines provided by the European Security Strategy (cf. creation of Civcom in 2000 stemming from recommendation by the PSC or establishment of the CivMil Cell in 2003).

The Treaty of Lisbon constituted a landmark development, because it instituted the comprehensive approach to crisis management and a holistic view of intervention in crisis situations, at the cornerstone of capacity-building and institutional reform processes. Accordingly, the Treaty envisaged a major reconfiguration of EU institutions in the CFSP and CSDP fields to achieve better internal coordination, management, efficiency and coherence among crisis-management structures. Changes included the creation of the post of High Representative of the Union for Foreign Affairs and Security Policy and Vice President of the Commission (HR/VP) and the establishment of the European External Action Service (EEAS).

Since its official opening (1 January 2011), the EEAS has integrated permanent civilian and military crisis management bodies as well as intergovernmental committees, including a new Crisis Management and Planning

Directorate (CMPD),[2] the Civilian Planning and Conduct Capability (CPCC) and the EU Military Staff (EUMS). According to the division of tasks among these three permanently-based structures, the CMPD deals with strategic planning for CSDP missions and operations, and is tasked with creating synergies between their civilian and military aspects; the CPCC covers operational planning and the conduct of CSDP civilian missions; the EUMS carries out early warning, situation assessment and strategic planning for CSDP activities; finally, the EU Operation Centre (OPCEN) was activated for the first time in March 2012 to support the EU's operations in the Horn of Africa. Intergovernmental committees were relocated inside the EEAS to bring together representatives from member states (diplomats, seconded experts and military representatives—chiefs of defence). These include Civcom, the EU Military Committee and the PSC, as well as the EU Special Representatives, the EU Delegations in third countries and the Politico Military Group (PMG).

A complete picture of security and defence structures should also take into account relevant Commissions DGs (e.g. DEVCO, ECHO, Justice and Home Affairs), the European Parliament's Foreign Affairs Committee and the Subcommittee on Security and Defence, the General Secretariat of the Council, and COREPER. Finally, the HR/VP and the Crisis Management Board (CMB), chaired by the HR/VP herself or by the EEAS Executive Secretary, is in charge of discussing organisational and coordination aspects of crisis response, crisis management and conflict prevention to ensure coherence in the EU external action.

Despite huge operational challenges and problems in implementation-effectiveness-efficiency, the institutional make up introduced by the Lisbon Treaty made the EU the home of the CA. It also revealed two inner peculiarities of the institutionalisation of EU security cooperation within CSDP.

First, the shape of the CSDP in the post-Lisbon era results from the internalisation of a new set of collective norms falling under the umbrella of comprehensiveness. Institutions, through the diffusion of norms, did shape states' interests and triggered further institutionalisation. States have not ceded interests to a supranational cause, but have reconstituted them in terms of European norms rather than just national ones (Smith 2004a, b).

Second, Brusselsisation (Nuttall 2000; Allen 1998) shows that, through the institutional nexus constituted by the vast number of committees, institutions did also play a role in shaping security identities (March and

Olsen 1989; Powell and DiMaggio 1991) towards new collective scopes for action—in our case, the call for a comprehensive understanding of EU security and defence policy.

The Brussels-based institutions created since 1999 facilitated the adoption of a comprehensive approach by the actors involved in the

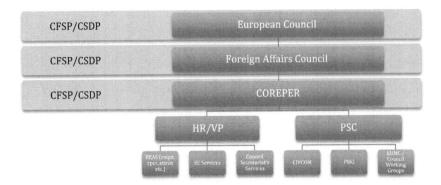

Fig. 4.1 Institutional structures in CFSP/CSDP (Rehrl and Weisserth 2010: 39)

Fig. 4.2 Bureaucratic actors in the CSDP and levels of governance (Vanhoonacker et al. 2010: 12)

CSDP. Institutions acted as socialising agents, and not just arenas for coordinated action. Let us now look at the actors and networks that form the CSDP institutional environment, so as to provide a morphology of CSDP and visualise the environment in which normative processes operate (Figures 4.1 and 4.2).

4.2   Comprehensiveness and Actorness: The Proliferation of Security Actors and Its Implications for the CSDP

With the adoption of a CA to security, security actors multiplied so as to include judges, police officers, private contractors or development agencies, as well as other private and public actors. EU decision-making has evolved not just in terms of bureaucratic structures, but also as far as the actors who interact within institutions (and produce policy outcomes) are concerned. Specifically, the objective of integrating long-term conflict prevention with short-term crisis management policies, resources and capabilities reduced the number of tasks carried out exclusively by states. Within the CSDP institutional set-up, a number of non-state actors offer advice or influence (formally or informally) security decisions, particularly in those contexts where member states lack sufficient information or expertise.

A typology of CSDP actors can be built across several dividing lines. A first one is between state and non-state actors. State actors include all member states bodies, representations, ministries in Brussels, capitals and on the ground. In addition to defence and foreign ministries, interior, finance and justice ministries also play a role, creating a need for coordination mechanisms (Vanhoonacker and Jacobs 2010).

Non-state actors constitute a complex galaxy. It is composed of permanent or temporary established supranational EU institutions and relevant units (Council of the EU, European Commission, European Parliament and EU agencies) and CSDP agencies (e.g. the European Defence Agency, the EU Institute for Security Studies and the EU Satellite Centre); but it also includes NGOs, think-tanks, research institutes and consultancies involved in CSDP, and the private sector (defence industry, private security and military companies).

The academic literature is divided over the real impact of the non-state actors on the CSDP policy-making. Some authors believe that supranational elements are creeping into the second pillar intergovernmental logic

(Allen 1998; Cross 2008). Others contend that, despite the existence of clear elements of transgovernmental and transnational cooperation along-side narrow intergovernmental relations, non-state actors in the CSDP remain in practice fairly marginal: in the end, a handful of state actors are really decisive and exert influence by reconstituting power at the suprana-tional level (Mérand et al. 2011).

The truth seems to be somewhere in the middle between these two viewpoints. Recent studies, particularly in the fields of governance and network analysis, have provided enough evidence that the CSDP has become a highly networked policy area. Therein, a variety of actors influ-ence the agenda and have to be taken into account when analysing the factors affecting policy outcomes. At the same time, it seems clear that the "supranational intergovernmentalist" vision of EU security (Howorth 2007, 2011) gets constrained, at all levels of policy-making, by the defi-nition of a strategic vision for the CSDP, which remains a prerogative of member states.

A second way to classify CSDP actors is by differentiating between mili-tary *vs* civilians. This stems from the traditional tension between civil and military cultures deep rooted in member states and uploaded at the EU level. From the time uniformed officers entered the Council's building in the early 2000s, professional and cultural barriers with civil servants have appeared. Problems of communication and coordination between civil-ians and the military have then become a distinctive feature of a CSDP viewed as flawed by design (Norheim-Martinsen 2010). Furthermore, the process set off since 2003 to enhance coordination in the EU's civil-military interface, after the "cultural revolution" initiated by the CMCO concept, was largely a result of the dialectic between civilian and military actors. This process can be seen as a struggle to find a balance of power for new structural and procedural arrangements. Under this perspective, the framework for crisis management structures and procedures should be viewed not only as the result of compromises between member states more or less influenced by non-state actors; but also, and perhaps most importantly, as a struggle between civilian and military inputs on how to structure strategic planning and ensure effective civil-military organisa-tion. In this struggle, the military has certainly been more influential than civilians (Khol 2006).

Third, CSDP institutions are part of a broader policy environment and are entrenched in a global network of inter-institutional relations and flows of influence. External players intervene in the policy debate and their influence cannot be underestimated. For instance, the EU and the UN have established mutually-influencing networks, which regularly engage in cooperative and supportive initiatives. The networks have shown a fair level of convergence on issues relating to peacekeeping and peacebuilding. Inter-institutional cooperation[3] between the two organisations resulted in the creation of an EU-UN Steering Committee. The relationship is even tighter with NATO, going well beyond the Berlin Plus capacity framework to include expanding security communities (Adler 2008) and institutional isomorphism (Koops 2012).

Fourth, and finally, individual leaders should be taken into account when mapping CSDP actors. Leaders are a precious—yet at times scarce—resource. EU security makes no exception, especially if one considers the tension between legitimacy (consensus and equality underlying decisions) and effectiveness at times when external and internal pressures are significant (Giegerich and Gross 2006). Besides the presence of *directoires* and the role of some member states in assuming control over planning and initiation of missions, individual leaders also count, as demonstrated by differences in the Solana (1999–2009), Ashton (2009–2014) and Mogherini (2014-present) mandates. This is particularly relevant in the EU, where the interactions between different levels of governance and the ensuing dispersion of authority/accountability can go to the detriment of efficiency and result in bad or ill-timed policies. Furthermore, in a social network, power is situational: it depends on one's position in the social structure, which grants the ability to control the flow of information or cooperation (brokerage). In a social structure, individual brokers (who are located at the very basis of the social structure) can be as influential as organisational units. Actors interact within institutional structures by means of transgovernmental and transnational networks. By introducing the concept of networked governance, the next section will track existing networks within the CSDP field.

4.3 Connecting the Dots: CSDP Networks and Communities

Between the micro-perspective (actors and structures shaping policies) and the macro-one (CSDP as a system producing a set of policy output) lies a meso-level, where interactions and processes take place. In this level, characterised by networked governance, the decision-making environment is influenced by the presence of different types of networks and communities that structure the relationships and the balance of power between actors.

Networked governance constitutes a step forward vis-à-vis traditional governance approaches. The latter stressed the existence of entry points allowing policy entrepreneurs to intervene in decision-making (Mérand et al. 2011: 123). In European security studies, they put emphasis on cooperation among a variety of state and non-state security actors, authorities and formal and informal arrangements that define institutional configurations (Krahmann 2005: 16; Kirchner and Sperling 2007) and policy outcomes (Webber et al. 2004: 4).

Networked governance introduces the configuration of ties between actors and EU structures, leading to the assertion that a policy area is embedded in a set of social—hence dynamic and evolutionary—relations. Ideas, knowledge, interests and preferences are contained in this fluid and inclusive environment surrounding the CSDP institutional nucleus, like molecules in the cytoplasm. Within this environment, socialisation processes induct actors into the norms and rules of the communities to which they belong (Checkel 2005). Socialisation is a widely-used approach in the recent IR literature, with a soaring number of studies addressing the role of institutions as sites of socialisation for individuals, and their consequences as regards the formation of preferences and policy decisions. Hence, as rules and norms become essential to maintain social order (Kratochwil 1989), the dynamic normative and epistemic interpretations of the material world are determinant of human action.

It is also important to differentiate analytically between networks and other knowledge and practice-based communities. Networks are constituted by actors who are formally equals (Lavenex and Schimmelfennig 2009: 797), whereas communities are studied on the basis of the practices and knowledge underpinning them (Bicchi 2011: 1119). In other words, whereas the core constituent of a network is the relationship (their depth and thickness) between nodes having equal rights, communities arise out of a shared activity that is narrowly associated with the exercise of power.

CSDP networks have first been detected (Smith 2004a: 118) from a national perspective. National agents do not just defend the national interest, but mediate between national capitals and the Brussels-based centres of foreign policy-making (Smith 2004a: 118). Some institutions, such as the Council Secretariat DG-E, facilitate socialisation as they instil a feeling of ownership in national civil servants seconded to CSDP bureaucracies of the Council. Once socialised, many of these agents import that spirit back to capitals. PSC Ambassadors adapt national positions according to what they deem appropriate as a result of the knowledge and interactions they had in the Brussels CSDP networks (Breuer 2012).[4] Duration of appointment might reinforce the impact of socialisation as those who have served for a longer time in Brussels may feel closer to PSC colleagues than other diplomats in national ministries.

Another way to detect CSDP networks is to pick up specific cases of intergovernmental agencies or transnational committees, such as the EUMC and Civcom (Cross 2010, 2011), the PSC (Howorth 2011; Juncos and Reynolds 2007), COREPER (Cross 2007, 2011), the Council Secretariat Working Groups (Juncos & Pomorska 2006; Beyers 2007) and the COREU (Bicchi 2011). Institutional boundaries simplify the task of detecting inner working processes, practices and knowledge flows. The downside, however, is that single institutions or groupings of professionals may say little about the causal force of ideas, except in those cases where a specific bureaucratic unit holds the monopoly of norm entrepreneurship and diffusion. Networks and communities, in fact, operate *across*, not *within* institutions. Analyses that take structures as isolated from one another fail to determine how social relationships are constructed (Hoffmann et al. 2005: 5).

According to Hoffmann et al., actors' collocation (centrality, or importance) within a network depends upon four variables: (1) presence in Brussels, with Brussels-based actors being more central than capitals-based ones; (2) professionalism (e.g. diplomats and military officers); (3) participation in transgovernmental groups (e.g. Franco-German group); (4) involvement in operations, as operational actors are more central than policy makers because their activity forges stronger common practices (Hoffmann et al. 2005).

My reading is different. In their working routine, EU policy-makers value the advice coming from organisations and individuals who are not, or not necessarily Brussels-based.[5] Practices are wide and stretch well beyond professionalism within a specific group. CSDP civilian and military staff are regularly in touch with professionals from other backgrounds or countries. Their perceptions are influenced by cross-fertilisation and knowledge-sharing (for instance, during international conferences), which contribute to their policy agendas.[6] The participation in field missions reinforces individual actors' beliefs and views on CSDP, for instance as far as more emphasis on the CA and integrated civilian/military crisis management tools are concerned.[7] Networks and communities within the

Table 4.1 CSDP levels of actorness

Entity/field	MILITARY	CIVILIAN	CIV-MIL	INDUSTRIAL	POLITICAL	Field/governance
STATE	E.g. MS Military Staff; Ministries of Defence; National Defence Colleges	E.g. MS National Police; Ministry of Interior/Justice;	Folke Bernadotte Academy; National Defence Colleges	E.g. BAE Systems, Finmeccanica, Airbus Military; EADS; Dassault Aviation	E.g. Ministries of Foreign Affairs, PM Cabinets; Parliaments' Committees; Political Parties	INTERGVT
NON-STATE	E.g. EDA; EUMS; EUMC;	E.g. CPCC; Civcom;	E.g. CMPD; ESDC; EU ISS; DCAF	E.g. EDA;	PSC; COREPER;	SUPRA/TRANS-national
THIRD PARTIES	NATO;	OSCE, UN, OECD, World Bank;	OSCE, UN;	Boeing;	US Government	–

CSDP field are therefore manifold and extend beyond the CSDP nucleus where formal institutional structures are located.

Moreover, networks have different configurations depending on the sector under study. As the two cases of seemingly overlapping policy agendas (SSR and CCM) will show, norm diffusion might follow similar patterns or originate in the same paradigmatic shift, but the communities as well as the actors affiliated to them are not quite the same. Analyses of the main agencies acting in the CSDP field (Cross 2010) tell us how socialisation affects decision-shaping and decision-taking. Nonetheless, they completely overlook how (and why) agencies are crafted in the first place; what (state, non-state) actors drove the institutionalisation of EU cooperation in specific security areas (civilian, military or the integration of both); and, most importantly, who or what shaped the views of these actors. Table 4.1 provides a useful template to locate the actors involved in the CSDP.

4.4   Conclusion

CSDP is characterised by a multitude of institutional structures, actors and networks. Previous academic works failed to provide an exhaustive overview of formal and informal relationships between institutions and other relevant stakeholders—although the governance-turn in EU studies was a big first step in dealing with the multi-level nature of decision-making in the hard case of security co-operation.

The rise of comprehensiveness and the push towards a more holistic approach in EU security policies, particularly after the Lisbon Treaty, have multiplied the actors influencing security decisions. As a consequence, networks and communities have proliferated beyond formal institutional structures or committees. With these considerations in mind, the next chapters look into the CSDP's cognitive architecture and the diffusion of SSR and CCM. The two case studies show that, as a result of the broadening security landscape, new actors, networks and communities emerged besides traditional ones and influenced, with different outcomes, the institutionalisation of security cooperation.

Notes

1. Cf. Rehrl and Weisserth (2010: 38).
2. On the creation of the CMPD, cf. Gebhard (2009).

3. On inter-institutional cooperation, cf. Tardy (2005), Hofmann (2009), Wouters and Ruys (2008), Duke (2008).
4. On the PSC, cf. also Duke (2005) and Howorth (2007, 2011).
5. Brussels Interviews, *European Commission* and *EEAS* (Spring 2012).
6. *Ibid.*
7. Interviews with policy-makers and practitioners in Brussels, Stockholm, London and Rome (Spring-Winter 2012).

CHAPTER 5

The EU's Engagement in Security Sector Reform and Civilian Crisis Management

According to the 2013 ENTRi's handbook on EU's crisis management, SSR is "based on the concept of human security, has formed part of the toolbox in international crisis management", and it is both "an operational as well as a normative concept" (ENTRi 2013: 81). Activities falling under SSR are cross-sectoral[1] and encompass the reform of institutional structures, the improvement of capabilities and the establishment of civilian offices for the supervision of security forces (ENTRi 2013: 82). CCM is also described in EU documents as "an important tool under the CSDP in support of international peace and security" (European Union 2008: 2). CCM activities cover the four priority areas defined by the 2000 Santa Maria da Feira European Council: police, rule of law, civilian administration and civil protection.

Innovative concepts providing new tools for the CSDP, SSR and CCM can best illustrate the empirical implications of the learning communities' framework. In both cases, ideas emerging in the post-Cold War setting led to the adoption, and subsequent implementation, of new policy frameworks. SSR and CCM are entrenched in the new understanding of security and crisis management involving the development of non-military approaches and tools for intervention (Table 5.1).

While CCM had a huge institutional and operational impact on the CSDP, EU-led SSR missions have been few and low scale, with uneven or disappointing results in the field. The next chapters will account for such difference in outcomes. This chapter illustrates the main characteristics of

© The Author(s) 2017
G. Faleg, *The EU's Common Security and Defence Policy*,
DOI 10.1007/978-3-319-41306-8_5

Table 5.1 Levels of analysis in EU crisis management

EU crisis management

Guiding principle	Comprehensive approach	
Tools	CCM	SSR
Activities	Four priority areas (Santa Maria da Feira European Council 2000): Police Rule of law Civilian administration Civil protection	Cross-sectoral and multidisciplinary activities. Holistic approach aimed at reforming the security system of a country, including institutional structures and operational capabilities: Defence and armed forces reform Security forces and services reform Judicial reform Police reform Prison reform Establishment of civilian authorities for the control of the security sector

the SSR and CCM policy frameworks, as well as all other relevant aspects such as structures, procedures and practices as they have developed from the late-1990s onward.

5.1   Introducing Security Sector Reform

Although SSR is not explicitly mentioned in the Treaties, its place in the EU security architecture is validated by two concept documents issued by the Council Secretariat (Council of the European Union 2005d) and the Commission (European Commission 2006), as well as by the *Report on the implementation of the European Security Strategy*[2] (2008). The development of SSR approaches to conflict resolution in general (Law 2006; Peake et al. 2006; Brozka 2006), and the EU's engagement in particular (Sheriff 2007; Spence and Fluri 2008; Law and Myshlovska 2008; Ekengren and Simons 2011) have attracted scholars' attention, particularly the practices and challenges arising from the implementation of SSR policies (Dursun-Ozkanca and Vandemoortele 2012). Theoretically, the debate on the emergence of SSR tends to be fenced off: studies emphasise the importance of development concerns (i.e. major donors)[3] or changes in the security/strategic environment (i.e., NATO or the OSCE).[4] The reason for this is the difficult (re)conciliation between security and development, resulting in an incoherent academic debate, in which SSR is considered the "bastard child of civil-military relations and development studies" (Chuter 2006: 3). Therefore, SSR studies show a significant variation as regards SSR definitions, objectives, processes, recipients, implementing institutions and methodologies so that is appears almost impossible, if not useless, to bring them under the same roof.

Against this backdrop, a striking feature of EU SSR is that the European Commission and some member states have been engaged for a long time in what can be defined as SSR policies *ante-litteram*. Even before the label "SSR" was created and the concept mainstreamed at the international level, the EU was involved in reconstruction and institutional reform policies, as part of its external action tools, that today fall under the conceptual umbrella of SSR. Different bits of the current SSR policies were operational well before the SSR concept was created.[5] In particular, the European Commission and member states were exposed to aspects of security sector reform through their membership in other international organisations active in the areas of human rights, conflict prevention, post-crisis reconstruction and rehabilitation and governance, such as the OSCE[6] or the UN (Law and Myshlovska 2008: 10).

Despite these examples of sectoral cooperation, security and development actors inside the EU hardly appreciated the importance of a comprehensive SSR framework. The nature of international relations during the Cold War was not conducive to the acknowledgment of this framework. Ideological enmity between the superpowers fuelled proxy wars and hence the re-emergence of conflicts between developing countries. Furthermore, donors' dogmatic view of aid policies was limited to economic growth, with no recognition of the mutual influences of security and good governance on development.

With the end of the Cold War, a window of opportunity opened up for the international community to adopt the paradigm of human security and paved the way for the emergence of SSR (Doelle and Gouzée de Harven 2008: 39). What changed the international security agenda in the 1990s towards a human security approach was the growing securitisation of sectors from small arms and light weapons to food, health and environmental security (Hanngi and Tanner 2005: 12). Before the mid-1990s, development agencies and security institutions (including the EU), despite the progressive acknowledgment that security had a crucial role in sustainable development, only focused on narrow sections of SSR (e.g. demobilisation or police reform) but did not look at the wider context through a long-term strategy connecting them (Hendrickson 1999: 18). From the mid-1990s, international organisations (particularly the OECD, UNDP and the World Bank) started profiling SSR, setting norm standards and promoting norm transfer (Hanggi and Tanner 2005). This process was driven by the emerging consensus that an unreformed security sector represented an obstacle to the promotion of sustainable peace, democracy and development.

Let us now turn to the existing definitions of SSR according to the context, implementing actors, operating principles and activities. The notion of SSR is associated with security sector governance:

> Security Sector Governance (SSG) *refers to the structures, processes, values and attitudes that shape decisions about security and their implementation.*[7]
>
> Security Sector Reform (SSR) *aims to enhance SSG through the effective and efficient delivery of security under conditions of democratic oversight and control. SSR offers a framework for conceptualising which actors and factors are relevant to security in a given environment as well as a methodology for optimising the use of available security resources. By emphasising the need to take a comprehensive approach to the security sector, SSR can also help integrate a broad variety of actors and processes.*[8]

The standard definitions of "security sector" and "security sector reform" are provided by the OECD Development Assistance Committee (DAC) and are today commonly used by international actors to formulate their SSR policies. According to DAC, the actors in the security sector are the security forces and the relevant civilian bodies and processes needed to manage them. Security sector reform involves "transforming the way the security sector is managed and monitored to ensure that the security organisations are accountable to democratic civil authorities and that sound principles of public sector management are applied to the security sector" (Ball 2002: 8). But what does security sector mean exactly, in other words what types of institutions and activities are covered when we use the term "SSR"?

The terminology note to the *OECD Handbook on Security System Reform* (OECD 2007: 5), which is based on the *OECD DAC Guidelines on Security System Reform and Governance* (OECD 2005), defines the security system as:

> *(…) including core security actors (e.g. armed forces, police, gendarmerie, border guards, customs and immigration, and intelligence and security services); security management and oversight bodies (e.g. ministries of defence and internal affairs, financial management bodies and public complaints commissions); justice and law enforcement institutions (e.g. the judiciary, prisons, prosecu-*

tion services, traditional justice systems); and non-statutory security forces (e.g. private security companies, guerrilla armies and private militia).[9]

The note adds that:

(...) this definition has become established internationally and so in the handbook, "security system", "security system reform" and "SSR" all refer to that broad range of security and justice institutions. The terms also denote activities sometimes referred to by international actors as "security sector reform", "security and justice sector reform" and "rule of law".[10]

Although the OECD guidelines allow the use of SSR for both security "system" and "sector" governance and reform, the gap between the systemic and sectoral approach triggered an intense debate in the expert communities on how to conduct SSR, with serious policy implications. When applying the OECD's systemic recommendations (OECD 2001b, 2005, 2007) some institutions continued to have a narrow understanding of SSR, limited to activities in the security sector. The systemic approach, instead, entails a fuller developmental and holistic viewpoint. The OECD has clarified this point:

security system includes the traditional security forces but indicates a broader approach: security system reform is understood as the transformation of security systems so that they are managed by, and operate in a manner more consistent with, democratic norms, rule of law – which includes well-functioning and just judicial and penal systems and sound principles of good governance. Therefore, the term security system reform no longer refers only to the reform of the armed forces, which is only one aspect or sector of security. The idea is to reform the entire security system.[11]

For instance, a joint paper by the U.S. Agency for International Development (USAID), the Department of State and the Department of Defence from 2009, fully takes on the systemic definition of SSR and defines it as:

the set of policies, plans, programs and activities that a government undertakes to improve the way it provides safety, security and justice. The overall objective is to provide these services in a way that promotes an effective and legitimate public service that is transparent, accountable to civilian authority, and responsive to the needs of the public. From a donor perspective, SSR is an umbrella term that might include integrated activities in support of: defence and armed forces reform; civilian management and oversight; justice; police; corrections; intelligence reform; national security planning and strategy support; border management; disarmament, demobilization and reintegration (DDR); and/or reduction of armed violence.[12]

The holistic provision of security along the OECD lines has a double meaning. First, it integrates all those partial reforms (such as defence reform, police reform and intelligence reform), which in the past were generally seen and conducted as separate efforts. Second, it puts the security sector and its components under democratic governance, given its normative commitment to the consolidation of democracy, promotion of human rights and implementation of the principles of good governance (Hanggi and Tanner 2005: 17). The EU has fully adopted this systemic and holistic approach at the declaratory level (Fig. 5.1).

Despite the existence of a standardised template for SSR, based on the systemic approach and codified by the OECD work, in practical terms SSR varies substantially according to factors such as the specific reform context,

---

Major Categories of Actors Influencing Security Sector Governance

- **Organizations authorized to use force** - armed forces; police; paramilitary forces; gendarmeries; intelligence services (including both military and civilian agencies); secret services; coast guards; border guards; customs authorities; reserve or local security units (civil defense forces, national guards, presidential guards, militias, etc.).

- **Civil management and oversight bodies** - the president/prime minister; national security advisory bodies; legislature and legislative select committees; ministries of defence, internal affairs, foreign affairs; customary and traditional authorities; financial management bodies (finance ministries, budget offices, financial audit & planning units); and statutory civil society organizations (civilian review boards and public complaints commissions).

- **Justice and public security bodies** - judiciary; justice ministries; prisons; criminal investigation and prosecution services; human rights commissions and ombudsmen; correctional services; customary and traditional justice systems.

- **Non-statutory security body actors:** liberation armies, guerrilla armies, traditional militias, political party militias, private security companies

- **Civil society actors: professional organizations,** including trade unions; research/policy analysis organizations; advocacy organizations; the media; religious organizations; non-governmental organizations; concerned public.

Fig. 5.1 Main actors in SSR and SSG (Ball et al. 2003: 32)

the implementing organisations, and has been shaped by several policy experiences and practices.

Many different sub-approaches have arisen and been developed by the several external actors engaged in SSR. These include state and non-state actors, NGOs and civil society organisations. Intergovernmental organisations have tended to play a leading role in conceptualising and implementing the SSR agenda (DCAF 2009). IOs approach SSR from either a development (i.e., World Bank), security (i.e., OSCE, NATO, EU) or democratic perspective (i.e. Council of Europe); have a global (i.e., UN, EU, OSCE), regional (i.e., African Union, Council of Europe) or sub-regional focus (i.e., the Economic Community of Western African States—ECOWAS); maybe active in field activities, such as capacity building and technical assistance (i.e., Council of Europe), norm development (i.e., OECD) or both (i.e., EU, OSCE); can operate in different country contexts, such as post-conflict (i.e., EU, NATO, OSCE), transition countries (i.e., Council of Europe) or developing countries (i.e., OECD, ECOWAS, World Bank). Although the overarching principle and framework of SSR remains the same, each IO has experienced SSR programmes in different ways, depending on its specific concerns (problem-solving), capabilities or geographical scope.

5.1.1   A Policy Framework for EU SSR

Since the early 2000s, the EU has constantly increased its focus on SSR as part of its external action. It has progressively internalised the SSR discourse and practice as part of the security-good-governance-development nexus. However, the rise of SSR did not come about from scratch. As a major provider of external assistance, the European Commission has been engaged in over 70 countries around the world in support of a wide spectrum of sub-sectoral SSR activities, several years before SSR entered the EU debate (Buxton 2008: 29). Activities included justice reform, capacity building for interior and justice Ministries, prison services, legal aid, human rights commissions and ombudsman functions, border guards and custom institutions and in some cases also the reform of armed forces.[13]

Similarly, both the CSDP and its predecessor, the Western European Union (WEU),[14] have been engaged in missions falling under the SSR template particularly police ones (van Eekelen 2006: 117). What the new SSR paradigm added to the pre-existing activities was not a simple re-labelling, but the more complex transformation of ad-hoc, sub-sectoral intervention scattered across a broad range of activities under different EU instruments to a holistic, coherent approach based on the "whole-of-government" and involving enhanced coordination between EU institutions as well as a comprehensive framework for action. The peculiarity of the EU's involvement in SSR and understanding of the security-developvcutting nature of the concept and the presence of several interlocking agendas, from development cooperation to enlargement, from conflict prevention to human rights.

Although the EU cannot be depicted as a leader in SSR (Dursun-Ozkanka and Vandemoortele 2012: 140), EU-led initiatives have gained momentum after the creation of the Union's SSR policy framework in 2005–2006. The DCAF's report on *Intergovernmental Approaches to SSR* identifies the EU as "potentially the most important resource provider for SSR programmes" (DCAF 2006: 9).

The European Security Strategy (2003: 2) underlines the importance of the security-development nexus and contains a reference to SSR as a means to "increase capabilities in different areas (…) in terms of a wider spectrum of mission" and as "part of broader institution building" in third countries (European Security Strategy 2003: 12–13). Two years later, in November 2005, the *EU Concept for ESDP Support to Security Sector Reform* was adopted (Council of the European Union 2005d) bringing into being the effective integration of the concept.[15] The document underlines the role of EU SSR in "…putting fragile states back on their feet…enhancing good governance, fostering democracy and promoting local and regional stability", placing special emphasis on local ownership and inter-institutional coherence with other areas of EU external action. In many respects, the concept adheres to the OECD DAC guidelines. For instance, the definition of security sector replicates the categories listed in the OECD DAC document, although it is stated that the guidelines do not "reflect the specificities of the EU, nor those security aspects that fall under the CSDP" (Council of the European Union 2005d: 5).

Six months after the Council's concept, in May 2006, the Commission issued its own framework document through a Communication to the Council and the European Parliament titled *A Concept for European Community Support for Security Sector Reform* (European Commission 2006), accompanied by annexes on previous areas of European Community support to SSR and international standards relevant for SSR activities. The document stated that "SSR is an important part of conflict prevention, peace-building and democratisation. SSR concerns reform of both the bodies which provide security to citizens and the state institutions responsible for management and oversight of those bodies" (European Commission 2006: 3). From a content analysis of the Communication it emerges that the Commission intended to stress more forcefully the "security system" (as opposed to "security sector") approach to SSR, underlining that reform should be part of a governance reform policy and public sector strategy (van Eekelen 2006: 115). Therefore, the Commission and the Council have articulated their approaches in slightly different ways, with the latter pursuing a narrower agenda based on security and crisis management, and the former relying on a broader one associated with good governance and conflict prevention.

Despite the scarce attention given by the Council Secretariat and the PSC to the Commission communication and differences between the two documents in terms of conceptual nuances, operational focuses and implementing bodies, a Council of Ministers' decision of 12 June 2006 resulted in the release of the *EU Policy framework for Security Sector Reform* (Council of the European Union 2006c). This third document pulled together the Commission's related activities and doctrines with the military route available to execute and support SSR through the common security and defence policy (Ekengren and Simons 2011).

The Commission and the Council have become active players in SSR. CSDP missions, the Community's Rapid Reaction Mechanism and the Instrument for Stability have contributed to this rapid development by complementing the adoption of an overarching holistic and coordinated framework. However, challenges for SSR implementation in the EU arise from an erroneous use of policy and operational instruments (Sheriff 2007). On the one hand, although developed with reference to the OECD model pledging effective cross-pillar mechanisms, the EU SSR policy framework has suffered from the EU institutional fragmentation and the presence of too many levels of governance (and hence too many bureaucratic structures snooping into decision-making about SSR). On the other hand, and partly as a result of the institutional framework, the EU has lacked common operational guidelines (Sheriff 2007: 98) to evaluate and assess SSR activities in order to improve conceptual, planning and implementation tasks.

5.2   INTRODUCING CIVILIAN CRISIS MANAGEMENT

The development of civilian crisis management in the EU is commonly seen as a process of capacity-building, aimed at equipping the Union with the instruments to carry out successful non-military peace-building and crisis response within the framework of the "Petersberg tasks" defined by the Article 17.2 of the Amsterdam Treaty (Nowak 2006: 17). No study, however, has approached the rise of CCM through the lenses of its conceptual evolution, and the resulting diffusion of norms and practices across EU member states. The genesis of CCM has been largely neglected or superficially regarded as a way to avoid the militarisation of the CSDP and draw a line between NATO and the EU's roles in global security. Although these factors have undoubtedly paved the way for the evolution of European security cooperation towards a non-military or civil-military approach, there is still no clear understanding of the drivers that have influenced EU member states' decision to move into this direction. This is a rather paradoxical situation given the prominence of civilian missions over military operations in CSDP.[16] Between 2003 and 2015, the EU has launched 32 operations and missions, 21 of which are civilian. As of 2016, 11 out of 16 ongoing CSDP operations are civilian, comprising 2,650 personnel deployed in theatre (Tardy 2015: 23). Previous works have mentioned, usually through a few introductory lines, the origins of EU CCM at the 1999 Cologne Council, propelled by policy failure over the Western Balkans and, in particular, by the trouble encountered by the United Nations Interim Administration Mission in Kosovo (UNMIK), NATO's Kosovo Force (KFOR) and the OSCE Mission in Kosovo (OMIK) to ensure peacebuilding in Kosovo. However, the processes through which policy failure turned into policy evolution, and hence the way non-military crisis management was adopted by EU policy-makers, lacked any systematic explanation.

Contextual factors and changes in the post-Cold War global security environment generated a momentum for non-military crisis management to become accepted as a key issue in the security policies of EU member states. The awareness that peacekeeping should go beyond the borders of military intervention spread rather fast. By the mid-1990s, an international policy consensus and convergence appeared on the need for more comprehensive, coordinated civil-military planning and intervention in crisis situations (Duke and Courtier 2010). The *Charter of Paris* (OSCE 1990) can be considered as the key document showing for the first time the relationship between the end of the Cold War and the implications for the future course of global security.

Systemic pressure alone would not have been enough to create the urgency for EU's involvement in civilian crisis management arising in the early 2000s. Focusing on cooperation between the EU and the UN,

Thierry Tardy (2011) argues that a fundamental reshuffle of the international security architecture, security governance actors and methods after the end of the Cold War led to the emergence of regionalisation—that is, international organisations that aspire to play a role in the security realm at a regional level. As a response to UN's inappropriateness or ineffectiveness in maintaining international peace (cf. policy failure in Rwanda, Bosnia, Somalia and Timor Este during the 1990s) the transformation of the EU into a regional peacekeeper was initiated by member states as a way to "overcome the rising distrust vis-à-vis UN crisis management" (Tardy 2011: 13). In addition to the EC's involvement in areas such as post- conflict recovery and humanitarian aid, the "CSDP increasingly engaged in peacebuilding and, in particular, CCM" (Tardy 2011: 16).

The internal politics of EU and its member states also pushed the EU towards civilian crisis management (Dwan 2002). The creation of an EU military rapid reaction force caused consternation to three overlapping constituencies: the neutral states (Austria, Ireland, Finland and Sweden), concerned about the prospects of military alignment that could follow the commitment to an EU military capacity; the smaller member states, fearing that a military *directoire* of bigger powers (Britain, France, Germany) would control the fate of the EU security and defence policy; and the anti-federalists (Denmark, the UK) willing to counterbalance the push towards military integration (Dwan 2002). For instance, the creation of the Civilian Military Cell—and its contribution to developing EU civil-military coordination—is explained by Quille (2006) an identity-driven struggle between Atlanticists and Integrationists over the EU's autonomy in defence planning and conduct (the autonomous operational HQ), particularly following the April 2003 initiative in Tervuren.

The CSDP's civilian identity can therefore be understood as a by-product of the controversy surrounding EU-NATO relationship and the degree of autonomy/complementarity of the newly created EU military identity. Combining civilian and military power in crisis management, however, cannot be seen as the sheer result of a package deal between member states' diverging national interests and visions of EU defence. The driving ideas behind civilian CSDP were rooted in the belief that the EU was better equipped than NATO to handle post-conflict reconstruction, namely in the Western Balkans (Chivvis 2010: 5).

Certainly, the strategic debate on the nature of EU power cannot be entirely neglected. According to Gross (2008: 9), the EU's comprehensive set of military, political and economic tools justifies the effort to put into practice the link between security and development and combine civilian and military instruments to meet the growing demand of civil-military planning.

In sum, the development of civilian aspects of crisis management in CFSP was "heavily reactive in nature" (Duke 2008: 90). Reactiveness can be interpreted in three ways. First, the need to respond to existing crisis situations, such as Kosovo. Second, the presence of inter-institutional forces (cf. EU-UN and EU-NATO relations) at play that shaped the way the EU built its identity in relationship to other international organisations. Third, the existence of a linkage between the internal politics (and cultures) of member states and the search for a common vision for CSDP, which ultimately enhanced civilian and civil-military structures and instruments for the conduct of crisis management.

5.2.1   The Rise of the EU as a Civilian Crisis Manager: Framework, Institutions and Capabilities

Since the beginning of its security and defence policy, the EU has been involved in the development of a civilian crisis management concept under the legal framework of Article 17.2 of the Treaty of the European Union (TEU): "*Questions referred to in this Article shall include humanitarian and rescue tasks, peacekeeping tasks and tasks of combat forces in crisis management, including peacemaking*".

The Lisbon Treaty has amended Article 17 TEU and the new formulation is now included in the Articles 28 A [42] and B [43] (cf. Table 5.2).

The EU involvement in civilian crisis management is distinctive and different from any other international organisation. First, the EU activities in crisis management and peacebuilding are divided into first-pillar Community actions and second-pillar civilian and military crisis management, with different actors, budget procedures and policies. Accordingly, the structures and resources for CCM are physically located both within the Community and the Council Secretariat and do not conform to the purely intergovernmental method of military crisis management.

Second, and unlike NATO or the OSCE, the EU has clearly declared its ambition to develop both military and civilian capabilities to support a comprehensive approach. Therefore, besides the adoption of a Civil-Military Co-operation (CIMIC) concept to ensure coordination with external actors (IGOs and NGOs) in EU-led operations, the Civil-Military Coordination concept (CMCO)[17] was produced to ensure effective internal coordination "of the actions of all relevant EU actors involved in the

Table 5.2 Extract from Art. 28 of the Treaty of Lisbon, the "Petersberg tasks"

"The common security and defence policy shall be an integral part of the common foreign and security policy. It shall provide the Union with an operational capacity drawing on civilian and military assets. The Union may use them on missions outside the Union for peace-keeping, conflict prevention and strengthening international security in accordance with the principle of the United Nations Charter (...)" {Art. 28 A [42(1)]}

"Member States shall make civilian and military capabilities available to the Union for the implementation of the common security and defence policy, to contribute to the objectives defined by the Council" {Art. 28 A [42(3)]}

"The tasks referred to in Article 28 A(1) [42(1)], in the course of which the Union may use civilian and military means, shall include joint disarmament operations, humanitarian and rescue tasks, military advice and assistance tasks, conflict prevention and peacekeeping tasks, tasks of combat forces in crisis management, including peace-making and post-conflict stabilisation (...)" {Art. 28 B [43(1)]}

planning and subsequent implementation of the EU's response to the crisis"[18] (Khol 2006). When accounting for the institutional genesis and evolution of CCM,[19] it is therefore important to bear in mind the broader civil-military developments, which are closely related to and often overlap with the question of purely civilian capacity-building.

The rise of CCM was characterised initially by three elements: under-thematisation, conceptual looseness and rapidity. First, the EU CCM was neither a policy priority, nor was it in the limelight of academic and media debates. In fact, while the Saint Malo Declaration and the proposed creation of rapid reaction corps for autonomous EU capacity in crisis management received media attention, the significance and potential development of non-military crisis response tools passed almost unnoticed.

Second, civilian crisis management has for a long time been an ambiguous and not clearly defined concept, which has led to conceptual confusion in international peacekeeping. The first definition was provided in March 2002 by a special report of the British American Security Information Council (BASIC) (Nowak 2006; Ioannides 2010), defining civilian crisis management as: "the intervention by non-military personnel in a crisis that may be violent or non-violent, with the intention of preventing further escalation of the crisis and facilitating its resolution" (Lindborg 2002: 4).

Third, institutionalisation of crisis management (including its civilian facet) in the EU has been remarkably fast. Such rapidity was made possible by a number of facilitating factors (lessons from the collapse of Yugoslavia, the Anglo-French Saint Malo declaration), among which the institutional precedent—the WEU—provided the new crisis-management structures with consolidated practices and experiences (Duke 2008: 76).

Contrary to what is commonly reported, the inception of the EU's CCM was not the Cologne Summit (June 1999), but, two years earlier, the inclusion of the Petersberg Tasks in the Amsterdam Treaty (signed on October 1997), as a result of the Swedish-Finnish initiative during the intergovernmental conference in 1996–1997. The initiative, which led to the adoption of the Article 17.2 TEU, was aimed at providing the Union with the tools to carry out peace support operations, arising from the realisation that the EU could not stand powerlessly in the event of situations like the violent conflicts that erupted in the Balkans.

At the Cologne Summit, one month after the entry into force of the Amsterdam Treaty, the European Council decided to mandate the upcoming Finnish Presidency to address non-military crisis management, besides the work undergoing on the military side. A "Security Working Group" (SWG) was tasked to deal with this question and produced a list of the existing instruments at the Union level, in cooperation with the Council Secretariat, the Commission and member states.[20] The result of this was an inventory of non-military crisis response instruments available in EU member states forwarded to Delegations on November 24, 1999.[21] As an example, Table 5.3 shows the list of pre-existing structures, instruments and expertise of civil police in some of the EU member states:

These inventories served as the basis for the *Action Plan for non-military crisis management* of the EU subsequently adopted by the December 1999 Helsinki European Council,[22] and designed to indicate the steps the Union should undertake to develop a rapid reaction capacity in the field of non-military crisis management. The Action Plan identified three objectives for the Union's approach to CCM:

- Strengthening the synergy and responsiveness of national, collective and NGO resources in order to avoid duplication and improve performance (…);
- Enhancing and facilitating the EU's contribution to, and activities within, other organisations, such as the UN and the OSCE whenever one of them is the lead organisation in a particular crisis, as well as EU autonomous action;
- Ensuring inter-pillar coherence.[23]

To that purpose, three tools were foreseen:

- An inventory of national and collective resources, to give an overview of resources that could be marshalled within a rapid reaction framework (…). In this process member states and the EU

Table 5.3 Non-military crisis management tools available in EU member states in the field of civilian police (1999)[a]

EU member state	Tools and resources available (Civil Police)
DK	Denmark participates in civilian police missions implemented by the UN, OSCE, WEU, as well as other multilateral and bilateral operations. Denmark at present participates in international missions with approximately 80 police officers (of whom 68 are deployed in various missions in the Balkans—IPTF, UNIP, ECMM, PMG, and MAPE). 50 of these officers are permanently at the disposal for international operations and are registered with the UN Stand-by arrangement system
ES	At present, 42 members of the Spanish national police and 188 members of Guardia Civil are serving in missions under NNUU, NATO, OSCE, and WEU. Tasks involve monitoring of human rights violations, local police forces, refugee/displaced persons movements, as well as control and police tasks of refugee camps, borders and embargoes
IR	Irish police have a long tradition of service as civpols in UN missions and have participated in a number of OSCE and EU missions. Coreu DUB109 sets out the position regarding the training of police officers in Ireland for such missions
IT	Italy has a territorial police, a state police and a custom police, which are autonomous forces that can and have been employed in crisis management. A school of advanced police studies offers two "stages" yearly to form around 70 international police trainers. This facility is at the disposal of international organisations (i.a. the EU)
NL	A total of around 70 military police officers from the Netherlands are currently deployed in various crisis regions, mainly in Bosnia-Herzegovina in IPTF, and some in Albania (MAPE). A group of civil police officers has been deployed on an ad hoc basis in crisis regions (e.g. forensic experts assisting the Rwanda Tribunal or the ICTY). The Government is currently looking into ways to enhance its capacity to deploy civil police in crisis regions to assist in the establishment of structures for democratic policing as an integral part of peace building
AUS	Long-standing experience for forces for international (especially UN) missions; for training: see coreu VIE 350/99
P	National civil police force (Polícia de Segurança Pública—PSP—depending on the Ministry of Internal Affairs) has been participating in international police missions (monitoring human rights and local police forces, refugee/displaced movements) humanitarian assistance to refugees, local police training, police counselling and consulting, voters registration and election monitoring
FIN	A rostrum of trained civilian police (CIVPOL) available. 110 trained experts in reserve. 16 civilian police at the moment in field operations (UN, OSCE, and WEU)

(continued)

Table 5.3   (continued)

EU member state	Tools and resources available (Civil Police)
SW	Currently about 180 Swedish police in international missions: 148 in UN, OSCE or WEU missions (IPTF, UNMIK, UNAMET, PMG, and MAPE).
	Before departure, training at the Swedish Armed Forces International Command (SWEDINT). Also bilateral missions (e.g. support for legal sector in Central and Eastern Europe).
	Responsibility currently shared between National Police Force and Swedish Armed Forces. Government proposal forthcoming that National Police Board takes a collective responsibility for all international police activity and creates a Foreign Force within the Police Force

ªSource: Council of the European Union (1999b: 3–4)

institutions could, if they wished, highlight sectors in which they find that they have acknowledged expertise;
– A database to maintain and share information on the pre-identified assets, capabilities and expertise within all areas relevant to non-military crisis management;
– A study taking into account lessons learned, to define concrete targets for EU Member States' collective non-military responses to international crises (e.g. the ability to deploy at short notice and sustain for a defined period a set number of civilian police as a contribution to civpol missions; to deploy a combined search and rescue capability of up to 200 people within twenty-four hours).[24]

The purpose of these three tools was to identify areas of relative strength and weakness to improve training standards, sharing of experience and best practices, as well as bilateral or multilateral projects between member states.[25]

The *Action Plan*, in turn, paved the way for the work undertaken by the Portuguese Presidency on the development of the CSDP civilian capabilities. In accordance with the recommendations contained in the Helsinki Presidency Report, the work of the Portuguese Presidency largely relied on the study that drew on "experience from recent and current crises, on the expertise of the Member States and on the results of the seminar on civilian crisis management in Lisbon on 3–4 April 2000", and "carried out to define concrete targets in the area of civilian aspects of crisis management".[26] The study concluded that four priority areas should constitute the bulk of EU civilian crisis management: police, rule of law, civilian administration and civil protection. It gave priority to the development of rapid reaction response capabilities "fully taking into account, and building upon, existing experiences, instruments and resources".[27]

The rationale for choosing these areas reflected a concern to pay particular attention to the fields where "the international community so far has demonstrated weaknesses", which hence would "provide added value as it would improve the Union's capacity to react as well as the Union's capability to meet the requests of the other lead organisations: they would be able to count—on a more systematic basis—on a sizeable quantitative and qualitative contribution which could represent the nucleus of some of their missions. This would, in turn, increase the Union's visibility".[28]

Therefore, capacity-building relied on the expertise made available by member states. Civilian police and, to a lesser extent, rule of law assumed a leading role in improving EU crisis response capabilities. The targets for the police were set by the June 2000 Santa Maria da Feira European Council: 5,000 police officers should be available for international police missions, with 1,000 of them deployable within 30 days.

The Gothenburg Council (June 2001) later adopted a *Police Action Plan* to further develop the planning capacity of police operations at the strategic level. The presence in some of the member states of specialised police forces ready to be deployed[29] facilitated the task of capacity building. In addition, the Gothenburg Council set up the targets in the area of the rule of law, with a commitment to 200 experts to train, advise and in some cases carry out executive tasks when local structures are failing or non-existent. Targets and guidelines for civilian administration and civil protection were also set, although in a less precise and sustained way compared to the other two priority areas. Member states committed to provide a pool of experts for quick deployment in civilian administration missions across a variety of functions, with emphasis on the promotion of a swift transition to local ownership. Targets for civil protection included intervention teams of 2,000 personnel and assessment teams to support humanitarian assistance (handled by the Commission).

From this inception phase (1999–2001) onward, conceptual, institutional and operational aspects of CCM made significant progress, sustained by those member states that were already disposing of expertise in the civilian aspects of crisis management. Institution building went in parallel with the creation of military structures. By a Swedish initiative, in May 2000, the Committee for Civilian Aspects of Crisis Management

(Civcom), composed of officials from the Commission and the Council Secretariat, mid-ranking national diplomats and a number of police experts (Cross 2011: 187) was formally established by a Council decision (it met for the first time on June 16, 2000). Civcom was to advise the PSC and other Council's bodies on civilian crisis management matters, therefore in parallel with the work of the European Union Military Committee (EUMC) for military affairs.

These improvements need to be understood in relation to the efforts to implement more coherent civilian military co-ordination as well as to an evolutionary path characterised by intense learning by doing. It began with the planning of the first civilian mission, the EU Police Mission on Bosnia and Herzegovina (EUPM) in early 2002[30] (EUPM was launched on 1 January 2003, taking over from the UN International Police Task Force).

5.2.2   Civilian Crisis Management After Lisbon

The last wave of institutional change occurred with the Treaty of Lisbon, as a result of two growing trends affecting the development of EU crisis management. The first trend was the continuing dissolution of the border between civilian and military intervention, which required a consolidation of the hybrid structures and procedures to implement the comprehensive approach. The second one was the demand for more sophisticated expertise and specialisation in the conduct of crisis management tasks.

In an attempt to complement the restructuring of the EU external action through the creation of the European External Action Service (EEAS), the Lisbon Treaty tried to further enhance civil-military co-ordination by integrating the former DG VIII (military) and DG IX (civilian) into a single new directorate, the Crisis Management Planning Directorate (CMPD). The CMPD, the CPCC and the EUMS are now placed under the same roof (the EEAS) and the authority of the High Representative. The restructuring was supposed, in theory at least, to enhance a culture of integration.

Between 2003 and 2015, civilian crisis management has become a central part of the CSDP, in institutional, conceptual, strategic and operational terms. Because of the expanding geographical and thematic reach, number of personnel deployed, growing complexity and scale of missions and institutional/conceptual innovation, CCM can be defined as the "ugly duckling" of CSDP: neglected at its origins and often overshadowed by the military debate, it constitutes nonetheless the bulk of the EU's role as a global security provider.

5.3 CONCLUSION

This chapter challenged the conventional wisdom on SSR and CCM on two grounds. First, it showed that the creation of an EU policy framework for SSR was more than a simple re-labelling of previous European Commission activities in post-conflict environments; as a matter of fact, framing SSR meant putting a wide range of sectoral and sub-sectoral activities under the same roof, with a specific emphasis on the holistic approach.

Second, as regards CCM, the chapter showed the existence of expertise and know-how, provided by member states, alongside a process of capacity-building. Accordingly it elucidated the relation between the conceptual efforts aimed at producing a CCM framework, and the expansion of structures and activities over time.

The following two chapters will explore the role of learning communities in shaping the evolution of SSR and CCM, moving from the conceptual framework to institutionalised and systematic practices.

NOTES

1. They include military, police and intelligence agencies, ministries, parliament, civil society organisations, judicial and criminal prosecution borders, paramilitary groups. Cf. ENTRi (2013: 81).
2. As regards SSR, the *Report on the implementation of the European Security Strategy* (2008: 8) states "Conflict is often linked to state fragility. Countries like Somalia are caught in a vicious cycle of weak governance and recurring conflict. We have sought to break this, both through development assistance and measures to ensure better security. Security Sector Reform and Disarmament, Demobilisation and Reintegration are a key part of post-conflict stabilisation and reconstruction (...)".
3. See, for instance, the bulk of the academic literature in the UK, which emphasises the role of DFID as the godfather of SSR and the central focus of this policy in poverty alleviation, hence upholding the view that development incorporated security concerns (and not vice-versa).
4. Cf. Schnabel and Ehrhart (2005), Brzoska and Heinemann-Gruder (2004). Cf. also the documents produced by the Geneva Centre for the Democratic Control of Armed Forces (DCAF).

5. Brussels and Geneva Interviews, (Summer/Winter 2011).
6. The Commission was among the signatories of the OSCE 1999 *Charter for European Security* and during the 1990s EU officials met regularly (both at the ministerial and lower levels) with OSCE colleagues to discuss common areas of action such as enlargement, stabilisation and association processes, ENP, the Western Balkans, South Caucasus etc. Similarly, the EU and its member states have traditionally provided support to UN agencies and programmes in fields that are now embedded in the SSR template.
7. DCAF (2009: 1).
8. *Ibid.*
9. OECD (2007: 5).
10. *Ibid.*
11. OECD (2001a: 35).
12. USAID, DOS, DOD (2009: 3).
13. These figures are drawn from a survey conducted by the Commission in the summer 2005, to map the past and current EC's activities in support of SSR related programmes in the period 2000–2005. The results are annexed to the EC Communication on Security Sector Reform of June 2006 (European Commission 2006).
14. The literature tends to downplay the WEU's engagement non-military missions before the transfer of its crisis management functions to the EU, particularly since, as noted by van Eekelen (2006) the WEU task of elaborating decisions concerning defence issues was, in its practical dimension, more often police-oriented than military. In this regard, it is worth reminding that, until 1995, Germany could not constitutionally contribute with military units to out-of-area operations: providing police, border-guards and custom officers was to a number of operations was then seen as a way to circumvent the problem (van Eekelen 2006: 117).
15. The draft concept document was produced by the Council Secretariat on the basis of a paper titled "Initial elements for an EU security sector reform concept" discussed by the Political and Security Committee (van Eekelen 2006: 113).
16. Such prominence reveals a striking (and unaccounted for) changing conception of CSDP, as at the time of policy creation member states intended to establish a European military capability in crisis management that would allow the Union to act independently from

NATO. This eventually changed as the value added of CSDP turned out to be civilian (Gross 2008: 314).

17. For a definition of CIMIC and CMCO, and the difference between the two concepts, see Khol (2006: 124).

18. Cf. Council of the European Union (2003).

19. When using the acronym CCM (whether preceded or not by EU) I refer to the civilian crisis management *framework* developed and used by the European Union only. When referring to the broader *concept* of civilian crisis management, also adopted by other international organisations, I will use the formulation "civilian crisis management", without acronym.

20. Cf. Council of the European Union (1999a: 2).

21. Cf. Council of the European Union (1999b).

22. Cf. Helsinki European Council (1999: 6).

23. *Ibid.* p. 6.

24. *Ibid.* p. 6.

25. *Ibid.* p. 7.

26. Santa Maria da Feira European Council (2000). Cf. also Nowak (2006: 19).

27. Santa Maria da Feira European Council (2000).

28. *Ibid.*

29. Gendarmerie-type forces were already present in France (*Gendarmerie Nationale*), Italy (*Arma dei Carabinieri*), Spain (*Guardia Civil*), The Netherlands (*Marechaussee*) and Portugal (*Guarda Nacional Republicana*).

30. The decision to deploy an EU police mission to Bosnia-Herzegovina was taken by the General Affairs Council on 18–19 February 2002.

CHAPTER 6

Learning Communities in EU Security Sector Reform

The EU developed the SSR framework to enhance its conflict prevention and post-conflict reconstruction capabilities, as well as to better address changing security threats. The learning process leading to an EU SSR policy was driven by transnational communities, who acted as agents of institutionalisation. Individuals belonging to these communities carried their expertise into the EU decision-making and mainstreamed a new security thinking based on the post-Cold War paradigm of human security and on the integration between security, development and good governance. EU SSR was hence a policy innovation process to enhance the Union's commitment as a security provider, by stressing the need for a holistic approach to security aimed at ensuring effective crisis management, conflict resolution and post-conflict reconstruction.

Three questions arise as to why, and how member states decided to institutionalise and operationalise the SSR guidelines, what influenced EU policy-makers choices and, finally, how a consensus on the

Some of the findings in this chapter were previously published as a book chapter in Dursun-Ozkanca, O. (ed) (2014) *The European Union as an Actor in Security Sector Reform*, Routledge (Chapter 2); and as an article in the special issue of *European Security* on "The European Union and Security Sector Reform: current practices and challenges of implementation": see Faleg, G. (2012) "Between knowledge and power: epistemic communities and the emergence of security sector reform in the EU security architecture", in *European Security*, 21:2, Routledge, April 2012.

© The Author(s) 2017
G. Faleg, *The EU's Common Security and Defence Policy*,
DOI 10.1007/978-3-319-41306-8_6

EU approach to SSR emerged and turned into a policy framework? A trickier question has to do with the outcomes of this diffusion process. Despite the growing recognition of the EU as a SSR provider, SSR programmes have been very far from ensuring effective implementation and a coherent management of the available mechanisms. Pure EU-led SSR missions have been few and low scale, with uneven or disappointing results in the field. SSR seems to suffer from a "firefly complex": whereas EU officials acknowledge its presence, the actual impact on institutional structures and procedures is hardly detectable when compared to other policies.

To address these questions, the chapter explores the pathways of influence triggering the dynamics of policy failure, policy paradigm innovation, emulation and learning (McNamara 1998; Adler and Haas 1992). It explains why the SSR framework did not generate learning by doing through systematic practice. Accordingly, the next section goes through the process of SSR formation and its diffusion in the EU, outlining the structure of learning communities and assessing SSR persistence. Section 6.2 discusses the EU's operational experience in the field of SSR. It shows that the lack of a fully developed SSR practice resulted in shortfalls in the learning process. The conclusion summarises the key challenges for the evolution of EU SSR in light of the empirical findings.[1]

Unpacking the construction of the EU approach to SSR bears two important normative implications. First, a deeper understanding of the genesis of SSR would allow us to better capture the distinct features of the EU's involvement, and achieve a more rigorous assessment of its SSR practices. This can positively contribute to identifying useful lessons to improve the coordination between EU external action instruments and procedures. Second, this exercise also sheds light on the complexities of the SSR concept and, potentially, clears up the confusion that obstructs effective international cooperation in this field. In fact, SSR activities take place in different contexts (transition and developing countries, post-conflict situation but also developed countries) and encompass a wide array of dimensions (defence, justice, development, governance etc.), making it difficult to delimit their conceptual and operational borders, and hence the division of tasks among international actors.

6.1 LEARNING COMMUNITIES AND EU SSR: BETWEEN KNOWLEDGE AND POWER

The EU SSR framework originates in policy failure and in an effort to merge different perspectives into a single *episteme*, prompting a holistic understanding of security, development and good governance. The conceptualisation of EU SSR was an attempt to gather different sub-communities in order to form, through socialisation and knowledge sharing, a new epistemic community of SSR. This attempt has been only partly successful. To account for this outcome as well as for the genesis of SSR as a process of learning, this section is structured in three parts:

1. the attempt to form an SSR epistemic community, bridging previously separated communities and building a new cognitive architecture;
2. the influence of the SSR concept on the CSDP, through the analysis of the four pathways of influence and intervening factors;
3. SSR policy outcomes, addressing whether the diffusion of ideas has led to policy evolution as learning by doing.

6.1.1 The Learning Communities of SSR

The conceptualisation and consolidation of security sector governance and reform have been influenced by three factors: first, a structural change in the nature and scale of conflicts characterising the post-Cold War period; second, the emergence of human security as a new thinking linking security to development and good governance; and third, the consequences of the traumatic experience of the conflicts in the Western Balkans, which eventually reinforced the need for a more coherent and integrated approach to security including civilian and military aspects.

Linked to these major systemic events, three epistemic communities flourished in the 1990s: the security policy community, the development cooperation community, and the one dealing with the promotion of democracy, good governance and justice. Although the three communities had varied discourses and slightly different focuses and causal beliefs, their policy enterprise was based on the common assumption that a well governed and transparent security sector and/or system is a key factor to ensure socio-economic development, conflict prevention and peacebuilding.

The genesis of SSR is deep-rooted into the interaction between these three communities. Security sector governance and reform are in fact bridging concepts joining distinct fields of expertise and, as a consequence, experts who are not used to talking to each other. Therefore, when the need for a holistic approach to crisis management and conflict prevention began making headway at the international stage, the idea of integrating security/development/good governance into a single policy framework was advocated by untied networks of individuals, who did not necessarily share the same view on the terms of this integrative process. As a result, much of the efforts that underlie the promotion of SSR were aimed at addressing the cleavages between independent epistemic communities, by having people sit around the table in view of setting up expert consensus around the new norms.

The Security/Defence Community

Since the end of the Cold War, the concept of security has widened and deepened. Systemic factors led to the proliferation of failing states and intrastate wars, entailing the progressive blurring of the boundaries between external and internal security. Declining military expenditures and downsizing state armies (SIPRI Yearbook 2006) also played an important role in opening a window of opportunity for a change to the old notion of security. In practical terms, this meant understanding peacekeeping as going beyond military intervention, leading to a blossoming debate on civil-military relations and, at a later stage, on governance issues as well. As non-military security issues (i.e. political, economic, judicial and societal aspects) were adopted by the global security agenda, the practices of IOs switched towards a comprehensive approach tackling a wide range of activities within the broader security sector (Hänggi and Tanner 2005). The endorsement of the United Nations Development Program (UNDP) notion of human security, encompassing the broader and non-military nature of security concerns (UNDP 1994), spurred the affirmation of the security-development nexus (Williams 2002; Chandler 2007) as the absolute protagonist of the peacebuilding discourse.

As a result, a new thinking regarding security emerged during the 1990s (Barbé 1995) and can be divided into three major strands. First, the call for democratic control of armed forces as well as oversight of the defence sector and, to a broader extent, of the whole spectrum of security forces, emerged. These norms were first adopted by the OSCE in the

1994 *Code of Conduct on Politico-Military Aspects of Security*, followed by the *Charter for European Security* agreed at the OSCE Istanbul Summit in November 1999. A second major strand was connected with NATO's emphasis on civil-military relations during the enlargement process to the post-Communist countries of Eastern Europe. The promotion of defence and security sector reform was one of NATO's central goals in the post-Soviet, new NATO candidate countries. Therefore, NATO became the first and most active provider of external assistance in SSR (though with a different label) under the Partnership for Peace (PfP) framework launched in 1994. A third strand of the debate, connected to the previous two but less transnational in focus, centred on the "new defence diplomacy" implemented by Western governments to ensure conflict prevention and stable relationships with other countries through bilateral and multilateral agreements, in order to make armed forces democratic and accountable. Members of the security/defence policy community were military and civilian staff from the Ministries of Defence, diplomats and officers seconded to security organisations (mostly NATO and OSCE) and the network of strategic studies institutes (academia and think-tanks) dealing with defence matters.

The Development Cooperation Community
A new paradigm also developed in the development discourse, stressing that security and stability, including the transformation of ineffective, inefficient and corrupt security forces, would become a necessary pre-requisite for development and aid delivery (Abrahamsen and Williams 2006). The security-development nexus stimulated multilateral and bilateral donors to embrace SSR as an instrument to improve the effectiveness of development assistance. Development experts and practitioners acknowledged that the foundation for sustainable development is in the capacity to address the root causes of conflict, hence integrating development aid with a new hybrid sphere of intervention called "post-conflict peacebuilding".

In May 1997, OECD countries' Development Ministers issued the *Policy Statement on Conflict, Peace and Development Co-operation on the Threshold of the twenty-first Century*, stressing that the "development co-operation efforts should strive for an environment of 'structural stability' as a basis for sustainable development (…), embracing mutually reinforcing objectives of social peace, respect for human rights, accountable military forces and broadly-shared social and economic development" (OECD 1997: 2).

This first policy statement initiated the process leading to the adoption of the OECD guidelines, which set the standards for SSR implementation and mainstream the security-development nexus into the development discourse. European donor states headed by the United Kingdom and operating under the institutional umbrella of the EU, were the first to embrace the concept, concerned about the effectiveness of their development policies in post-conflict situations and with significant impact on their policy preferences (Sabiote 2010). Much of the debate initially revolved around military spending: that is, on the way governments would be expected to control and administer the security sector and the difficulties in managing the accountability of institutions. The enlargement of the Euro-Atlantic institutions as well as the "baptism by fire" (Ginsberg 2001) for the EU in the Western Balkans dramatically accelerated the development and diffusion of the security-development nexus. The EU and NATO's support to the transition from authoritarian rule in Eastern Europe empirically demonstrated that good governance in the rule of law and defence sectors are crucial for sustainable economic and social development. The link between development and security became mainstream in the Balkans as well (Spence and Fluri 2008). The EU's South-eastern neighbourhood, pretty much like the Eastern, was composed of states having serious deficits in security, development and democracy, with regime types ranging from new but weak democracies to regimes with authoritarian features and limited political participation (Hänggi and Tanner 2005). The challenge for European donors was to prevent conflicts in the Balkans from undermining their own security, and to ensure the effectiveness of the stabilisation mechanisms (i.e. the Stability Pact for South Eastern Europe).

The Genesis of SSR

Against this backdrop, the conceptual roots of SSR are twofold. First, they arise from what was described as a "developmentalisation" of donor countries' security discourse.[2] The increasing influence of the development community in security affairs was aimed at emphasising transparency, comprehensiveness and a system-wide approach to the establishment of good governance starting from the security sector. Second, a "securitisation" of the development assistance also came about.[3] This process sought to make aid and state building more effective in the long-term, by integrating the conflict-peace-development agenda and reduce the security threats associated with state failures. Mainstreaming the security-development nexus and achieving a whole-of-government approach to SSR is therefore a complex process of knowledge formation, whereby security and development experts came to talk to each other intensively, in order to strengthen linkages between the two communities, produce consensus over the trajectories of policy change and instil a culture of integration.

This peculiar structure of SSR communities is reflected in their shape and extension. First, no institutionalised body has been tasked with advancing the SSR agenda transnationally, yet SSR actors are easily identifiable and in many cases receive strong financial and political support from Governments. SSR experts were very likely to be affiliated or associated, if not employed in, a relatively small batch of organisations. Second, expertise does not overlap with practice: there are no pre-existing, shared experiences within the same or contiguous organisational unit (a network of professionals) that generate a change of habitus. SSR practitioners generally deny having been involved in a working relationship with SSR professionals before the term "SSR" was created, as shown by differences in their backgrounds, in the jargon used and in their professional output.[4] Working routines were restricted to the defence or development community, with very few individuals operating in the middle-ground and no or a very poor sense of belonging among individuals committed to advance SSR principles. Experts working for DFID had a radically different view of the subject matter than those working for EPLO. Similarly, their account of the origins of SSR as more security or defence-focused differed substantially. A "wall" had to be torn down between the vision of SSR as strictly relating to the defence sector and a more systemic understanding, which should take into account development as well as good governance challenges and closer inter-institutional cooperation.[5]

The SSR genesis is therefore associated with a new vision of a specific social reality, namely the idea that the security sector or system is crucial to improve donors' operational outreach. Practitioners describe the relationship with other SSR experts as the explicit attempt to forge a new understanding of things, beyond the simple sharing of knowledge. Intense collaboration took place from the early-2000s among the individuals belonging to the organisations in all the five areas listed in the table. Individuals met frequently during conferences and seminars organised or co-organised by these institutions. Their participation in conferences is associated with the objective of promoting a mutual understanding, aimed at the achievement of a common policy goal. Table 6.1 shows the participants' list to four selected conferences on SSR that took place between

Table 6.1 SSR conferences 2005–2007

The EU and security sector reform (3–4 May 2007, Stockholm)	Security sector governance and reform: a challenge for the European Union (30 September 2005, Brussels)	Coordination or confusion? The integration of security and development in EU policy (29 November 2005, Brussels)	Security sector reform in peacebuilding: towards an EU-UN partnership (28 June 2006, Brussels)
Organiser: DCAF Venue: Swedish National Defence College	Organiser: DCAF Venue: CEPS	Organisers: Egmont Institute (Brussels), International Peace Information Service (IPIS, Antwerp) and DCAF Venue: Chateau de Val Duchesse, Brussels	Organisers: DCAF, EPC, King Badouin Foundation Venue: Residence Palace, Brussels
Expert Defence (DCAF) Scholar Security/Defence (Bristol University) EU Official (European Commission) Expert Security (EPC) Diplomat (SNDC) UN Official (UN, Disarmament Affairs) Expert Defence (Defence Academy of the UK, Conflict Studies Res. Centre) EU Official (Deputy Director General for Political and Military Affairs, Council EU) Former Minister Defence (The Netherlands)	Expert Defence (DCAF) Diplomat (EU PSC) Expert Defence (DCAF) Expert Defence (DCAF) Expert Security (GCSP) Expert Defence (EU ISS) NATO Official (NATO PA) Expert Security (CEPS)	Expert Defence (Egmont) Expert Defence (IPIS) Scholar Development (Oxford) Expert Development (German Development Institute) Expert Development (Sussex IDS) Expert Security/ Defence (DCAF) EU Official (DG RELEX, European Commission) EU Official (EUMS)	Expert Security (EPC) Expert Defence (DCAF) EU Official (UN DPKO) EU Official (EUSR) Expert Defence (DCAF) EU Official (Council EU)

2005 and 2007, gathering experts and officials with different backgrounds (security and development). Table 6.2 provides a list of the institutions that form the epistemic communities of SSR, divided into five areas: (1) Education/Research (University departments, think-tanks, research institutes); (2) Government (Ministries, Agencies, national defence colleges); (3) Training centres; (4) NGOs; (5) IOs (and related bodies).[6]

Table 6.2   SSR epistemic communities

Institution	Sector	Country	Function
Scuola Superiore Sant'Anna	1, 3	Italy	Training
Netherlands Institute of International Relations—Clingendael	1	The Netherlands	Research, consultancy, training
European Union Institute for Security Studies	5	–	Research
European Peacebuilding Liaison Office	4	–	Advocacy network
Austrian Study Center for Peace and Conflict Resolution	1	Austria	Research, training
Institute for Peace Support and Conflict Management—National Defence Academy	2	Austria	Research, training, political advice
UK Department for International Development (DFID)	2	UK	Government
Global Facilitation Network for Security Sector Reform	1	UK	Research, advocacy, knowledge sharing
Conflict, Security and Development Group—King's College London	1	UK	Knowledge sharing, research
Geneva Centre for the Democratic Control of Armed Forces	1, 5	Switzerland	Training, research, advocacy, knowledge sharing
International Security Sector Advisory Team	1,3	Switzerland	Training, mentoring, networking
Association for Security Sector Reform Education and Training	1, 3	Switzerland	Training, capacity building, networking
Geneva Centre for Security Policy	1	Switzerland	Research, training
OECD—International Network on Conflict and Fragility (INCAF), previously Conflict Prevention and Development Co-operation Network (CPDC)	5	–	Advisory, networking, Decision-making
Zentrum für Internationale Friedenseinsätze	3	Germany	Training
German Institute for International and Security Affairs	1	Germany	Research
Folke Bernadotte Academy	3	Sweden	Training
Crisis Management Centre	3	Finland	Training
Swedish National Defence College	2	Sweden	Research and development
Deparment of Peace and Conflict Research, Uppsala University	1	Sweden	Research, education

(*continued*)

Table 6.2 (continued)

Institution	Sector	Country	Function
Swedish International Development Cooperation Agency	2	Sweden	Government— Development co-operation
Forum Syd	4	Sweden	International development cooperation, research and advocacy
Saferworld	4	UK	Research, consultancy, advocacy
EU—Council Secretariat EEAS, EUSRs, EUMS, EUMC, CMPD, CPCC, CIVCOM, PMG, PSC	5	EU	International organisation
European Security and Defence College	3	EU wide	Training
EU—Member States Ministries of Foreign Affairs, Ministries of Defence, DGs Development Co-operation, Ministries of Justice, Ministries of Interior	2	Sweden, Finland, Denmark, Germany, Italy, Netherlands, France, Portugal, United Kingdom, Austria	Government
European Centre for Development Policy Management	1	Netherlands, Belgium	International development think and do tank
Overseas Development Institute	1	UK	Research
NATO	5	–	International organisation
OSCE—Organisation for Security and Cooperation in Europe	5	–	International organisation
Crisis Management Initiative	4	Finland	Advocacy
International Alert	4	UK	NGO, advocacy
International Crisis Group	4	–	NGO, research, advocacy
Council Secretariat DG-E External	5	–	*IGO*
High Representative's Office	5	–	*IGO*
DG RELEX	2	–	*EU—Policy-making*
Downing Street	2	UK	*Government*
UK Foreign Secretary's Cabinet	2	UK	*Government*
Foreign Office's Security Branch	2	UK	*Government*
UK PR (PSC Ambassador)	2	UK	*Government*
UK Foreign Office's CFSP Unit	2	UK	*Government*
UK Defence Ministry's Policy Staff	2	UK	*Government—Military*
UK Defence Ministry's EU/NATO Division	2	UK	*Government—Military*

6.1.2   The Dynamics of SSR Diffusion: Does Knowledge Matter?

This section explains how the EU elaborated its approach to SSR in the mid-2000s, showing that a set of constituencies (the UK and other member states; the OECD) backed it up, and that the creation of a policy consensus emerged from policy failure, emulation and innovation.

The rise of SSR in the EU was expert-driven. Specifically, it relied on the elaboration of the *OECD-DAC Guidelines on Security System Reform and Governance*, published since 2004 (OECD 2004), and on the *Handbook on Security System Reform* (OECD 2007), which served as a vehicle for the "multilateralisation" of the EU variant of SSR (Albrecht et al. 2010). It is therefore crucial to understand how the OECD guidelines were developed and framed and what were the flows of influence and networks involved in different phases of policy innovation, diffusion, selection, persistence and evolution. SSR conceptual foundations are rooted in the attempt to forge a Europe-wide policy consensus that emerged gradually among national think-tankers, political actors, pressure groups, research centres and NGOs belonging to the security and development communities.

Policy Innovation, Selection, Diffusion and Emulation
Learning from policy failure, national epistemic communities from major aid donors provided the boost for policy innovation. The UK communities were in the frontline of this development, supported by the British government.[7] Actually, British policy-makers did not reinvent the wheel when launching the SSR agenda in 1998/1999. Tony Blair's—and the Labour Party's—internationalist agenda relabelled and reformulated concepts that had already been introduced in the policy arena (including the EU and the European Commission) but lacked a comprehensive policy framework and, most importantly, could not get enough drive to spread transnationally. It is therefore important not to overemphasise the role of the UK as the pioneer of SSR, but to stress the fact that specific ideas and norms already circulating in the international system were picked up and reframed as part of a broader agenda sustained by EU member states. The UK advanced the SSR agenda first at the national level, then through the OECD DAC forum before SSR norms reached the EU, at a crucial stage where comprehensive and civilian crisis management principles were gaining ground.

The vision of SSR as a new instrument for the foreign/security policy of donor countries was laid out by Clare Short, the UK Secretary of State for International Development, through a policy statement in

March 1999. Short's understanding of future SSR activities reflected an emerging government-wide consensus on a new rationale for increasing foreign-security-development policies coordination, as a result of recent experiences in developing countries such as Cambodia or Sierra Leone.

The Department for International Development (DFID) got that vision off the ground (Hendrickson 2000). The UK's role as a promoter of SSR relied on a tight network of expert communities, who were tasked with assisting the wider overhaul of DFID's humanitarian policies, procedures and organisational structures. This process started with the creation, in April 1998, of the Conflict and Humanitarian Affairs Department (CHAD). CHAD replaced the Emergency Aid Department and its action was aimed at monitoring and providing advice to DFID on conflict prevention, peacebuilding, human rights and migration, as well as to liaise with government departments and conflict departments of other governments, NGOs and academic groups (Gibbons 1998). It is within CHAD's institutional framework that SSR policies started to be addressed as a tool to increase effective implementation of the security-development nexus. Shortly after the creation of CHAD, DFID commissioned a number of research projects to further develop the SSR agenda. Among these projects, a paper written by Nicole Ball for *Saferworld* and funded by DFID, titled *Spreading Good Practices in Security Sector Reform: Policy Options for the British Government* (Ball 1998) was published in March 1998 and steered the definition of an UK approach to SSR.

Another important step towards concept-building was the establishment of the Conflict, Security and Development Group (CSDG) at King's College London in 1999, supported by a three-year grant awarded by DFID. The rationale for the establishment of the CSDG was to examine policy challenges associated with the linkage between security-development and good governance, and to provide support to the UK's government policy development in the field of SSR and conflict prevention. Neither DFID, nor the Ministry of Defence (MoD) had in fact sufficient capacity/ expertise to deal with the emerging SSR/good governance agenda and thus needed to rely on external advice to set up a coherent policy framework.

In February 2000, a DFID-sponsored symposium on security sector reform and military expenditure constituted the first attempt to mainstream SSR across the development and security communities. It served also as an opportunity for Claire Short to announce the DFID-CSDG joint initiative to create an information network, in order to enhance the sharing of information and analysis (Short 2000).

As a result, in the first semester of 2000, DFID commissioned CSDG to produce a set of security-sector assistance guidelines identifying the ways in which development assistance could help countries strengthen their security-sector governance and pointing out the ways in which DFID itself, the Foreign and Commonwealth Office (FCO) and the MoD could find synergies (Hendrickson 2000). By allocating funds to networks such as the GSDG, DFID promoted knowledge-sharing and gathered expertise on SSR that subsequently fed back into DFID structures and triggered policy development.

The Global Facilitation Network for Security Sector Reform (GFN-SSR) was another DFID-funded initiative. Initially hosted by Cranfield University and subsequently managed by the University of Birmingham, the GFN occupied a prominent position in promoting SSR. The epistemic mission of the GFN is stated in the network's principal aims listed in the website: to "promote a better understanding of security and justice sector reform through the provision of information, advice and expertise to practitioners, academics and policy-makers through the world". The FCO also defined the objective of the network as "to provide knowledge management and network-facilitation services to an international network of SSR practitioners".

The role of the DFID in SSR shows that the formation of consensual knowledge to diffuse transnationally depends upon national backup. There is an overwhelming agreement that the UK is a leader in the field of SSR, and DFID is described as the "Godfather of SSR", exerting a significant influence on *fora* such as the OECD DAC and the UNDP (Sudgen 2006).

Other EU member states jumped on the bandwagon. The Netherlands became involved in the development of SSR to enhance civil-military cooperation. In the early 2000s, close cooperation between the Dutch Ministry of Foreign Affairs and the Clingendael Institute produced an intense exchange of information allowing decision-makers to understand how to take up and implement SSR-related policies. In 2004 an SSR team located in the Ministry of Foreign Affairs and composed of one expert from the Ministry of Foreign Affairs and one from the Ministry of Defence was established. The team was tasked with identifying specific SSR activities that Ministries could be involved in, such as training, policy support and the provision of material/infrastructures (Ball and Hendrickson 2009). In January 2005, a development advisor was seconded to the Ministry of Defence after a pool of some 30 military SSR specialists was created within the same Ministry. The pool also included highly qualified staff in the field of policy, judicial issues, finance, logistics etc. Germany also started promoting a holistic approach to SSR, although more focused on internal security structures (Albrecht et al. 2010).

In parallel with the creation of the Western-based networks, an African effort to conceptualise SSR according to the developing countries' perspectives led to the creation of the African Security Sector Network (ASSN), initially supported by South Africa, Ghana and Nigeria. The institutionalisation of a regional network on the recipients' side promoted the debate among African parliamentarians, military officers, and policy analysts leading to SSR norm development and feeding back into the reflexion taking place at the donors' level.

How do these norms convey into the EU security architecture? SSR policy diffusion and persistence within the EU institutional framework (CSDP/Commission) see networks come into play in addition to existing national constituencies, through emulation processes. The OECD-DAC, and in particular its Conflict Prevention and Development Co-operation Network (CPDC)[8] was a leading cross-national forum for epistemic communities to sit around the table and share their views on SSR. As a matter of fact, the UK (and DFID in particular), following the conclusion to the February 2000 symposium on security sector reform, increased its contribution to the DAC in order to shape the international agenda and influence other member states. So did the Netherlands and other interested donors. This resulted in the expansion of the CPDC's mandate and in the recruitment of new consultants.

Chaired by the DFID Senior SSR adviser, the CPDC's *modus operandi* was designed to forge a common, transnational understanding of the security-development nexus through the adoption of standardised guidelines (OECD 2005). It led to the coordination of a team of consultants (by and large including members involved in CSDG and GFN activities) that produced a conceptual framework for the OECD's initial engagement with SSR (2001), a global survey on SSR covering 110 developing and transition countries (2004) and a policy report on SSR and Governance (edited by Nicole Ball and Dylan Hendrickson), constituting the basis for the OECD-DAC 2004 Guidelines (OECD 2001).[9] The CPDC's mission was not only to achieve a clearer understanding of SSR and provide guidelines for policy implementations, but also to coordinate and bring together the SSR experts from different backgrounds and organisations.

At the same time, mainstreaming SSR cannot be defined as a one-way flow from norm setters (the UK and the OECD) to norms takers (other states and IOs, including the EU). It was, instead, a complex and multi-dimensional process, characterised by intense socialisation and multiple flows of influence. Although some countries promoted norm creation by investing financial resources, it would be misleading to conclude that the EU was passively delivered norms.

On the one hand, representatives of EU member states and Commission/Council officials seconded to the OECD were socialised as a result of their participation in CPDC meetings.[10] Evidence of this influence is reflected in the European Commission's 2004 annual report on development aid and external assistance, which promotes an holistic approach to governance, peace, security and development according to the OECD guidelines (European Commission 2004: 130). On the other hand, fifteen EU member states and the Commission actively contributed to the same debates leading to the adoption of the OECD 2004 Guidelines: that is, the very document the EU policy framework on SSR was modelled on.

The conclusion to be drawn is that in the phase of policy innovation, selection and diffusion, the EU was both a norm taker and a norm maker. Another important implication is that multiple influences have arisen across different communities (security, development and democracy promotion) shaping the debate at different stages. The construction of networks around centres of expertise and knowledge-sharing sought to achieve the creation of consensual knowledge, raising awareness by "setting up useful meetings at useful times".[11]

The Geneva Centre for the Democratic Control of Armed Forces (DCAF) was also in the frontline of this development and was outsourced by the EU with the task of spurring on the conceptualisation of SSR.[12] Outsourcing implies the existence of a convergence between the EU's need to develop a policy framework from scratch and other actors (such as DCAF) with the goal, mandate and capacity to fill such gap providing the right input at the right time.[13] Policy-makers drafting the *Concept for ESDP support to Security Sector Reform*, adopted by the Council of the EU in November 2005, relied on the policy recommendations advanced in the *Chaillot Paper no. 80* published by the EU Institute for Security Studies and DCAF in July 2005 and co-edited by Hänggi and Tanner (2005).[14] Further conceptual development of SSR was also fostered by experts communities through networking and training activities between 2006 and

2009, promoted by the "pool" of member states favourable to the new approach and exploiting the rotating presidency of the Council of the EU to shape the security agenda. Austria and Finland, who held the Council presidency in the first and second semester 2006, provide a good example of this. Both states, traditionally committed to non-military crisis management, took advantage of the six months presidency to further refine the SSR concept.[15]

This policy enterprise contributed to change the perceptions and behaviour of some member states, who had been reluctant to adopt the security-development nexus. The Europeanisation of France's attitude towards SSR is an interesting case, since it demonstrates the power of knowledge to shape the security agenda of a "big" member state. The French government was initially very sceptical about an approach that implied bridging the gap between the Ministry of Foreign Affairs (specifically l'*Aide au développement et gouvernance démocratique*) and the Military. The French involvement in SSR comes directly as a result of the pressure of OECD DAC on French policy-makers.[16] The French policy framework on SSR followed the OECD DAC guidelines and was released in August 2008, to "board the train before it leaves" as reported by a French official.[17]

The persistence of SSR norms in the EU was made possible by two factors. First, the constant networking and cross-fertilisation activities operated by the emerging epistemic community of SSR, divided into different sub-communities. Second, by the "Presidency factor", which allowed some EU member states to push forwards the SSR agenda. In the period between 2002 and 2006, favourable circumstances encouraged a prioritisation of the EU SSR agenda, as the rotating presidency was held by major donors such as Denmark (second semester 2002), The Netherlands (second semester 2004), the UK (second semester 2005) or by countries supporting the development of non-military crisis management tools such as Ireland (first semester 2004), Austria (first semester 2006) and Finland (second semester 2006). A conference on SSR in the Western Balkans held in Vienna and organised by the Austrian presidency of the EU (in association with DCAF and the EU Institute for Security Studies) on February 2006 took forward the work done by the previous British presidency to further mainstream the SSR conceptual basis, coherence and coordination among different institutional, governmental and non-governmental actors (Batt 2006) (Table 6.3).

Table 6.3   Timeline for SSR conceptual development

Date	Main SSR-related initiatives/documents	Actors concerned
January 1994	Partnership for peace (PfP) launched	NATO
December 1994	Code of conduct on politico-military aspects of security	OSCE
May 1997	Policy statement: conflict, peace and development co-operation on the threshold of the twenty-first century	OECD
March 1998	Publication "Spreading Good Practices in Security Sector Reform: Policy Options for the British Government" (by Nicole Ball)	Saferworld
April 1998	Conflict and Humanitarian Affairs Department (CHAD) established at UK Department for International Development (DFID)	United Kingdom
March 1999	Conflict, Security and Development Group (CSDG) established at King's College London	United Kingdom
March 1999	Speech by Clare Short, UK Secretary for Development, at King's College London: "Security Sector Reform and the Elimination of Poverty"	United Kingdom
June 1999	Stability Pact for South Eastern Europe launched	EU
February 2000	DFID-sponsored symposium on security sector reform and military expenditure	United Kingdom
October 2002	Publication "Enhancing Security Sector Governance: A Conceptual Framework for UNDP" (Paper prepared by Nicole Ball)	UN
2003	Global Facilitation Network on Security Sector Reform (GFN-SSR) created	United Kingdom
2003	African Security Sector Network (ASSN) created	Africa
2003	European Security Strategy: "A Secure Europe in a Better World" released	EU
2005	DAC guidelines on security system reform published	OECD
July 2005	Chaillot Paper n. 80 "Promoting security sector governance in the EU's neighbourhood" (by H. Hanggi and F. Tanner) published	EU ISS
July (→ Dec) 2005	UK Presidency of the EU begins	EU
October 2005	EU Concept for ESDP support to Security Sector Reform (SSR) released	EU/Council of the European Union
January 2006 (→ June)	Austrian Presidency of the EU begins	EU
February 2006	EU Presidency seminar on security sector reform in the Western Balkans (Vienna, Austria)	EU/Presidency

(*continued*)

Table 6.3 (continued)

Date	Main SSR-related initiatives/documents	Actors concerned
May 2006	Communication from the Commission to the Council and the European Parliament: "A Concept for European Community Support for Security Sector Reform" issued	EU/European Commission
June 2006	Council conclusions on a policy framework for security sector reform released	EU
2007	DAC handbook on security system reform published	OECD
2008	UN Secretary-General's report on "Securing peace and development: the role of the United Nations in supporting security sector reform" released	UN
2008	International Security Sector Advisory Team (ISSAT) created within DCAF	DCAF
2008	Association for Security Sector Reform Education and Training (ASSET) created	Global
June 2008/ September 2010	EU SSR mission in Guinea-Bissau launched/ completed	EU/CSDP
August 2008	French policy framework on SSR released	France
October 2008	First pilot training session for practitioners on SSR in CSDP missions organized at European Security and Defence College (ESDC) by France and the Netherlands	EU/ESDC
2009	EU member states' decision to create a permanent pool of SSR experts	EU
December 2010	Selection process for the EU SSR Pool completed	EU
January 2011	Europe's New Training Initiative for Civilian Crisis Management established	Europe

6.2   SSR in Practice

The EU SSR practice has displayed a gap between what was stated in the policy frameworks and what was actually being achieved on the ground. SSR remains in the mind of the EU policy-makers a fuzzy concept, difficult to implement and assess, with disappointing operational results and no systematic lessons learned that exercise to underpin policy evolution. Therefore, the question arises as to why did the EU adopt SSR, but failed to implement it? The next section discusses the operational experience of the CSDP as far as SSR missions are concerned. As operations represent the learning environment in which the learning by doing process should occur, it is important to analyse how the EU has practically implemented SSR.

6.2.1 Operational Experience

The EU has positioned itself as a key actor in the promotion of SSR activities, within the framework of its crisis management operations (Sedra 2006; Dursun-Ozkanca and Vandemoortele 2012). However, the EU SSR strategy underlines a fragmentation of competences within the EU and, in operational terms, a cultural gap between a development-oriented and a security-oriented community (Weiler 2009: 27). The confusion existing between different perspectives (e.g. systemic *vs* sectoral, development *vs* security, civilian *vs* military) and responsibilities (e.g. Council Secretariat *vs* Commission) have affected the EU's performance on SSR. As a consequence, learning has been poor essentially because the EU struggled to implement SSR.

Dursun-Ozkanca and Vandemoortele (2012: 145) distinguish three aspects of the EU SSR policies: (1) the rebranding under SSR of a number of existing policies; (2) the integration of other policies to bring them in line with SSR principles; (3) the creation of new instruments and actions emerging from the SSR agenda. Despite some clear progress, the EU has not completely redone the scope of its activities in post-conflict reconstruction under the SSR guidelines.

Two types of EU SSR missions can be identified. The first type includes civilian CSDP missions addressing the transformation of one or more parts of the security sector, such as police reform, training and capacity-building in relation to police forces, border guards and security forces, or development of the culture and institutions of the rule of law (Dursun-Ozkanca and Vandemoortele 2012: 140). Among the EU missions and operations launched between 2003 and 2015, seven involve aspects of SSR, namely: EUPM Bosnia and Herzegovina (BiH), EUPOL COPPS (Palestine), EUPOL Afghanistan, EUTM Somalia, EUJUST-LEX Iraq, EUPOL DRC, EUAM Ukraine (Bloching 2011: 2; Gross and Jacob 2013: 14).

The second type includes, instead, missions that are explicitly labelled as SSR-support activities and build on a comprehensive and holistic approach to the provision of advice and assistance to the reform of the security sector in a given country (Derks and More 2009: 20). There have been only two missions that were launched with the explicit objective to reform all the major state security institutions, in line with the holistic understanding of SSR: EUSEC RD Congo and EU SSR Guinea-Bissau (Derks and More 2009: 20).

A "knowledge-practice" gap explains the predominance of the first type of mission, targeting an individual agency or institution, over those implementing a multifaceted and integrated approach to SSR. The emergence of SSR in the international conflict prevention and peacebuilding agenda has pushed the EU to integrate the SSR knowledge into its system. However, the implementation has been predominantly sectoral, in spite of the fact that the EU policy framework defines SSR as systemic in line with the OECD-DAC guidelines.

When operationalising SSR, EU officials have been confronted with a new, complex policy area, requiring the integration of different crisis management tools, without a track record of collaboration on this matter. A common repertoire on SSR programme design, planning and delivery was missing in the Council Secretariat, and the majority of staff lacked expertise or training.[18] In the first five years of SSR implementation (2005–2010), the Council Secretariat has had only three full-time SSR officials within DG E VIII and DG E IX and some rule of law experts (Derks and More 2009: 20). The design of CSDP missions covering SSR has overlooked the core holistic component because of the lack of SSR expertise, aggravated by the high turnover of the Council Secretariat staff. Even when created, expertise struggled to be retained in EU bureaucratic units (Derks and More 2009: 21). This has also affected evaluation and assessment works, which often misconstrue the SSR objectives in what are, in reality, civilian missions. These problems have been worsened by an absence of comprehensiveness in the way EU institutions deal with planning aspects of SSR missions. In the case of the SSR mission in DRC, attempts to merge the Council and Commission strategies for SSR were unsuccessful. Similarly, there has not been a framework bringing together First and Second pillar approaches to SSR in Guinea Bissau.

Troubles in planning, resulting from bad conceptualisation, had consequences on the implementation of the EU SSR-support activities. Neither EUSEC DRC, nor EUSSR Guinea-Bissau, have lived up to their ambitious agenda, as they focused almost exclusively on the security side of the security-development nexus (Bloching 2011: 4). As a result, learning by doing in SSR fell short of a correct, holistic implementation on the ground, and was hence hampered by the EU's failure to set up a sufficient number of missions of the second type described above.

That being said, it is worth reviewing the assessments on holistic CSDP SSR missions and the major challenges associated with them: coordination, management, financial, leadership, staffing and training.

EUSEC DRC (June 2005–June 2016)

EUSEC DRC is the first, ground-breaking EU mission addressing security sector reform in a post-conflict environment, through the adoption of comprehensive, coordinated and multilateral responses. Launched in 2005, it is the first mission of its kind and reflects the growing importance of army reform in the EU's approach to peacebuilding. Originally aimed at providing advice in support of army integration, compatible with the principles of human right, good governance, international humanitarian law, transparency and the rule of law, the mandate evolved over time, according to the inclusion of other strands of activity in line with the evolving EU objectives in SSR (Clément 2009a: 245). As of July 2015, EUSEC was made of 51 staff, not counting the 17 police officers deployed under the EUPOL mission.[19]

EUSEC's main achievement has to do with the mission's advice role on army reform, in cooperation with the United Nations, resulting in the adoption by President Kabila of the "Revised Plan of Army Reform" in May 2009 (Clément 2009b: 97). The mission also addressed the problem of the Congolese soldiers' low pay—to prevent widespread corruption in the army—and achieved several small initiatives in the fields of human rights training, IT network, and flanking measures designed to improve the life of the military (Bausback 2010: 158).

Five big challenges are associated with the mission: the EU's internal organisation, the missions' ability to engage non-military actors, the coordination with non-EU donors, and difficulties in implementing SSR when security forces were fighting a protracted conflict (Clément 2009a: 247). The unclear division of labour among EU actors has certainly been a major one and has affected the mission from the early stage. Three separate budget lines were created and two different missions set up: military activities were part of the EUSEC mandate, while police activities fell under the responsibility of EUPOL; finally, REJUSCO, under the Commission's Directorate General for Development, addressed the programme for justice reform (Froitzheim and Soderbaum 2013: 175). Unclear division of labour resulted in the Commission and the Council squabbling over their respective responsibilities, which ultimately undermined the credibility of the EU vis-à-vis local authorities (More and Price 2011: vii). Poor division of labour also occurred between the EU and external actors, in particular coordination with MONUC was difficult as competition developed between the two missions, because of a fundamental disagreement over who and how should take a lead in promoting SSR in the DRC (Clément

2009a: 251). The lack of political expertise was another important setback. Mission's members were hired for their technical/military skills, with little consideration of their political ability to engage Congolese actors in devising the Strategic Plan for SSR (More and Price 2011: 20).

Overall, a limited number of lessons have been learned from EUSEC. The gap between the EU's ambitions in SSR and the modest means (financial, capabilities) available has probably been the most evident one. Internally, it is noted (Clément 2009a: 253) that as the mission represents the first EU attempt to implement SSR under the OECD-DAC rules, it allows member states with less operational involvement in the region to attract new SSR players, such as Germany and Italy, in addition to the early supporters (Benelux, France, the UK and Sweden). However, evaluations of the mission describe the overall EU coherence as suboptimal. Beyond the general principles enunciated in the EU SSR policy frameworks, there has been no guiding framework or common EU objectives that were feasible in the Congolese context (More and Price 2011: 23).[20] Tensions between member states further fragmented the EU's approach to SSR. The launch of two separate missions—EUPOL and EUSEC—results in part from the reluctance of some member states to be engaged in defence reform (Bausback 2010: 159), which came at the expense of an integrated approach. Furthermore, little or bad coordination existed between CSFP actors and the Commission, among different EU missions (EUPOL, EUSEC) in the field, as well as between the headquarters and the field.

With the launch of EUSEC, expectations for the implementation of other comprehensive SSR initiatives were relatively higher, as the EU seemed able to carve out a niche role (Law 2007) in stabilizing fragile post-conflict states through an emphasis on training, institutional reform and governance of the security sector. Those expectations were in fact disappointed by the lack of coherence and the implementation of EU SSR in Congo. Most importantly, the learning curve slowed down dramatically after EUSEC, as most of CSDP SSR missions continued focusing on specific sectors, rather than a comprehensive approach, with the exception of SSR Guinea-Bissau.

EU SSR Guinea-Bissau (June 2008–September 2010)
Guinea-Bissau provides another example of the challenges of SSR in conflict-affected contexts. It has been one of the smallest CSDP operations, with 21 advisors deployed and a budget of less than €6 million.

The mission had a relatively ambitious mandate. It was to assist the local authorities in developing implementation plans on the basis of the national SSR strategy; prepare donors' engagement on capacity building, training and equipment for the security sector; and, to achieve these two objectives, it relied on a comprehensive SSR approach linking with regional and international donors and partners (e.g. UN agencies), as well as with several long-term EC instruments (Helly 2009: 371).

Staff recruitment proved extremely difficult due to member states' reluctance to send civilians into a country with poor strategic importance and language requirements in a Portuguese-speaking country (Helly 2009: 371). As a result, EU SSR in Guinea-Bissau ended up understaffed and overstretched, hampering the ability of EU officers and advisers to take the lead on key issues (Bloching 2010). Growing instability in the country and political violence (Helly 2009: 375) also undermined the missions' ability to carry through its mandate and the effectively liaison with local authorities. It also made it harder for EU advisors to grasp the specificities of Guinea-Bissau's state fragility and to foster local ownership.

Coordination within the EU and with other international organisations proved loose, and envisaged synergies with EC-funded long-term programmes (European Development Fund and the Instruments for Stability) failed to take off (Bahnson 2010: 270), although the logistical and political support provided by the EC delegation proved crucial to ensure the deployment and implementation phase.

Several lessons learned have been identified. Matching mission's mandate with adequate capabilities and human resources was widely seen as a prerequisite for future SSR missions, based on the shortfalls experienced in Guinea-Bissau (Bahnson 2010; Helly 2009). This, in turn, is a function of the political will of Member States to supply the mission with appropriate staffing and equipment (Bloching 2010). A sustainable basis for long term SSR assistance would have also been required— because member states showed no willingness to deploy another CSDP mission in the country. Some authors have noted that the military mutiny of April 1, 2010, which triggered the EU's decision to terminate the mission at the end of September, provided member states with a good opportunity to exit Guinea-Bissau without loosing face (Bloching 2010: 8).

To conclude, Table 6.4, based on the report by Gross and Jacob (2013), overviews the common lessons learned and challenges for SSR implementation. The table shows that failure to implement the holistic, long-term approach to SSR, confusion or lack of expertise among staff and persisting

Table 6.4   SSR operational experience, main lessons and challenges

Lessons	A holistic and comprehensive approach to SSR is needed to engage with institution-building in the long-term;
	Mission planning revolves around the identification of appropriate mission mandates and civil-military coordination where both aspects of crisis management are present;
	Staffing should be improved in selection aspects as well as training standards, especially in the pre-deployment phase;
	Common training standards should also facilitate the dissemination of a common understanding of SSR activities (currently missing);
	Civil-military coordination structures have been insufficient and underutilized; planning and oversight mechanisms continue to function separately (CPCC vs EUMS) also after the creation of CMPD;
	Civilian and military planners should share lessons learned and the contacts between them should be intensified.
	Cooperation with partner (UN, NATO) should go beyond framework agreements and involve strategic discussions on the entire conflict cycle to develop joint guidance;
Key hindering factors	Inter-institutional competition between EU actors with SSR-related competences has negatively affected the implementation;
	Budgetary procedures and financial instruments are insufficient and inflexible, which explains delays in the implementation of missions or the achievement of their mandates;
	Working approaches and culture remain distinct as coordination between EEAS and Commission (entailing diverging planning and funding cycles) is problematic

Source: Gross and Jacob (2013: 23–26)

differences among organisational cultures (civilian, military) as well as EU bureaucratic actors (EEAS, Commission) influenced operational performance and constituted an obstacle to lessons drawing.

6.2.2   *Why Has the EU Failed to Implement Holistic SSR?*

To summarise, three factors explain the EU's poor performance in SSR and consequent lack of learning by doing: (1) the absence of a consensus among expert communities scattered across the development, cooperation and security areas; (2) the complexity of the EU bureaucratic politics and the cleavage between supranational and intergovernmental governance, involving confrontation between the Commission and the Council Secretariat and member states, which has not been solved by the creation of the European External Action Service; (3) shortfalls in terms of capacity building, training and recruitment. These three aspects are intertwined.

The failure to create an overarching epistemic community, which would mingle the security and development discourses, is evident. SSR is by its nature a bridging concept: the success of diffusion, persistence and evolution of holistic norms hinges on the degree of consensus among experts on how concepts shall be interpreted and implemented. As experts held different meanings, values and beliefs about SSR, according to the lenses they use, a strong normative force could not fully drive forward. The most notable divisions have emerged across systemic and sectoral approaches to SSR. Language also restricted access to the community, producing a gap between English speaking and non-English-speaking individuals. As a result, expertise has been translated into policy framework, but failed overall—the EU is a case in point—to be turned into something governments and organisations can use at the practical, operational level.

The intricacy of EU decision-making, characterised by multi-level governance and the confrontation between supranational and intergovernmental institutions, did not help. Although it provided epistemic communities with multiple access points to influence decision-making, EU bureaucratic politics has overall proceeded to the detriment of SSR policy implementation. This triggered further conceptual confusion, as well as coordination and organisational problems arising between the Commission and the CSDP-led activities. It also exacerbated critical cultural gaps, such as divergent national approaches towards areas of intervention (i.e. police reform), not to mention the broader issue of civilian vs. military structures and expertise within the Council Secretariat.

Finally, the training-recruitment-deployment gap has been a significant practical problem. Challenges can be divided into four categories: finance, procurement, staffing and training.[21] Lack of sufficient financial support to SSR-related missions hindered effective implementation, together with the shortage of or the inadequacy of the equipment for civilian personnel. Procurement has thus far been cumbersome, slow and ineffective, for both regulatory and financial reasons, hence reducing freedom of movement, operational flexibility and increasing reliance on external actors (UN, NATO) for protection in dangerous places such as Afghanistan or Iraq. Understaffing and a general lack of training and knowledge of the areas of intervention are other important shortcomings. Despite the launch of initiatives aimed at developing international SSR training standards,[22] EU member states have struggled to recruit or second deployable personnel and, when they managed to, officers were not sufficiently prepared for the task or did not have a cultural understanding of the context in which the mission takes place (Bloching 2011).

To fill these gaps, recent initiatives have attempted to enhance strategic training, pre-deployment specialisation and permanent expertise for EU SSR civilian and defence missions. The establishment of the European Security and Defence College (ESDC), the launch of Europe's New Training Initiative for Civilian Crisis Management (ENTRi) and the setting up of the permanent pool of SSR experts (or Deployable European Expert Teams) are three significant examples. These initiatives are expected to promote shared expertise and contribute to the reflection on the development of SSR theory and related matters within the EU, by submitting analyses and reports to the Council and Commission.

6.2.3   Appraising SSR's Robustness

Let us finally turn to the robustness of SSR, on the basis of Legro's (1997) criteria of *specificity*, *durability* and *concordance*.

First, how well are SSR guidelines grasped by EU actors? A major lesson learned from the institutionalisation of SSR into the EU is that mainstreaming does not necessarily mean "understanding". And even if there is understanding, it does not necessarily mean "being able to do". Although SSR has been mainstreamed in the EU through the creation of three policy frameworks, the process has been anonymous and bureaucratic, with no specific institutions or individual that can be recognised as truly responsible and accountable. When the EU approach to SSR was carved out in 2005, under the UK Presidency's push, the questions of who in Europe was to deal with SSR, how and with what instruments was left open. EU policy-makers were not in the position to do much about it due to their lack of expertise in this area. Governments and institutions preferred to hire external consultants to outsource studies and evaluations for SSR activities. In the long run, however, outsourcing makes obstacles to the development of expertise and know-how within bureaucracies. An exception in this regard is the *Swedish guidance document for Security Sector Reform* (2007), outlining the overall approach and assessment framework for Swedish actors' engagement in SSR processes. The document was produced by the Contact Group of the national SSR Steering Committee composed of representatives from the Swedish International Development Cooperation Agency, the National Defence College, The National Police, the Armed Forces and the Folke Bernadotte Academy. Unfortunately, this best practice developed at the national level to create synergies and convergence among agencies has not been replicated at the EU level.

Second, is the legitimacy of SSR durable? The young age and the confusion over its exact meaning, coupled with the fact that many policy-makers see it as a slogan rather than a credible—and implementable—policy agenda have an obvious effect on the durability of SSR. Missed opportunities—such as the reluctance to launch an SSR mission in Libya after the fall of the Gaddafi regime in 2011 and in support of the Libyan Political Agreement in 2016—seem to confirm these feelings. Poor durability results from the fact that the EU is far away from a true implementation of SSR as a whole of government approach.

Poor durability is linked to low concordance. SSR ideas in the EU could flow within a limited time frame (2005–2009), after which information exchange and constructive debate has stopped, blocking further conceptualisation (and consequently, evolution as learning) of SSR: a normative downturn occurred. All in all, the norm development behind the EU SSR framework fails to meet the Legro's criteria of robustness.

6.3   Conclusion

It can be concluded that EU and national decision-makers sought the support of experts to develop a framework for SSR. Norms were set and diffused out of a complex interplay between knowledge and power nested in epistemic communities. This chapter outlines a co-constitutive relation between ideational factors and state interests in accounting for the choices made by the EU and its member states in the security domain. Policy convergence and European cooperation in the field of SSR was driven by epistemic communities conveying new ideas and operating in the grey area between changing structural conditions of the post-Cold War era and domestic/EU political processes. Support from national constituencies (the UK in particular) and the presence of a guiding model or template for implementation (the OECD handbook) contributed to the persuasiveness of epistemic communities.

However, policy consensus on the SSR framework failed to turn into a real convergence in the outcomes and into policy evolution. SSR remains embroiled in conceptualisation: confusion among experts creates confusion among policy-makers, ultimately resulting in confusion in policy. Different lenses, through which SSR policies are visualised, persist as *epistemes* are neither coherent, nor truly dominant and consensual.

Notwithstanding strong backing from constituencies, wobbly cognitive cohesion hampered effective persistence and policy evolution. This reinforces the view that ideas, interests and power are deeply inter-related in a co-constitutive relationship when it comes to shaping security policies.

The question hence arises as to why the SSR community lacked cohesiveness, especially since, as it was argued in the previous chapter, learning communities tend to be congenitally heterogeneous. A first explanation has to do with inconsistencies in the SSR debate itself. Neither the expert communities nor the policy communities have made enough effort to sort out the disagreement between different approaches over security. The divide between sectoral and systemic SSR is a case in point.

EU bureaucratic politics has triggered further confusion, for instance by exacerbating critical cultural divides. Shortfalls in capacity and standardised training could only make the situation worse by clogging up implementation and assessment. Obvious as it may seem, ideas are powerful yet fragile drivers of change: like interests, their impact on the social reality relies on context, timing and, most importantly, on the actors' ability to consolidate consensus underlying action. The institutionalisation of SSR diffusion shows that the EU policy environment is open for norm entrepreneurship—in fact, the EU did grab SSR shortly after the OECD guidelines came out. However, it also indicates that implementation can become problematic if concepts are not pinned down as clear targets compatible with states' capabilities and interests.

6.4   NOTES

1. Research for this chapter is based on a content analysis of official documents and reports on SSR as well as on interviews with more than 25 officials from the Council Secretariat, the European Commission and member states as well as experts from leading European think-tanks and NGOs. Interviews were carried out between March and December 2011 in Brussels, Geneva, Paris and London, as part of the author's doctoral thesis.
2. Brussels Interview, *European Think-Tank* (January 2012).
3. *Ibid.*
4. Conclusions based on answer to semi-structured questions posed during in-person interviews and via telephone.
5. Brussels Interviews, *European Think-Tanks* (December 2011).
6. A methodology based on the criteria of position, participation and reputation was used to map the population of SSR communities. Data

gathered from semi-structured interviews were cross-checked with the analysis of reports/documents/publications of relevant individuals and organisations on SSR, as well as with research on open sources (institutions websites and available contact lists).

7. I am grateful to Dylan Hendrickson and Nicole Ball for their comments on the development of SSR in the UK.

8. Now the International Network on Conflict and Fragility (INCAF).

9. London Interview, *UK Think-Tank* (September 2011). Cf. also the acknowledgment page of the *OECD DAC Guidelines on Security System Reform and Governance* (2004: 5). See also OECD (2001).

10. London Interview, UK Think-Tank (September 2011).

11. Brussels Interview, European Commission (March 2011).

12. Geneva Interview, *DCAF* (April 2011).

13. See previous note.

14. Brussels Interviews, European Commission and EEAS (Spring 2011).

15. Geneva Interview, *DCAF* (April 2011).

16. Geneva Interview, *Swiss Think-Tank* (April 2011).

17. Geneva Interview, *Swiss Think-Tank* (April 2011).

18. Brussels Interview, *EEAS* (22 February 2014).

19. Sources: European External Action Service, EUSEC RD Congo Factsheet, updated July 2015, p.1; International and German Personnel in Peace Operations 2013–14, Berlin: Center for International Peace Operations, (p. 4).

20. In their study, More and Price (2011: 23) note that a 2006 classified document entitled "A Comprehensive Approach to SSR in DRC" and a 2010 "Roadmap on EU Engagement in DRC" actually existed, but only a handful of headquarters staff were aware of them. Field staff were not familiar with these documents and acted on the absence of an overarching framework and without evidence-based strategic direction on SSR support.

21. For a more detailed account of operational and implementation challenges to EU SSR, see Bloching (2011).

22. Organisations such as the Geneva-based International Security Sector Advisory Team (ISSAT) and the Association for Security Sector Reform Education and Training (ASSET), established in 2008 within DCAF, were in the frontline in promoting training, education and networking activities to foster a transnational understanding of the issue and facilitate coordination among different actors on the ground.

CHAPTER 7

Learning Communities in EU Civilian Crisis Management

EU civilian crisis management has produced policy evolution through learning by doing. This is especially true in the Western Balkans, where the EU experience with crisis management, catalysed by the policy failure in the 1990s, produced a sort of "laboratory for learning" (Gross 2008: 311). Lessons learned have been applied to enhance command and control structures (cf. through the creation of the Civilian Planning and Conduct Capability) or to improve internal/external coherence and coordination with the military, thanks to the implementation of civil-military coordination and cooperation (CIMIC-CMCO). Therefore, by showing a clear evolutionary pattern, norm diffusion in the case of CCM has led to very different outcomes in comparison with SSR. Why has this policy area persisted and evolved?

A policy consensus laid at the core of the institutionalisation of CCM in the EU produced profound implications on the EU role as a global security provider during the first decade of the 2000s. The chapter shows the impact of CCM learning communities on the CSDP, demonstrating that communities are more persuasive when practice and knowledge intertwine.[1]

© The Author(s) 2017
G. Faleg, *The EU's Common Security and Defence Policy,*
DOI 10.1007/978-3-319-41306-8_7

7.1   Bridging Practice, Knowledge and Power: Learning Communities and the EU Way to Civilian Crisis Management

Is there such a thing as a "learning community" promoting the institutionalisation of CCM in the EU? To what extent has learning from others (by emulation) and from experience (by doing) been facilitated by transnational networks of experts and practitioners? Finally, how do ideas translate into institution-building, leading to the establishment of new civilian and civil-military structures such as Civcom, or the CPCC?

The following sections will explore how learning communities contributed to a civilian CSDP by looking at three factors:

1. the type of CCM communities, namely their structure, boundaries and cohesiveness, and the overall cognitive architecture of CCM;
2. the diffusion of CCM in the CSDP;
3. the policy outcomes and the expansion of CCM practices by experiential learning;

The analysis of CCM diffusion focuses, in particular, on the contribution of the Nordic countries, namely Sweden and Finland, in defining the crisis management agenda. It argues that a Nordic constituency of member states allowed transnational communities to become persuasive and influence the EU policy-making. Out of Nordic initiative, ideas spread across the EU decision-making process, facilitated by multiple points of access within the EU institutional structure and by the presence of networks of practitioners, who had experienced the importance of a new approach to crisis management during previous field operations.

The conclusion accounts for the structure and outreach of learning communities in civilian crisis management, with special emphasis on the mechanisms of policy evolution by learning and the impact of EU policies in conflict and post-conflict situations.

7.1.1   Learning Communities in Civilian Crisis Management

The EU's decision to develop a civilian crisis management capacity is linked to member states' domestic politics, as the CCM agenda was supported by three overlapping constituencies: neutral, small and anti-federalist states

(Dwan 2002: 2). Major donor countries (the Nordics, The Netherlands and the UK) can be considered another constituency in support of CCM, motivated by their need to reframe aid strategies in a changing international system.

Springing from the international debate on the new dimensions of peacekeeping and peacebuilding, national and transnational communities of practitioners and experts, supported by these four constituencies, started prioritising CCM in the debate on the future of European security, bolstered by the Cologne European Council's decision (June 1999) to mandate the Finnish Presidency to address non-military crisis management. The rotating presidency of the European Council between 1999 and 2003[2] was particularly favourable to CCM conceptual development.

The composition and membership of those CCM communities can be identified on the basis of the three criteria already used by Mérand et al. (2011: 126) to delineate the boundaries of CSDP networks: *position, participation* and *reputation*. The first criterion (position) permits to map government departments, decision-making units or interest groups having a stake in security policies and CSDP issues, namely those who are related to civilian crisis management; the second criterion (participation) pinpoints the actors who took a major stand on CCM issues on the basis of their attendance to conferences, seminars or summits; finally, through the third criterion (reputation) members of the learning communities were invited to cross-check the list of key CCM actors and add/subtract other individuals or institutions they considered important/marginal in the CSDP debate.

Based on these criteria, Table 7.1 provides a list of actors divided into five areas: (1) Education/Research (University departments, think-tanks and research institutes); (2) Government (Ministries, Agencies and national defence colleges); (3) Training centres; (4) NGOs; (5) International Organisations (and related bodies).

The universe of CCM learning communities appeared, at its early stage (late-1990s, early-2000s) heterogeneous and somewhat mutable. Relations between experts, practitioners and decision-makers mostly occurred through private or informal channels and were dominated by a few key, influential individuals closely connected to governments or international institutions. This phase was also characterised by terminological confusion and inflation, through the blossoming of several new, ill-defined terms (Blockmans 2008: 8), owing to the re-conceptualisation of security in the new international system.[3]

Table 7.1 Learning communities (expertise and practice-based) of EU CCM, overview of the main national and transnational actors involved (1999–2002)[a]

Institution	Sector	Country	Function
Istituto Affari Internazionali	1	Italy	Research, consultancy
Scuola Superiore Sant'Anna	1, 3	Italy	Training
Netherlands Institute of International Relations – Clingendael	1	The Netherlands	Research, consultancy, training
European Union Institute for Security Studies	5	–	Research
European Peacebuilding Liaison Office	4	–	Advocacy network
Austrian Study Centre for Peace and Conflict Resolution	1	Austria	Research, training
Institute for Peace Support and Conflict Management— National Defence Academy	2	Austria	Research, training, political advice
British American Security Information Council	1	UK/USA	Research, advocacy
UK Department for International Development (DFID)	2	UK	Government
Global Facilitation Network for Security Sector Reform	1	UK	Research, advocacy, knowledge sharing
Conflict, Security and Development Group—King's College London	1	UK	Knowledge sharing, research
Geneva Centre for the Democratic Control of Armed Forces	1, 5	Switzerland	Training, research, advocacy, knowledge sharing
International Security Sector Advisory Team	1,3	Switzerland	Training, mentoring, networking
Association for Security Sector Reform Education and Training	1, 3	Switzerland	Training, capacity building, networking
Geneva Centre for Security Policy	1	Switzerland	Research, training
OECD—International Network on Conflict and Fragility (INCAF), previously Conflict Prevention and Development Co-operation Network (CPDC)	5	–	Advisory, networking, decision-making
Zentrum für Internationale Friedenseinsätze	3	Germany	Training

Table 7.1 (continued)

Institution	Sector	Country	Function
German Institute for International and Security Affairs	1	Germany	Research
Folke Bernadotte Academy	3	Sweden	Training
Stockholm International Peace Research Institute	1	Sweden	Research
Swedish Institute of International Affairs	1	Sweden	Research
Crisis Management Centre	3	Finland	Training
Finnish Institute of International Affairs	1	Finland	Research
Institut français de relations internationales	1	France	Research
Swedish National Defence College	2	Sweden	Research and development
Department of Peace and Conflict Research, Uppsala University	1	Sweden	Research, education
Swedish International Development Cooperation Agency	2	Sweden	Government— Development co-operation
Forum Syd	4	Sweden	International development cooperation, research and advocacy
Royal United Services Institute	1	UK	Think-tank, research
Centre for European Reform	1	UK	Think-tank, research
Saferworld	4	UK	Research, consultancy, advocacy
EU—Council Secretariat EEAS, EUSRs, EUMS, EUMC, CMPD, CPCC, CIVCOM, PMG, PSC	5	EU	International organisation
European Security and Defence College	3	EU wide	Training
EU—Member States Ministries of Foreign Affairs, Ministries of Defence, DGs Development Co-operation, Ministries of Justice, Ministries of Interior	2	Sweden, Finland, Denmark, Germany, Italy, Netherlands, France, Portugal, United Kingdom, Austria	Government

(*continued*)

Table 7.1   (continued)

Institution	Sector	Country	Function
European Centre for Development Policy Management	1	Netherlands, Belgium	International development think and do tank
Overseas Development Institute	1	UK	Research
Egmont Institute, Royal Institute for International Relations	1	Belgium	Research, think tank
Security & Defence Agenda	1	Belgium	Think-tank
European Policy Centre	1	Belgium	Think tank
Centre for European Policy Studies	1	Belgium	Think tank
International Relations and Security Network—Swiss Federal Institute of Technology Zurich	1	Switzerland	Research, think-tank
RAND Europe	1	UK	Consultancy
NATO	5	–	International organisation
OSCE—Organisation for Security and Cooperation in Europe	5	–	International organisation
Crisis Management Initiative	4	Finland	Advocacy
International Alert	4	UK	NGO, advocacy
International Crisis Group	4	–	NGO, research, advocacy
Council Secretariat DG-E External	5	–	*IGO*
High Representative's Office	5	–	*IGO*
European Defence Agency	5		*IGO*
German PR (PSC Ambassador)	2	*Germany*	*Diplomacy*
DG RELEX	2	–	*EU—Policy-making*
Downing Street	2	*UK*	*Government*
UK Foreign Secretary's Cabinet	2	*UK*	*Government*
French Defence Ministry DAS	2	*France*	*Government—Military*
German Chancellery	2	*Germany*	*Government*
German Defence Ministry	2	*Germany*	*Government—Military*
German Foreign Ministry's Policy Staff	2	*Germany*	*Government*
European Parliament SEDE	5	–	*EU*
Foreign Office's Security Branch	2	*UK*	*Government*

Table 7.1   (continued)

Institution	Sector	Country	Function
French PR (PSC Ambassador)	2	France	Government
UK PR (PSC Ambassador)	2	UK	Government
German PerRep NATO	2	Germany	Government
French Defence Minister's Cabinet	2	France	Government—Military
French Defence Staff's Euroatlantic Division	2	France	Government—Military
UK Foreign Office's CFSP Unit	2	UK	Government
UK Defence Ministry's Policy Staff	2	UK	Government—Military
German Defence Ministry's Policy Staff	2	Germany	Government—Military
German Foreign Ministry's Political Directorate	2	Germany	Government
French Foreign Ministry's Political Directorate	2	France	Government
French Defence Staff	2	France	Government—Military
UK Defence Ministry's EU /NATO Division	2	UK	Government—Military
NATO Secretary General	5	–	IGO
NATO International Staff	5	–	IGO
German Foreign Ministry's EU Correspondent	2	Germany	Government
German Foreign Minister's Cabinet	2	Germany	Government

[a]In *Italic*: actors in the CSDP network according to the list produced by the "ESDP network project" (Mérand, et al. 2011: 130). The table shows that the "traditional" CSDP actors and the communities of CCM do not fully correspond

Despite the absence of a formal CoP, practitioners had a record of a working relationship with colleagues from other ministries, or international organisations.[4] They did not perform collaborative work within the same office or unit, but were reported to be frequently confronted with the same operational challenges and to collaborate during multi-national missions in the field (e.g. United Nations peacekeeping missions). The expansion of these practices progressively led to the formation of a fully-fledged civilian crisis management CoP.

7.1.2   The Dynamics of CCM Diffusion

Knowledge rooted in practice and backed by the strong support provided by the Nordic member states, prompted capability generation and institution-building for EU civilian crisis management since its inception at Cologne in 1999. The linkage between *epistemes* and *habitus* propped up policy evolution, facilitating patterns of learning from experience and from emulation. As a result, the evolution of consensual and background knowledge on crisis management fostered what the literature erroneously conceived as the sole matter of capabilities. Quite the contrary, the very act of integrating non-military tools, resources and procedures in the EU crisis management mechanisms denotes a deeper process of conceptual evolution aimed at changing the EU and its member states' role as providers of regional and global security. The process arose in response to changed structural conditions that tailed off the effectiveness of pure military interventions. It involved the creation of a Europe-wide consensus based on intense knowledge sharing and socialisation, both inside and outside the EU institutional setting.

Policy Failure, Innovation, Diffusion, Selection
The use of civilian means in the conduct of the Petersberg tasks originated in a systemic fracture—the end of the Cold War—as a result of which Europe was confronted with a number of important political developments (De Zwaan 2008: 23): the fall of the Berlin wall and the unification of Germany; the demise of the Soviet Union; the collapse of communism in Central and Eastern Europe and the rise of new fully independent states; finally, a high-risk and unstable area in its south-eastern neighbourhood (the Balkans). These and other factors (see Chapter 3) gradually transformed the international security discourse towards a rising role for humanitarian and peacekeeping tasks beyond classic defence and security doctrines.

Civilian crisis management is, against this backdrop, a tricky concept. On the one hand, the implementation of a CCM doctrine is exclusively an EU prerogative, as no other international organisation has formally adopted a similar concept, with the exception of the UN's executive policing. On the other hand, its genesis is closely linked to the debate arising in the 1990s at the international level on the future of military expenditures; on how to improve civil-military operations on the ground; and the increasingly relevant linkage between governance, development and security in a developing world whose political and economic destiny was unshackled from the constraining forces of a bipolar system.

At the time, EU security and defence was framed by the article J.4 TEU, stating that CFSP included "all questions related to the security of the Union, including the eventual framing of a common defence policy which might in time lead to a common defence". The security landscape was still dominated by NATO, with the Western European Union (WEU) and the OSCE as important players. Therefore, policy innovation for civilian crisis management eventually came about in a period when EU security institutions, procedures and policies were not yet in place. It stemmed out of the need by member states to address two fundamental questions: a broader one concerning the future trajectories of global security and the looming need to integrate civilian and military means of intervention; and a narrower one concerned with the shape and the room for manoeuvre of the security/defence dimension of the CFSP.

With the entry into force of the Treaty of Amsterdam (1999), a consensus developed between the three constituencies composed of neutral, small and anti-federalist on the fact that civilian crisis management could yield a weighty value-added element for the EU. Nordic countries advocated the development of CSDP towards a civilian crisis manager (Rieker 2004; Bailes 2006; Jorgensen 1999).

A number of factors explain the active stance of the Nordic countries' in this domain. Sweden's commitment to the civilian dimension of EU crisis management has at least six explanations: (1) the peculiarities of Swedish society, namely an inclination to look at conflict through civilian lenses, rooted in the fact that the country has not been at war for more than 200 years; (2) political and ideological proximity of the ruling social democratic government with a non-military (or not just military) development of EU security cooperation; (3) the imperative to demonstrate, domestically, that EU was well suited to fulfil civilian tasks and was hence different from NATO; (4) the *élites'* awareness of new patterns of conflicts that arose at the end of the cold war; (5) the Ministry of foreign affairs' conflict prevention agenda driving the debate on Sweden's international role, particularly considering Sweden's allegiance to the UN; (6) the strong concern that CSDP could lead to a mutual defence agreement (unacceptable for a non-aligned country) and that CSDP development could be to the detriment of NATO's role in Europe's defence.

Finland's position was similar to Sweden's. All the way through the Cold War, the idea of neutrality has been deep rooted in the Finnish strategic culture, a characteristic labelled as "Finlandisation". Finland's decision-makers were also aware that with the end of the Cold War and the new emphasis on the comprehensive approach to security which gradually spread in the 1990s there would be a reformulation of the country's strategic posture, pretty much as any other Western nation. This triggered a change of mindset, entailing the switch from a broad notion of neutrality to a narrow notion of military non-alignment (Ojanen 2008: 56). The end of the Cold War and the accession to the EU pushed Finnish decision-makers to adopt a more flexible strategic doctrine, to "constantly re-assessing its military non alliance and the functioning of crisis management and security cooperation in Europe, taking into consideration changes in the regional security environment and developments in the European Union".[5] Ideology, leadership and party politics counted too. Martti Athisaari, previously a diplomat and UN mediator, was elected President of Finland in March 1994, remaining in office until March 2000. His personal engagement with crisis management, mediation and human rights undoubtedly contributed to shape Finland's security policy preferences.

Against this backdrop, the paradigmatic shift in security turned shortly into policy consensus in Sweden and Finland, facilitated by two factors. First, previous experience with crisis management arises from Swedish and Finnish involvement in UN peacekeeping, which contained a civilian element although it could not be labelled as CCM; second, a strong presence of non-state actors, knowledge-based community in these two countries, exerted a substantial influence in policy-making through institutional and informal channels. The former constitutes a community of practice; the latter is an epistemic community, clustered around the idea that addressing the roots of conflict should involve the use and development of civilian instruments. Overlapping communities of practice and epistemic communities characterised the Swedish and Finnish approach to crisis management. These, in turn, impacted on the conceptualisation and capacity-building at the EU level.

The resulting policy innovation and diffusion were accompanied by patterns of Europeanisation, causing the Nordics to move away from the strategic Cold War thinking. In the Nordic region, the 1990s came as an opportunity to rethink their strategic choices and posture, in particular the choice of neutrality (Bailes 2006). From a theoretical standpoint, the influence of Europeanisation processes is perfectly compatible with transnational learning communities, which are understood as flexible entities that produce institutional change, and do not oppose it. As the wind of change was blowing from outside the EU (the demise of the Soviet Union led to a reconsideration of the Nordic balance and opened a new course in defence policy), the accession to the EU and the progress towards a common security policy in the late 1990s accelerated these transformations.

In Finland, due to geopolitical (e.g. the proximity with Russia) and historical considerations, the traditional need to maintain a strong territorial defence capacity merged with an increased commitment to international crisis management (Ojanen 2008). From the late 1990s, civilian crisis management and civilian military integration and coordination entered the security discourse. The debate involved Ministers and Government officials, but most importantly relied on practitioners previously involved in the UN system and in peace operations. The White Book on Finnish national defence (2001) has an entire section dedicated to civilian crisis management, as opposed to the previous documents of 1995 and 1997. Before and during the drafting phase of the White Book, multiple flows of influence were at play, spurred by key individuals (e.g. the Ministers of Foreign Affairs Paavo Väyrynen and Erkki Tuomioja) as well as external institutions (e.g. the Finnish Institute for International Affairs).[6] In the years preceding the adoption of the White Book, open seminars and regular meetings were held between representatives of the Government, the Ministry of Foreign Affairs and the expert community in the security and strategic fields.[7] Finland's previous engagement within the UN in support of the Agenda for Peace and the Brahimi report was beneficial to forge this consensus.

In Sweden, the modernisation of the national defence forces began in 1992, although more concrete steps were taken in 1995 through the establishment of a permanent Defence Commission (*Forsvarsberedningen*). The Commission's proposals gave high priority to an increased role for Sweden in international crisis management, which would entail changing the country's strategic doctrine from territorial defence to flexible forces well equipped to be deployed in multilateral operations (Rieker 2004). The Swedish Parliament ratified these measures on March 2000.

In substance, the debate that set off in 1995 had mostly to do with enhancing the comprehensive approach to conflict through new training facilities for peacekeepers, taking care of those aspects such as logistics, division of tasks, effective recruitment etc. It became clear very soon that a crucial aspect of civilian crisis management has to do with "individuals", a "pretty rare and pricey resource" in this field.[8] Accordingly, the key lesson ensuing from the debate was that effective civilian crisis management missions would depend on the states and international organisations' capacity to recruit, train and raise funds for deployment.[9] In parallel with the reorientation of Swedish defence forces, the Ministry of Foreign Affairs (MFA) was also developing a doctrine for conflict prevention in an attempt to increase the commitment to civilian police within UN missions, therefore with a strong emphasis on non-military crisis management. To this purpose, the Council for Peace and Security Initiatives (RFSI) was created within the MFA and remained operational between 1995 and 2002. This body was composed of individuals from several backgrounds, including national and transnational NGOs and think-tanks, scholars and representatives of the Swedish MFA, MoD and the Swedish International Development Cooperation Agency (SIDA). The Council was tasked with three aims: (1) informing the Government about crisis management, sharing knowledge and fostering cross-fertilisation; (2) from a Government perspective, it was also a way to inform (and get feedback from) non-governmental actors on a wide range of policies regarding security; (3) the body also gathered and produced policy recommendations, acting as an informal think-tank.[10] It led to the publication of a number of papers on the subject of the new dimensions of security and crisis management, ultimately resulting in the Government's White Paper for defence reform in 2004. The paper stressed the importance of Sweden's role in civilian crisis management, as a way to support international security. It also pointed out how national capability would benefit from participation in international civilian crisis management, particularly at the EU and UN levels (Wedin 2008). Members of the Council were exposed to a significant amount of internal and external influences, through interactions with key experts and practitioners who influenced the way conflict prevention was conceptualised and, as a consequence, would be institutionalised.[11]

The creation of the Folke Bernadotte Academy (FBA), the first international centre dedicated to training aspects of crisis management provides another good example of the role of learning communities in shaping institution-building and the conceptualisation of crisis management at the national, then international level. Mandated by the Swedish MFA and the MoD, a training coordinator for international missions was appointed in 1997 with the aim of conducting an inquiry and developing an integrated civilian and military training system for international conflict management.[12] The task involved both civilian and military aspects of training for humanitarian or peace support mission, which corroborates the centrality of expertise and human resources in the civilian crisis management capacity building. The inquiry was explicitly set to be "open both to broad international participation and the NGO community".[13]

The report concluded that the training platform for civilian and military crisis management should become a reference point for all the actors in international conflict management to meet, regardless of their affiliations—military and police officers, representatives of humanitarian agencies, diplomats etc.[14] An integrated and multidisciplinary approach, dialogue between different sectors and close contacts with international and regional actors were set as key items of the Institute's agenda. The design of the new institution was inspired by the Lester B. Pearson Canadian International Peacekeeping Training Centre in Nova Scotia. A number of institutions and individuals external to the Swedish government were consulted to produce the report, and hence, the design of the new institution.

The launch of the FBA, as well as the process leading to its creation, also affected the definition of crisis management and Sweden's policy preferences in this domain. At the time (1997–1999) there was in fact no finished notion of what civilian crisis management meant. Swedish diplomats and officials engaged in lobbying and knowledge exchange activities between 1997 and 2003, supported by the diffusion of a number of reports and working papers produced by experts and academics affiliated to research centres—Table 7.2 lists the relevant institutions in Sweden.

Lobbying and exchange of knowledge were also facilitated by the fact that many of these practitioners shared the same field experiences—and failures—in the Balkans (Kosovo, Bosnia, Timor Este) in the framework of UN or NATO missions. A "loose and informal network" composed of officials previously seconded to multilateral missions helped the diffusion of ideas and proposals.[15] Back from the field, those officials would keep in touch and meet up in Brussels, when working for EU institutions or for their respective MFAs.[16] Bonds of friendship and acquaintances, developed through shared practices, enabled a shared assessment of policy failure (what lessons to be drawn?), a consensus over paradigm innovation (how to design/change institutions resolved to deal with crisis management?) and, as a consequence, reinforced and made a positive impact on decision-making.

Members of the CCM learning community agreed on two fundamental priorities for the EU agenda: first, that above the policy or strategic aspects, recruitment should be seen as the main challenge to future CCM initiatives; second, that implementing the CA is necessary to reduce the gap between different organisational cultures and improve inter-institutional collaboration.

Table 7.2 CCM, the knowledge community in Sweden

Institute	Sector	Country
Swedish International Development Cooperation Agency (SIDA)	Governmental	SE
University of Lund	Academia	SE
Uppsala University—Department of Peace and Conflict Research	Academia	SE
Stockholm International Peace Research Institute (SIPRI)	Think Tank	SE
Forum Syd	NGO	SE
Swedish Red Cross	NGO	SE
Swedish Fellowship of Reconciliation (SweFOR)	NGO	SE
National Defence College (FHS)	Military (Civilian management)	SE
Folke Bernadotte Academy	Training	SE
Ministry of Foreign Affairs	Governmental	SE
Ministry of Defence	Governmental	SE
Swedish Armed Forces International Centre (SWEDINT)	Military	SE
Swedish EOD and Demining Centre (SWEDEC)	Military/Civilian	SE
National Board of Health and Welfare (Socialstyrelsen)	Governmental	SE
Swedish Institute of International Affairs (UI)	Think Tank	SE

Policy selection was positively influenced by three factors: timing, national cultures and EU governance structures, all compatible with a high degree of persuasiveness of learning communities. Undoubtedly, the support provided by shared practices to the development of a consensual knowledge (that is, the overlapping of epistemic communities and communities of practice) made it possible to crystallise ideas and turn them into institutions. So did the backing of countries such as Sweden and Finland, in terms of political and financial investment. At the same time, ideas were heard and promoted because they arose in a period of momentous international change and reconfiguration of European security cooperation. Activists and NGOs had been championing greater civil-military cooperation for at least a decade in the late-1970s to late-1980s, without producing any significant change in policy cooperation. Conversely, a stronger demand for a new paradigm existed in the mid to late 1990s.

National cultures and some institutional practices of the Nordic countries' political systems were also conducive to letting ideas circulate freely. In Sweden, for instance, consultation between governmental agencies, research centres and other actors is an institutionalised practice, partly because of the reduced size of the Ministries. External ideas can therefore easily shape policy-making. *Gemensam beredning* (joint drafting procedure/joint preparation) is a system of inter-governmental coordination that occurs "when a government matter impinges on another ministry's area of responsibility or involves another minister within the same ministry, the matter is dealt with in consultation with the other ministers concerned".[17]

Interestingly, a similar openness to the circulation of ideas exists in the EU multi-level governance structure. In the EU decision-making, in fact, the presence of multiple access point due to the intergovernmental/supranational divide and the multi-level governance seem to magnify the impact of expert communities and communities of practice. The EU's "field", in Bourdieu's understanding of the term, prompts learning since ideas, particularly those ones that are not or are less politicised, are allowed to blossom and influence policy-making. The presence of the Commission as a supranational architect in shaping policies[18] mitigates the impact of the intergovernmental method of negotiation, which tends to be constrained by member states' politics.

Policy Emulation
Emulation from EU military crisis management, as well as from other international organisations (UN, OSCE) and NGOs fulfilled an important task, providing a successful model and organisational blueprint for the new-born civilian crisis management.

By looking at how EU military structures and procedures worked, civilians tried to learn from and, in some cases, effectively replicate what they considered as a successful organisational model. Indirectly, this meant copying from NATO: EU military crisis management, in fact, largely reproduced NATO's structures[19] and procedures to set up its configuration, through institutional isomorphism.[20] Accordingly, the decision-making procedures (planning, implementation and evaluation) to launch civilian missions were designed on the basis of the Crisis Management Procedures for military crisis management, which in turn were modelled on those of NATO (Juncos 2010: 88). The Civilian Headline Goal 2008 followed the same planning methodology used under the Military

Headline Goal 2010, based on virtual planning scenarios (the "illustrative scenarios"), listing of available personnel required for mission deployments and comparison between member states' indications and capabilities required to achieve operational preparedness (Schuyer 2008: 136). As far as institutional structures are concerned, the CPCC reproduced the organisational logic and template of the EUMS (adapted to its civilian tasks); similarly, the creation of Civcom was proposed in the course of the negotiations for the establishment of new military CSDP structures (early 2000), namely the EUMC, and out of the need to find similar institutional solutions for the civilian track (Rieker 2004).

From a procedural standpoint, the debate about the establishment of a formal lessons-learned management process, particularly within the CPCC, followed a similar emulation model. The current conceptual framework aimed at setting the standards for knowledge management and lessons learned procedures[21] builds on existing practices for military operations of the EUMS (European Parliament 2012: 20), such as the Lessons Learned Cell. The Civilian Lessons Management Application (CiLMA) was developed following the model of the European Lessons Management Application (ELMA), the database for military lessons learned created within the EUMS. These tools were established in emulation of the NATO Joint Analysis and Lessons Learned Centre (Council of the European Union 2007c).

Nonetheless, the standard military approaches, which assume strictly separated crisis management phases, failed to reflect the more long-term ambitions of civilian interventions. The EU hence looked at other examples of civilian intervention or administration to consolidate its framework for CCM. The UN and OSCE's experiences with international civilian administration, particularly in the Balkans (e.g. UNMIK), served as a reference for the first wave of civilian missions.[22] The Civilian Response Teams (CRTs) followed the model of the United Nations Disaster Assessment and Coordination capacity (UNDAC) (Schuyer 2008: 138).

Finally, cooperation with NGOs proved to be useful to enhance capacity building, based on the experiences of these actors on the ground. The role of the European Peacebuilding Liaison Office (EPLO) in advising EU policy-makers on sustainable peacebuilding policies during the formulation of the CHG 2008 can be cited as an example in this regard.

Table 7.3 displays some examples of policy emulation that helped design EU civilian crisis management. It also highlights the nexus between

Table 7.3   EU civilian crisis management, learning from others

Organisation	Structure/procedure/framework	EU (military)	EU (civilian)
NATO	Joint Analysis and Lessons Learned Center	European Lessons Management Application (ELMA)	Civilian Lessons Management Application (CiLMA)
NATO	NATO Crisis Management Process (NCMP)/ NATO Crisis Response System (NCRS)	EU Crisis Management Procedure	EU Crisis Management Procedure
NATO	Military Committee (MC)	EUMC	CIVCOM
NATO	International Military Staff	EUMS	CPCC
UN	UNDAC	–	CRTs
UN	UNMIK	–	EULEX

the EU civilian/military structures and the organisations that provided the model inspiring EU structures, procedures and frameworks.

7.2   CCM in Practice

This section discusses the operational experience of CCM and the ensuing process of learning by doing. The section does not to review all the civilian missions, but identifies key areas within the experiential learning process that demonstrate the evolution of the CCM practice.[23]

A total of 21 CCM missions have been launched since 2003. 11 are ongoing as of 2016.[24] They cover a wide range of activities in several operational theatres, under the umbrella of advice, assistance for conflict-prevention and peacekeeping tasks provided by Article 43 TEU. They can be divided into strengthening missions, monitoring missions and executive missions. Strengthening missions are mostly focused on capacity-building, such as EUBAM Libya or EUCAP Nestor; monitoring missions provide third-party observation, such as EUBAM Rafah or EUMM Georgia; executive missions perform certain functions as a substitution for the recipient state, such as EULEX Kosovo (Tardy 2015: 23–24).

Those operational environments generated a learning dynamic, which included the recruitment of the professionals and experts within EU institutions; a progressive standardisation and formalisation of the learning process; and the implementation of the lessons, creating evolution in areas such as capabilities and training.

7.2.1   Professionalism and the Policy Consensus on CCM

An important side effect resulting from the creation of a policy consensus and subsequent institutionalisation of civilian crisis management is the expansion of the learning communities of EU CCM, particularly the practice-based ones. The emerging CCM policy framework, in fact, created the need for new experts to join new units, both in national capitals and in Brussels, to sustain the extended set of security policies—which had been built from scratch—and contribute to their improvement through providing input for experiential learning.

Therefore, as a result of the process of institution building (from 2001/2002 onward), new seconded and contracted officers, experts and consultants joined the Directorate for civilian crisis management (DG E IX) of the General Secretariat of the Council as well as other new born structures such as CIVCOM or the CivMil Cell.[25] Recruitment increased as a result of the 2004 enlargement to Central and Eastern Europe. The enlargement, in fact, made new expertise available. The latter was welcomed in Brussels as new member states had direct experience of the Post-Cold war systemic shift. Their experts offer the know-how acquired during a decade-long period of institutional reform covering critical aspects of CCM such as the reform of the police sector, the rule of law and the transition towards transparent and accountable armed forces. New expertise also mushroomed in non-institutional settings, as the new policy area magnetised the attention of Brussels and member states-based think-tankers, academics, NGOs etc. CCM's policy persistence is hence characterised by an attempt to enlarge the communities through new recruitment inside and outside EU institutions.

The unclear scope of civilian peacekeeping and peacebuilding at the international level (Nowak 2006: 16) did not hamper the emerging consensus on the definition of civilian crisis management within the EU. Despite some degree of terminological confusion, a broad convergence developed between experts and practitioners on the definition and purposes of the EU way to CCM.[26] The Security Working Group established after Cologne settled on the broad definition of EU CCM as all non-military instruments and policies of the EU dedicated to Crisis Management (Nowak 2006: 17). The identification of the four priority areas agreed upon at Feira (2000) allowed them to further narrow down the definition. Specifically, they provided the Union with a niche differentiating the EU's activities in the four areas from other international actors. At the same time, the EU also acquired its own way to design and operationalise crisis management missions, placing the emphasis on the cooperation (CIMIC) and coordination (CMCO) between civilian and military aspects also known as CA. This too contributed to the consolidation of a common view of CCM.

In sum, CCM learning communities display a reasonable degree of cohesiveness. Civilian crisis management in the EU is consensually understood as: (1) non-military crisis management activities, instruments, resources and policies; (2) covering the four priority areas established at Feira; (3) complying with the logic of a CA to security provision integrating civilian and military means; and (4) firmly entrenched in the process of institutional reform (e.g. the creation of integrated institutional structures such as the EEAS or the CMPD) and the build-up of capabilities.

7.2.2   *Main Lessons from Operational Experience*

A shared view on CCM allowed EU policy-makers to identify common lessons, adopt new procedures to manage the feedback flowing from the missions and improve the effectiveness of the crisis management machinery. CCM operational activities encompass monitoring, substitution, mentoring, training and assistance in the following areas: policing, rule of law, human rights, gender, civil administration, mediation and border support (Blair and Gya 2010: 118). These field operations provided the Union with a large amount of lessons learned, to improve its institutional structures, procedures and capacities.

Police missions have been the largest deployment so far. Police advisers deployed on the ground outnumber any other type of personnel.[27] The initial orientation was towards executive policing, defined as missions that "include the responsibilities for law enforcement in unstable situations" (Dwan 2002: 9). Subsequently, the focus of EU police missions moved to include training and advisory tasks. The EU has helped host nations improve the quality and professionalism of their forces, fighting organised crime and developing confidence building between clashing ethnic groups. The key geographical focus has been in the Balkans (Bosnia, Macedonia and Kosovo), but major missions have been deployed also in Afghanistan and in the Democratic Republic of Congo (DRC). In the rule of law field, the EU missions in Iraq, Georgia and Kosovo have a focus on training for judicial and prison officials, and support to the democratisation processes.

As a result of the early assessments, specific recommendations were made to improve strategies and capacities for civilian and civilian—military crisis management. Bossong (2012) distinguishes between four phases of learning: (1) learning from others (2000–2002), when officials and international experts developed a first wave of planning documents for civilian missions following previous examples of civilian administrations under the UN and OSCE (Bossong 2012: 14); (2) early learning by doing (2003–2004), resulting from the police missions in Bosnia and Macedonia and characterised by experimentation and improvisation, at least if compared with the long-standing templates for planning, conduct and assessment of the military staff; (3) proliferation of missions (2005–2005), with operational (i.e. lack of human resources), bureaucratic (i.e. turf wars between the Council and the Commission) and political (lack of agreement on the creation of an EU operational headquarters) shortfalls hampering learning; (4) build-up of infrastructures and processes for regular organisational learning (2007–2009), which followed the formal lessons-learned process established by the EUMS and was characterised by the establishment of the Civilian Planning and Conduct Capability (CPCC), operational since 2008.[28]

The lessons learned matrix (Table 7.4) provides a list of the main lessons that have been identified over a decade of operational experience.

7.2.3   Formal and Informal Mechanisms for Lessons Drawing

The CPCC structure is conceived as an upgraded version of the Civilian/Military Cell (Civ/Mil Cell). The latter was created in 2005[29] within the EUMS, serving as a planning body to enhance the capacity to deliver early warning, situation assessment and strategic planning for conflict prevention and post-conflict stabilisation, with particular emphasis on management of the civilian/military interface.[30] With a 70 + civilian experts staffed structure, the CPCC keeps operating as a formal chain of command (a headquarters) for EU civilian mission by providing planning and operational support (Chivvis 2010).

Further institutionalisation of the lessons-learned process for civilian crisis management was possible thanks to the creation of new structures and procedures, such as the IT-based system "Crisis Management GOALKEEPER"[31] to ensure more effective knowledge and resource

Table 7.4   Overview of the main lessons learned in civilian crisis management

Lessons	Type	Details	Missions affected[a]
Inter-pillar Coherence and institutional coordination	O/P	Institutional disconnect between First and Second Pillar, hampering effectiveness on the ground (e.g. difficult transition between short and long term programmes)	EUPM BiH, EUPAT-EUPOL PROXIMA, EUSEC-EUPOL RD Congo, EUBAM Moldova, EUPOL COPPS, EUPOL Afghanistan, EU SSR Guinea Bissau, EULEX Kosovo, EUMM Georgia
International coordination	O/P	Lack of "effective multilateralism": challenges of coordination with international partners, namely IOs (UN, OSCE, NATO), affecting the implementation of the comprehensive approach	EUSEC-EUPOL RD Congo, AMM Aceh, EUPOL COPPS, EUPOL Afghanistan, EUMM Georgia, EUTM Somalia
Capability: Training and Deployment	O/P	Deficiencies in mission leadership and in the delivery of adequate or standardized training to seconded staff during the pre-deployment phase	EUPM BiH, EUPAT-EUPOL PROXIMA, EUSEC-EUPOL RD Congo, AMM Aceh, EUPOL COPPS, EUPOL Afghanistan, EU SSR Guinea Bissau, EULEX Kosovo, EUMM Georgia
Capability: Recruitment and Staffing	O/P	Reluctance of MS to meet promised personnel contributions. Deficiencies of seconded civilian experts, judicial staff and police officers. EU positions often not attractive to qualified national staff	EUPM BiH, EUPAT-EUPOL PROXIMA, EUSEC-EUPOL RD Congo, AMM Aceh, EUPOL COPPS, EUPOL Afghanistan, EU SSR Guinea Bissau, EULEX Kosovo, EUMM Georgia
Budget and Finance	O/P	Need to increase the speed and flexibility of finance mechanisms (e.g. ATHENA)[b] for crisis management missions	AMM Aceh, EUBAM Moldova-Ukraine, EULEX Kosovo,

(*continued*)

Table 7.4 (continued)

Lessons	Type	Details	Missions affected[a]
Mandate, Planning, Command and Control	O/P	Insufficient planning and conceptualisation of missions, lack of proper command and control structures resulting in missions' design not being appropriate for the task, both at the operational and political level	EUPM BiH, EUSEC-EUPOL RD Congo, EUJUS-LEX Iraq, AMM Aceh, EUBAM Rafah, EUBAM Moldova-Ukraine, EUPOL COPPS, EUPOL Afghanistan, EULEX Kosovo, EUMM Georgia, EUTM Somalia
Comprehensive approach CIV-MIL	S/P	Absence of predefined procedures to harmonise CIV and MIL planning. Gaps in planning capabilities, with overly complicated procedures scattered over different political and military actors not willing to cooperate intensively. Insufficient national efforts to increase coordination	EUTM Somalia
Scale	S/P	Small scale of operations with limited impact on country context	All missions except EULEX Kosovo and EUPM BiH
Strategic Vision	S/P	Lack of an overarching strategy and common vision as to what missions should achieve. De-link with European Security Strategy	All missions

[a]*Source*: Lessons Overview Matrix (European Parliament 2012: 113–114)

[b]It is worthwhile noting that ATHENA has itself an internal lessons learning cycle. Because of the small size of the mechanism (10 staff), the learning process is considered fairly agile, informal and direct (European Parliament 2012: 25)

O/P operational and procedural lessons

S/P strategic and political lessons

management; or the institution of best practice units across missions and the revision of the methodology for lessons learned reports so as to make recommendations less mission than thematic-specific (Bossong 2012: 24).

Since 2009, in line with the recommendations of the 2008 Guidelines on lessons learned (Council of the European Union: 2008b), a comprehensive report has been produced annually to review ongoing CSDP missions and identify the key lessons. The first edition (2009) focused mostly on the strategic and operational planning levels, namely on the type of mission (with a special emphasis on rapid deployment), mandates (police, rule of law and monitoring) and mission support issues (European Parliament 2012: 20). The report also highlighted the need to pay more attention to identifying and implementing lessons in the following areas: chain of command, co-operation between actors, training, rapid deployment, operational planning phase, conduct, finance and procurement, training and recruitment, press and public information, logistics and communication and security (European Parliament 2012: 21). The second annual report (2010) shifted instead its attention towards broadening and improving the system of learning, through the introduction of benchmarking at the operational level and the conduct of impact assessment for each mission (European Parliament 2012: 21).

In addition to the establishment of formal and standardised processes, informal practices (including personal relationships, corridor talks) have been a pragmatic if not essential way to disseminate and integrate new knowledge into the system. This is due to the wide use of informal mechanisms—such as information sharing through personal or professional networks and knowledge exchange with external experts—to capture and report lessons (European Parliament 2012: 21). Through informal channels, communities of knowledge and practice helped convey lessons to foster policy evolution.

For instance, the process aimed at strengthening CMCO in EU crisis management occurred ad hoc, before systematic structures for learning were established. Much of the EU operational lessons in the first deployments were based on the cross-fertilisation of expertise of individual officials and the rotation of key experts from one EU mission to the next. These individual initiatives led to institutional learning at the operational level (Ioannides 2010: 45). Examples of lessons gathered through those ad hoc mechanisms include the need to strengthen evaluation mechanisms (EULEX Kosovo); the problem of the apolitical character of missions, hampering the development of long-term strategies linking CSDP operational results to CFSP goals (also EULEX Kosovo); the importance of engaging the entire spectrum of the rule of law—including police, justice and customs—rather than individual components (EUPOL Proxima, EUPAT Macedonia, EUPM Bosnia-Herzegovina). In particular, the operational experience in Bosnia[32] (EUPM, EUFOR) revealed the need for increased internal coordination between the civilian and military aspects of CSDP. Building on the work of the Danish (2002) and Greek (2003) EU presidencies, the CA of all EU actors in the planning of crisis management missions was adopted,[33] and the concept of CMCO created, thus leading to a new template for the EU Crisis Management Concept.[34] The CMCO's culture of coordination "builds into the EU's response to a crisis at the earliest possible stage and for the whole duration of the operation", relying on "continued co-operation and shared political objectives" as well as on "detailed preparations at working level involving relevant Council General Secretariat/Commission services".[35]

Further operational experience, particularly in Bosnia, consolidated CMCO. In line with the CHG 2008,[36] the UK, Austria and Finland produced a non-paper on enhancing the EU CMCO, based on the conclusions of a seminar organised by the UK Presidency on the 17th of October 2005. The non-paper stressed the need to improve comprehensive planning and management of capabilities, with special emphasis on three key issues: comprehensive analysis (shared understanding of the causes of a crisis); comprehensive planning (to refocus the Civ/Mil Cell on new procedures and methods, in order to ensure the participation of all relevant EU actors in the mission planning phase, and encourage a joined-up vision of strategic aims); joint review and lessons learned process (to provide continuous evaluation of individual missions according to the strategic objectives of the EU).[37]

7.2.4   *Improving Civilian Capabilities and Human Resources*

The two major shortfalls arising from the civilian missions deployed under the CSDP from 2003 onwards have been the absence of adequate training and, as a consequence, severe shortfalls in recruitment (Ioannides 2010; Blair and Gya 2010; Bossong 2012).

The Civilian Headline Goal (CHG), elaborated in December 2004, built on "what was achieved in civilian crisis management since 1999"[38] and out of the awareness that EU's ambitions in global security lay on enhanced civilian capacities. Official EU documents also underline that, in developing the CHG, "the Lessons Learned from EU-led operations and exercises should be taken into account".[39] Key aspects of the CHG included the development of integrated civilian crisis management packages; the ability to conduct concurrent civilian missions, to deploy at short notice and to work with military missions; as well as the issue of inter-pillar coherence between CSDP actions and long term EC programmes (Gross 2008: 16). A new Civilian Headline Goal 2010 was approved by the Civilian Capability Improvement Conference in 2007, building on the results of the Headline Goal 2008 and on the growing body of CSDP crisis management experience.[40] As highlighted by the Headline Goal process itself and by several reports from field missions, challenges to CCM capacity building pertained to the lack of personnel and expertise available for CCM missions: costs of recruitment, bureaucratic hurdles, training, replacement and domestic shortage.

In 2005 the Civilian Response Team (CRT) concept was launched, tasked with creating a pool of civilian experts (pre-selected by member states) ready for deployment within five days and for up to three months. The CRTs objectives included assessment and fact-finding missions, logistical support, early presence following the adoption of a Joint Action and assisting the EUSR function (Gross 2008: 17).

The availability of technical expertise and the deployment of staff depends on training. Lessons from CCM missions underscored differences between Member States in training standards for civilian personnel, which jeopardised an effective and coordinated pre-deployment strategy (Bloching 2011; Korski and Gowan 2009).

To patch up this aspect of the crisis management machinery, a Commission's funded pilot project, called the *Training for Civilian Aspects of Crisis Management*, was launched in October 2001. From November 2002, due to the positive assessment it received, it evolved into a more structured initiative, the European Group on Training (EGT).[41] This open and informal network of training experts and centres was tasked with delivering a common approach and harmonised training programmes across EU member states. Its activities expanded fast, becoming a reference for the identification of joint standards and requirements for both civilian and civilian military training. The latter included the implementation course for the Civilian Response Team (CRT), the EU civilian stand-by force created to solve staffing problems in individual crisis missions (Gross 2008). All through its nine years of activity, it activated courses focused on the rule of law, civilian administration and civilian crisis management, with over 1,200 member states' experts getting trained by the members of the network. Three centres have been more actively involved in the development of the network since its inception: the Scuola Superiore Sant'Anna (Italy), the Austrian Study Center for Peace and Conflict Resolution (ASPR, Austria) and the *Zentrum für Internationale Friedenseinsätze*

(ZIF, Germany). The Crisis Management Center (Finland) and the Folke Bernadotte Academy (Sweden) joined this core group shortly after the creation of the network.

Despite a promising start, insufficient linkage between training, recruitment and deployment as well as the lack of institutionalisation of arrangements among the members constituted a heavy burden for the EGT'S mission (Bloching 2011). As a result of these flaws, a new network, the Europe's New Training Initiative for Civilian Crisis Management (ENTRi), was created and coordinated by ZIF. As the successor of the EGT, ENTRi was designed to address previous gaps, namely by intensifying pre-deployment and specialisation courses for civilian experts and issuing standardised certificates for training courses to improve the quality of formation. In 2005, another attempt to deepen and increase the know-how and expertise for CCM missions led to the establishment of the European Security and Defence College (ESDC). A Brussels-based virtual network college comprising civilian and military academies, universities and colleges, the ESDC was mandated with the task of fostering a European security culture within CSDP and disseminating a common understanding of CSDP activities, including the civilian aspect of crisis management.

Notwithstanding these efforts and the intense network-building, however, staffing and training still constitute, even after the entry into force of the Lisbon Treaty, the main obstacles to the delivery of effective civilian crisis management in the framework of CSDP operations. The persistence of these problems can be accounted for as follows.

To start with, it is worth reminding that a convergence in policy actions does not necessarily lead to a convergence or effectiveness in policy outcomes (McNamara 1998). Consensus building and cohesiveness of the members of learning communities stimulates the institutionalisation of new norms. However, policy change may take longer to occur and the lag between intentions and deeds can be substantial. Furthermore, the learning aspect of policy evolution is a much more expensive and time-consuming step than the previous steps of the norm/practice evolution models, especially in terms of resources for training and coordination to achieve the desired operational results and improve the efficiency of institutional structures and procedures. In fact, member states' civilian cultures vary greatly and, although CCM became institutionalised relatively easily, a proper culture of coordination involving civilian and military tools is much harder to instil as civilian and military structures are subject to centrifugal forces and tend to remain "separate worlds" (Drent 2011). Finally, one should not forget that civilian crisis management structures, despite drawing from models through policy emulation and institutional isomorphism, have been built from scratch, as opposed to the much longer history of military cultures and organisation—including international security cooperation (cf. NATO-EU relations).

7.2.5   CCM's Robustness

Let us conclude by assessing the institutionalisation of CCM according to the criteria of norms' specificity, durability and concordance (Legro 1997).

According to Legro, *specificity* refers to how well the guidelines for restraint and use are defined and understood: do countries argue about what the norm entails in terms of behaviour or implementation? Are guidelines simple and clear enough to be correctly understood by actors?

Although conflict exists between the Council and the Commission on the division of tasks for civilian missions and inter-pillar coherence[42] (Hoffmeister 2008), and member states maintain different strategic cultures,[43] organisational structures and procedures for deployment (Biava et al. 2011; Howorth 2002; Meyer 2006; Baun 2005), civilian crisis management has found its own niche in the EU institutional structure, associated with the development of non-military crisis response capabilities. The EU specificity and specialisation as a civilian crisis manager is well known and acknowledged both inside and outside the EU institutional setting.[44] Furthermore, in comparative terms, the objectives and instruments of civilian CSDP are much better defined than those of military CSDP, given the enormous divergence among key member states as regards a common vision of European defence—for instance, the political barriers to the creation of a common defence market.[45]

The second criterion is *durability*, which denotes how long the rules have been in effect and how long-standing is their legitimacy. In this regard, civilian crisis management has, since its inception, produced an ever-growing amount of missions and, over ten years, left a strong mark on the operational contours of the CSDP. Despite the shortcomings outlined in the previous section, the CSDP has unquestionably gone civilian, developing an international reputation as a provider of non-military security services. One of the key characteristics of the institutionalisation of crisis management within CSDP has been the rapidity with which it has blossomed, boosted by previous (learning from others) and new (learning by doing) experiences as well as from the competence and know-how provided by those practitioners who operated in national and international (NATO, OSCE, UN) contexts (Duke 2008). At the same time, civilian and civil-military aspect of the institutionalisation of EU security cooperation is not complete and remains, by and large, a story to be written, particularly taking into account the quest for a clear strategic vision for the future of CSDP (Biscop and Coelmont 2010).

Finally, *concordance* is the degree of intersubjective agreement, which denotes how widely accepted the rules are in diplomatic debates, treaties and formal and informal settings. A consensus emerged on a common definition of what the EU's involvement in civilian crisis management amounts to, based on the guidelines set up at Feira. CCM has become part of the EU jargon, with no equivalent in the lexicon and practices of other IOs. Swedish, Finnish and Czech practitioners working in the EEAS converge on a definition of the EU's involvement in CCM, with no substantial dissimilarity between their views.[46] Similarly, think-tankers working on EU matters seem to have few problems locating the conceptual boundaries of EU CCM, whereas complexity arises when experts are asked to comment on civilian crisis management outside the EU setting.[47]

Legro's expectation is that the clearer, more durable and widely endorsed a prescription is, the greater will be its impact. Consistent with this vision, it can be concluded that norm robustness and the progressive creation of an EU way to civilian crisis management, driven by learning communities, accounts for the persistence of CSDP as a civilian security actor. The policy and expert consensus underlying the robustness—and hence the impact—of CCM did not spring up overnight, but progressed as part of an evolutionary process through which knowledge and practices became shared, consensual and dominant, thus influential within the EU decision-making process.

7.3   Conclusion

Learning communities influenced the creation of a civilian crisis management capacity within the CSDP. EU decision-makers and member states' governments sought the support of a body of experts and practitioners to develop a policy consensus in support of their security choices towards a non-military understanding of the EU's role as a security provider.

Through an in-depth analysis of the learning communities of CCM, this chapter has answered some crucial questions about (1) the relationship between state interests and ideational factors in accounting for EU security cooperation; (2) the factors that influenced the overall impact and policy evolution of civilian crisis management in comparison with other new, post-Cold War security policies (such as SSR); (3) the conceptual and empirical link between knowledge and practice.

With regards to the first question, findings suggest that cognitive and ideational forces conveyed by learning communities stand neither above nor below interstate bargaining and power struggles between nation-states.[48] Instead, they are to be located at the same level of policy-making, as they provide domestic political élites and decision-makers in Brussels with an essential normative underpinning, without which the creation of policy convergence and hence cooperation could not occur. Learning communities intervene in the grey area between structural factors (i.e. the end of the Cold War) and domestic political processes (at the EU or member states levels) to influence decision-makers' perceptions and value-based judgements about the necessity and/or the type of policy responses envisaged.

This co-constitutive relation between state interests and ideational factors also accounts for the central role of national constituencies—in particular, Nordic EU member states—in supporting the process of norm diffusion. The persuasiveness of CCM learning communities depends on the resources and political backing provided by those constituencies. Indeed, ideas and knowledge do not float freely (Risse-Kappen 1994). In the case of the CSDP, the demand for non-military instruments championed by some member states as well as the opening window of opportunity to provide the Union with an added value in the global security arena facilitated the progress towards CCM and the Feira decision to develop a specific range of civilian tools.

The chapter has then presented the main institutional and bureaucratic factors hampering policy evolution as learning by doing. In this regard, the potential of learning communities is to maximize EU CCM as a "know-how asset" aggregating knowledge, experience and lessons learned that are lacking in other international organisations (Chivvis 2010: 46).

Finally, the chapter demonstrates that the presence of a practice in the formative stages of knowledge, and its expansion through communities, positively affects norm diffusion. The narrower the disconnect between *habitus* and *episteme*, or between professionalism and expertise, the more likely the possibility that norms will impact on decision-making and generate a convergence in policy objectives. In other words, ideas have better chances of becoming dominant and consensual if they are rooted in overlapping practices and beliefs.

NOTES

1. The empirical analysis is based on desk research, experts and élites interviews carried out between March 2011 and April 2012, as part of the author's doctoral dissertation, with officers from the Council Secretariat, the European Commission, and member states as well as experts from leading European think tanks and NGOs and at the UN.
2. The list of member states holding the rotating Presidency of the European Council between 1999 and 2003 includes: Germany-Finland (1999), Portugal-France (2000), Sweden-Belgium (2001), Spain-Denmark (2002), Greece-Italy (2003).
3. See Chapter 3.
4. Source: answers to standardised questions during fieldwork research in Brussels, Stockholm, New York and Rome (2011–2012).
5. Council of State, 2001. The Finnish Security and Defence Policy 2001, Report to parliament 13 June 2001. Helsinki: Edita, p. 7, 39. Aka the White Book (2001). Cf. also Ojanen (2002: 162).
6. Phone Interviews with Finnish policy-makers and experts (March 2012).
7. Phone Interviews with Finnish policy-makers and experts (March 2012).
8. Stockholm Interview, Swedish Ministry of Foreign Affairs (March 2012).
9. Stockholm Interview, Swedish Ministry of Foreign Affairs (March 2012).
10. Stockholm Interview, Swedish Ministry of Foreign Affairs (March 2012).
11. Stockholm Interview, Swedish Ministry of Foreign Affairs (March 2012).
12. Statens offentliga utredningar, 1999. *Internationell konflikthantering—att förbereda sig tillsammans*, Stockholm: SOU, p. 15 (Summary in English). This document contains the final report of the commission of inquiry.

13. *Ibid.*
14. *Ibid.*, p. 17.
15. Stockholm Interview, Swedish Ministry of Foreign Affairs (March 2012).
16. Stockholm Interview, Swedish Ministry of Foreign Affairs (March 2012).
17. Cf. Swedish Government, Glossary of Government's terms: http:// www.svet.lu.se/links/Svenska_sidor/ord/wordlistgov.pdf.
18. On this point, cf. Rhinard (2010) and Lavallée (2011).
19. Previous studies have shown that EU member states took NATO's decision-making structures into account when creating a politico-military body at the ambassadorial level (PSC), assisted by a military committee composed by the representatives of the Chief of Defence (EUMC) and supported by a military staff (EUMS). Cf. Koops (2012: 68) and Juncos (2010).
20. Institutional isomorphism posits that organisations within the same field tend to look alike. Cf. Powell and DiMaggio (1983).
21. The *Guidelines for identification and implementation of lessons and best practices in civilian ESDP missions* (Council of the European Union, 2008b) and the document *Towards an architecture for evaluation of civilian ESDP missions* (Council of the European Union, 2008a).
22. Cf. Council of the European Union (2008a).
23. There is a growing body of secondary literature dealing with the nitty-gritty of individual CCM missions, both in terms of evaluation and lessons learned. A comprehensive review is provided by the European Parliament's report on CSDP missions and operations (European Parliament, 2012: 34–101).
24. Ongoing civilian missions as of 2016 are EUBAM Rafah (launched Nov 2005), EUPOL COPPS Palestinian Territories (launched Nov 2005), EUSEC RD Congo (launched June 2005), EUPOL Afghanistan (launched June 2007), EUMM Georgia (launched Oct 2008), EULEX Kosovo (launched Dec 2008), EUCAP Nestor Horn of Africa (launched July 2012), EUCAP Sahel Niger (launched July 2012), EUBAM Libya (launched May 2013), EUBAM Ukraine (launched December 2014), EUCAP Sahel Mali (launched Jan 2015).
25. The creation of the Civilian Response Teams (CRT) as a pool of experts rapidly deployable to conduct a wide range of missions is a particularly interesting development in this respect.

26. Asked about how they would define CCM, and what they saw as the main challenges of implementation, interviewees' answers revealed a shared understanding of the subject matter, detectable from the language and example used, and references to the same keywords—namely in terms of policy documents, frameworks and initiatives (Feira, CHG, main missions such as EULEX Kosovo). Shared lessons also emerged—cf. Section 7.2.2.

27. For an updated count of CSDP missions' personnel, see the CSDP MAP website: http://www.csdpmap.eu/mission-personnel.

28. Cf. Bossong (2012).

29. Before the Civil-Military Cell was launched, two concepts had been instated to deal with coordination during the actual crisis management: an ad hoc Crisis Response Co-ordination Team (CRTC) responsible for a draft of the crisis management concept at the political-strategic level and a Crisis Action Team within the EUMS (operational-tactical level).

30. A reference document on the creation of the Civ/Mil Cell is the Italian Presidency Paper "European Defence: NATO/EU consultation, planning, operations" (2003).

31. The Goalkeeper system is composed of the "Governor" and "Schoolmaster" databases and it is available online at: https://esdp.consilium.europa.eu/StartApp.aspx.

32. Here, in fact, a police mission (EUPM) and a military operation (EUFOR) were operating simultaneously.

33. Cf. Council of the European Union (2002b).

34. Cf. Council of the European Union (2002c).

35. Council of the European Union (2003: 2–3).

36. CHG 2008 envisages CCM missions deployed either jointly or in close cooperation and coordination with military operations throughout all phases of the operation (Khol, 2006: 137).

37. See Khol (2006: 137).

38. Council of the European Union (2004: 2).

39. *Ibid.* p. 7.

40. Council of the European Union (2007b: 2).

41. EGT is the phase II of the project, launched in November 2002 after the enlargement of the core group (Austria, Denmark, Finland, Germany, Italy, Netherlands, Spain and Sweden) to additional EU member states (Belgium, France, Greece, Ireland and the UK).

42. In several instances, in fact, the EU deploys several civilian crisis management tools at the same time and under different frameworks: in general, it has been noted (Hoffmeister, 2008) that when CSDP civilian crisis management operations (defined as short term actions in response to acute crises) intrude on institution building and long-term conflict prevention, serious questions of delimitation of competences between the Community method and intergovernmentalism arise.

43. According to Howorth, six types of divergences can be identified across EU member states national security cultures: allied/neutral, Atlanticists/Europeanists, professional power projection/conscript-based territorial defence, nuclear/non-nuclear, military/civilian instruments, large/small states and weapons providers/consumers (Howorth, 2002: 15). Cf. also Biava et al. (2011: 1231).

44. Cf. Jacobs (2011).

45. On such divergence, cf. Bono (2002), Faleg and Giovannini (2012).

46. Brussels Interviews, *EEAS* (Spring 2012).

47. Brussels Interviews, *EEAS* (Spring 2012).

48. A similar point is made by Verdun (1999: 323).

CHAPTER 8

The EU's Common Security and Defence Policy: Learning by Doing

Over more than a decade of operational experience (2003-present), the EU has successfully established the institutional and policy means to become a modern crisis manager. It has adapted to a changed security demand of the post-Cold War international system, requiring the development of non-military and integrated crisis response capacities to better address complex security environments. Since the early 1990s, new agendas and approaches to interventions aimed at achieving sustainable peace have arisen in global *fora* (e.g. the UN). This policy consensus involved the diffusion of concepts such as democratisation, good governance, human rights and the security-development nexus. The CSDP is partly the result of this diffusion process. EU actors' responses to structural changes are the product of community-clustered, socially constructed learning.

Civilian crisis management has provided a significant drive for institutional reform, shaping the policies governing EU operations towards the four priority areas (police, rule of law, civilian administration and civil protection) and producing impact on the ground. The institutionalisation of security sector reform has instead been less notable. Why?

Policy consensus (McNamara 1998) is a necessary, but not sufficient condition to redefine cooperation between states. Consensus, driven by the emergence of new, shared beliefs emerging from innovation or failure, can redefine states and actors' interest towards new forms of cooperation. However, it does not automatically result in successful policy

© The Author(s) 2017
G. Faleg, *The EU's Common Security and Defence Policy,*
DOI 10.1007/978-3-319-41306-8_8

outcomes or institution building. For that to occur, knowledge needs to be solidly and coherently secured to a power system, and anchored in practice. These two characteristics define the dominance of a certain type of knowledge over others. CCM found a secure harbour in the EU power system as well as in the pre-existing shared practices of non-military crisis response developed by other international actors. SSR, instead, was thwarted by divergent interests, perspectives and organisational cultures.

The first section of this chapter summarises the main findings of the comparative analysis between CCM and SSR. The second section engages the debate on the persuasiveness, cohesiveness and impact of learning communities on policy structures. Finally, the last section assesses the relative significance of this approach vis-à-vis the alternative explanations of EU security cooperation.

8.1   Summary of Findings

8.1.1   Learning Communities and Formative Interactions

Despite overlapping transnational actors (cf. Tables 6.2 and 7.2), different learning communities can be discerned in SSR and CCM. In both cases, knowledge generation and community formation run almost in parallel, as transnational communities advocating paradigm innovation were missing. Formal communities such as the Delors Committee (Verdun 1999) were absent in the early development of SSR and CCM. The role of the Delors Committee as the epistemic community behind the creation of the EMU relied on an explicit mandate by the European Council. The committee was formally tasked with addressing monetary issues, in view of creating a consensus and achieving a targeted policy result. The constitution of the EMU epistemic community preceded the policy action associated with it. Conversely, the learning communities in CCM and SSR did not match with a formal institutional body.

A main point of differentiation between the two cases has to do with the relationship between the notions of *episteme* and practice. The genesis of CCM provides evidence of common practices, albeit informally diffused and not structured. Those practices, arising in member states' involvement in field operations with other international organisations (e.g. UN missions), supported the formation of a new *episteme* and the work carried out by experts.

On the contrary, the conceptualisation of SSR was not associated with a specific *habitus* or background knowledge provided by the actors involved. Knowledge sharing and socialisation were an important part of the purpose of bridging different approaches into the new SSR vision. However, individuals who influenced the debate on SSR, although exposed to practitioners, were not part of the same community of practice. Development and security professionals did not share field experiences. They did not have a sense of common routine that would facilitate their interaction. EU SSR remains today an innovative crisis management tool that lacks a back-up empirical basis. Furthermore, SSR is a *chapeau*, integrationist concept, which includes very different types of activities and an intense coordination of effort, in order to provide long-term systemic reform. This makes it easier for existing and competing organisational cultures/behaviours to resist the merger.

The case of SSR displays, in this regard, a particularly strong divide between the security/defence and development communities, differences in the terminology used, as well as over the definitions and means to achieve policy ends. Experts working for DCAF do not share the same concept of SSR as colleagues from development agencies such as the ODI or DFID. Their sense of belonging to an SSR community reflects different visions of what SSR should achieve, or how it should be operationalised in the field. Because SSR is the "bastard child" of the security-development nexus, norm entrepreneurs have struggled to set up expert consensus around the new norm, which explains much of the fuzziness resulting in vague policy objectives and a lack of awareness between policy-makers.

Civilian crisis management shows a different picture. Involvement in previous experiences shaped actors' perceptions and reinforced the move towards a new episteme. For instance, actors socialised by meeting regularly during peacekeeping missions, or contributing to conceptual preparatory works, such as the Agenda for Peace or the Brahimi Report. Shared practices of crisis management led to traceable personal and informal relations. Going back to their capitals after a mission in the field, national diplomats and civil servants maintained professional links with colleagues with whom they shared a working routine or an occasional task.[1] These experiences contributed to the construction of a background knowledge. As a result, CCM is not built from scratch, but can be better understood by looking at the conceptual and operational work being done in other international contexts such as the UN's integrated missions, or the OSCE's civilian administration. The relationship between *habitus* and *episteme* allowed CCM to be diffused at the national and transnational level. The learning communities in Sweden and Finland are composed of both practitioners with extensive field expertise in the civilian aspects of crisis management, and experts sharing new principled beliefs relating to the multi-dimensional nature of interventions in response to crises.

Conversely, the conceptual work required to create a policy framework on SSR, in the UK and The Netherlands, is less rooted in shared practices and more focused on the epistemic attempt to bridge distinct policy fields.

8.1.2   Pathways of Influence and the Diffusion of Ideas

Both SSR and CCM were generated by the recognition of policy failure that emerged throughout the 1990s. The consensus on failure was facilitated by ineffectiveness in UN peacekeeping missions as well as by growing instability in the EU's South-eastern neighbourhood, which European member states were unable to tackle. The two policies hence stem from a process of paradigm innovation, whereby start-up communities initiated the conceptual work with a shared enterprise of updating the security discourse—and policies.

There are some noticeable empirical differences. SSR innovation was channelled through the growing debate on the future of governments' military spending and, in parallel, through the debate on the need to redesign aid policies, to address interrelated problems of conflict and fragility more efficiently and to avoid a waste or bad allocation of resources. Pioneers of SSR found fertile ground in traditional security providers (e.g. states having a significant military apparatus) and major donors.

CCM entrepreneurs intersected the debate on European—and, in particular, Nordic countries' post-Cold War strategic posture, and hitched their ideas to the future of major international organisations in a transformed international system: the UN, in a quest for legitimacy as a peacebuilder; and NATO, engaged in the overhaul of European security institutions—meaning, essentially, the need to avoid duplications with the new-born EU security policy.

The way constituencies of interested state actors supported the diffusion of the two concepts through sponsorship was similar. The constituency factor is prominent in the diffusion of CCM and SSR. Learning communities define the boundaries of the space in which states reconstitute behaviours and interests as EU norms, and not just national ones (Smith M.E. 2004a). What enables institutions to shape interests, and identities, is the formation of a set of consensual and dominant norms emanating from a shared background (practices) or *episteme* (value-based judgment) clustered in communities. Learning communities are therefore pivotal insofar as they are within the state (they are tightly connected with state interests) and, at the same time, they carry ideational content inside national, intergovernmental and supranational bureaucracies. For this reason, they can be considered as a thermostat of power, regulating the balance between actors' material interests and cognitive/ideational inputs. Accordingly, national actors—the UK in SSR and the Nordic countries in CCM—acted as "godfathers" of the new approaches. At the constituency level, advocacy through workshops, conferences, studies and publications (white and non-papers, editorials) characterised the emergence of ideational relations between actors, leading to the creation of ad hoc institutional structures tasked with dealing with the emerging paradigms—such as the Swedish Council for Peace and Security Initiative (RFSI) for CCM and the UK's Stabilisation Unit (FCO, MoD, DFID) for SSR.

During the policy selection process, timing, national cultures and EU governance structures facilitated the emergence of new ideas, although with some differences between the two cases. As regards the cultural factors, both CCM and SSR diffused first in those countries (UK and Nordic states) where a culture of "openness" was present; where the political system was particularly conducive to letting ideas circulate; where consultation with non-governmental bodies (academia, think-tanks, agencies and NGOs) as well as across the institutional spectrum was part of the country's political culture.

The role of ideology and party-based policy networks should not be neglected. The presence of progressive, social democratic governments in both Sweden and the UK when the CCM and SSR agenda were presented, gave impetus to the debate. In the first case, the Swedish and Finnish Social Democratic parties (and influential individuals, such as Ministers of Foreign Affairs Anna Lindh and Tarja Halonen) were keen on showing their electorate that the new-born CSDP would not open a season of militarisation of security co-operation in the EU (hence duplicating NATO), but conflict prevention and non-military crisis management tools would be included in the basket. Similarly, in a way, the UK Labour Party had a stake in enhancing Britain's outreach and a more efficient planning and conduct of overseas international development policies.

Emulation, as an intervening factor facilitating the institutionalisation of CCM/SSR through persistence and evolution, shows instead two

different patterns. EU CCM was modelled on a reliable set of successful experiences and practices, providing a blueprint for the organisational,
conceptual and procedural aspects of the new policy realm. Cooperation
with other actors (OSCE and UN), NGOs and institutional isomorphism—replication of EU military structures, procedures and capability
generation for crisis management –facilitated the implementation of the
CCM agenda. Operationally, experiences of UN and OSCE with civilian administration in the Balkans provided CCM with a useful model.
Emulation of military lessons learned procedures also contributed to
create a conceptual framework for knowledge management and lessons
learned gathered on the civilian side.

For SSR, emulation acquires a different meaning. Mainstreaming and
institutionalising SSR in the EU was not inspired by a model, as no other
actor had been previously involved in comprehensive SSR activities and,
most importantly, had been labelling its efforts in the security-development-
good governance nexus as "SSR". Emulation came in terms of guidelines
for adapting SSR to individual actors' need, with the OECD DAC acting
as the agent of standardisation. Almost all international actors involved in
SSR adhered to the OECD guidelines on security system reform, although
in reality policy documents displayed a degree of variation: jargon, objectives and means for SSR policies still vary substantially across organisations
and European policy-makers seldom agree on what SSR implies as they are
asked to go into detail, beyond the OECD principles.

Finally, SSR and CCM differ strikingly in terms of evolution as
learning by doing. Despite some common challenges, such as the
training-recruitment-deployment gap and the practical inadequacies
of financial, logistical and regulatory support for SSR and CCM missions, one can hardly argue that the two norms face the same destiny
when turning into real policies. The EU commitment to CCM has
been vast, whereas pure SSR missions can be counted on the fingers
of one hand. Asked about the definition of EU CCM, practitioners in
Brussels respond quickly and precisely, making explicit references to
the Feira priorities or to the experience in the field.[2] Instead, discussions on the notion (and application) of SSR generally end up in stam-
mer. Similarly, the EU as a civilian power has consolidated over the
past ten years, whereas SSR security provision has been systematically
criticised as lacking both impact on the ground and sufficient coordination, in spite of the relevance of the norm for current crises in the
southern neighbourhood (e.g. Libya). Lessons learned are abundant

on the CCM side—although procedures to collect and elaborate lessons learned are far from being faultless; they are scattered and ineffective on the SSR side.

8.1.3   Outcomes: Explaining Policy Change and Variation

The reason why the CSDP has gone civilian, and that some policies (e.g. police and rule of law) had a more successful and committed implementation record than others (e.g. SSR and DDR) can be explained by looking at the relationship between interests and ideas.

To begin with, the clearer, more durable and widely endorsed a norm is, the greater will be its impact (Legro 1997). CCM evolution corresponds to a relatively robust norm, as opposed to a relatively weak one in the SSR case.

Another explanation can be deduced from the comparison of the two processes of diffusion through the pathways of influence. By cross-checking the Adler and Haas (1992) model of policy evolution (diffusion, selection, persistence and evolution) with the elements of the pathways that define how learning occurs (innovation, socialisation, emulation and sponsorship), one can conclude that CCM and SSR share all but three (emulation, persistence and evolution). Since evolution is the outcome, then emulation and persistence are responsible for variation.

Emulation and persistence are directly linked. The persuasive example of the potential merits of an idea gives a strong impetus to forge consensus and maintain it across time. Economic theory also suggests that once a policy is introduced, it is likely to persist and its removal proves hard (Coate and Morris 1999). As a matter of fact, SSR has not entirely disappeared, hence a certain level of persistence can be acknowledged. It has not, however, produced enough persuasive power to influence the design of EU institutions or the nature of missions.

Explanations can be manifold. Timing was certainly an intervening factor according to Fullan, "terms travel easily…but the meaning of the underlying concepts do not" (Fullan 2005: 67). An SSR expert said that "mainstreaming (SSR) does not necessarily mean understanding; and if there is understanding, it does not necessarily mean being able to deliver. Perhaps SSR has been mainstreamed too early".[3] Theoretical, conceptual and analytical embedding for SSR did not lead to the creation of appropriate means to implement SSR programmes. SSR and CCM have also been problematised (Rose and Miller 1992) differently. CCM has acquired political salience, thanks to states' interest in avoiding the militarisation of CSDP and maintaining NATO's primacy as Europe's defence organisation. Shortly before the development of the CCM framework, the St Malo process created a unique window of opportunity for some countries to mitigate the push towards a common army or a mutual defence agreement vision of the CSDP, and to keep the United States involved in European defence by not duplicating or downgrading NATO.[4] SSR has not been subject to the same process of problematisation. It was less attractive for policy-makers than CCM, given the latter's contribution to differentiating CSDP from other security organisations, such as NATO or the UN.

Conceptual work for the EU approach to CCM followed a pragmatic approach, which started with an inventory on resources already available within member states and subsequently aimed at addressing the issues of how to develop (cf. headline goal process), apply (cf. learning by doing 2003-onward) and coordinate (cf. institutional build up and reform since 2001) them, on the template of parallel developments on the military side. SSR posed more serious conceptual challenges, and demanded profound institutional change at different levels. First, in the methodology of decision-making, since SSR entails unprecedented cooperation and exchange of information between institutions, up to the need to create a collegial collaboration between competing bureaucracies. Second, in the practices on the ground, for instance through the implementation of a systemic—as opposed to sectoral—approach, or by stressing the importance of local ownership. Third, in the troublesome partnership between technical, academic and policy/practice expertise. With regard to the last point, EU policy-makers knew little about SSR at the time it was introduced: SSR networks did not exist beforehand. On the contrary, CCM was supported by shared stand-by practices, and its conceptualisation came largely as a result of pre-existing informal networks between ministries and organisations "streamlining countries' positions and preferences".[5]

8.2   Persuasiveness and Impact of Learning Communities: Theoretical Implications

If learning communities are of any use to explain cooperation it is because the concepts they advocate have an impact. Academic research has tried to establish when and under what conditions epicoms, or CoPs are more likely to be persuasive. A number of alternative explanations have been offered: access to key decision-makers (Haas 1990a; Drake and Nicolaidis

1992), the compatibility of policy goals with institutional norms (Sabatier 1998), policy-makers' dissatisfaction with past policies (Hall 1993), political salience of the issue requiring expert advice (Radaelli 1995), and last but not least, the sharing of a high level of professional norms and status (Sabatier and Jenkins-Smith 1993). Communities of practice expand when they cross the cognitive threshold known as the "tipping point" (Gladwell 2002), which include the socially constructed definitions of novelty and the success of the practice, which in turn depend on individuals' expectations vis-à-vis their collective background knowledge (Adler 2008: 203).

The role of learning communities in the evolution of SSR and CCM suggests that:

1. A shared practice facilitates the emergence of a policy consensus, which constitutes the necessary basis to achieve progress towards a new policy orientation of security cooperation. New cognitive content is more easily learned if it comes as an expansion of a practice, as opposed to the attempt to bridge previously separated episteme. The capacity of institutions to learn by doing also depends on the presence of a fully-fledged CoP, since routines and a shared sense of belonging facilitates communication and understanding between actors on the benchmarks, the outcomes and the types of lessons to be learned—and how to learn them. Conversely, a policy framework not supported by an existing shared practice makes it difficult to overcome institutional and cultural barriers, which jeopardises policy evolution. As a result, this book demonstrates that the CSDP has learned by doing in areas where a common understanding on the "doing" was already present. Conversely, CSDP actors failed to improve their performance through experiential learning when trying to bridge previously compartmentalised sectors.

   A corollary of the previous argument is that the presence of a consensus does not automatically lead to the existence of a single dominant vision of what should be achieved. Learning communities may also co-exist at different levels of analysis like Matryoshka dolls: consensus can be reached at a broader and abstract level (e.g. on human security as a new paradigmatic approach, or on the necessity to introduce elements of peace-building in security cooperation), but it does not become dominant unless sub-communities agree on common standards, definitions and measures to achieve policy change. In the case of SSR, the emerging consensus on failure, innovation and diffusion was counterbalanced by disagreement across bureaucracies (defence and development), institutions as well as divergent national interests and perspectives over the policy instruments needed to sustain the new policy framework. Therefore, consensus is necessary to persuade decision-makers, but the impact on institutional change (involving goals, means and instruments) fundamentally depends on dominance. The relationship between consensual and dominant knowledge is what influences the robustness of learning communities and, as a result, robustness of norms (Legro 1997). In this regard, practice-based communities lead to a more effective policy and institutional evolution, whereas knowledge not supported by a shared practice may result in fragmented communities and, in turn, in dysfunctional policy outcomes. The comparison of SSR and CCM also demonstrates that the narrower and more technical policy consensus gets (e.g. how to operationalise CCM approaches and use scarce resources/develop new ones to this purpose), the higher the chances that a dominant vision emerges.

2. Power matters. Besides providing communities with financial and political backing, capitals can mobilise and steer them in order to match their interests. As Verdun observed, in her study of the role epicoms in the EMU process, epistemic communities do not stand "above the political struggle between nation states" (Verdun 1999: 323), but they are in a way part of it: they are given responsibility and power to shape decisions because lack of cooperation in a technical field would go against states' interests and members of the communities possess the exclusive access to information or knowledge needed to advance such cooperation.

3. Two intervening factors, national cultures and a certain permeability of EU institutional structures, facilitated policy diffusion, but they cannot be considered indispensable drivers (Cross 2011: 28).[6] First, the overlapping constituencies supporting CCM (neutral, small and anti-federalist states and donors) can hardly be included in the same cultural family, yet they forged a solid consensus on the need to conceptualise an EU approach to non-military crisis management. Bonds between practitioners rooted in practices and experience with previous organisations in the field (e.g. UN policing) arose from a common sense of engagement and not from a similar cultural background.

   Second, the EU's decision-making structure was conducive to norm diffusion, but it was not a sufficient condition per se for ideas to produce policy evolution. In general, as long as new ideas are not politically sensitive (both CCM and SSR can be considered as less sensitive from a political standpoint compared to, for instance, military crisis management), they can become institutionalised thanks to the relative permeability of EU decision-making. However, once they are mainstreamed or institutionalised, their destiny gets indeterminate: CCM and SSR are, as we have seen, two different stories in terms of practical impact.[7]

4. The cognitive architecture of the policy area influences the learning dynamics and, as a result, the outcomes of institutional change. A cognitive architecture can be defined as the type and structure of communities at the moment norm entrepreneurship starts; their place in the social environment; the boundaries between knowledge and practice, defining where an epistemic community ends and a community of practice begins.

    Many studies have investigated one community (e.g. a single Committee). However, multiple communities often co-exist and overlap, due to variation in expertise, cultures or professional norms. CSDP is an environment in which practices and expertise are arranged in multiplex social and cognitive ties, embedded in learning communities. Neither CCM, nor SSR diffusion results from a single epicom or CoP, but show a heterogeneous morphology of inter-connected or even competing communities. Learning communities are evolutionary and dynamic, and very rarely limited to a single committee because of the multiple flows of influence and socialisation across institutional borders.

5. Finally, it is important to specify how knowledge relates to practice. A consensual understanding about new, shared causal beliefs emerged both in CCM and SSR, even though the latter was not underpinned by shared practices. However, pre-existing shared practices determined the agreement over a dominant vision of appropriate policy goals. Dominance emerged in the CCM case only. Here, pre-existing networks of practitioners, having a common understanding of routines on the ground or in headquarters, reinforced the overall persuasiveness and impact of learning communities. When practice interfaces with knowledge, a dominating view or some kind of prioritisation within the means-ends relationship is more likely to emerge, thus reinforcing the long-term impact of the norm.

    In the case of SSR, the creation of a policy framework at member states (the UK and The Netherlands) and EU levels occurred before the first attempt to introduce shared protocol, procedures and professional routines leading to an SSR practice that was absent before-hand. On the contrary, the CCM framework comes as a result of the validation of new knowledge, which is vetted by practical change socially constructed by networks of practitioners. A common *episteme*, or information base on human interpretation of facts, is stronger and more dominant if it is supported by the practical routines and back-ground knowledge arising from CoPs.

CSDP missions show that the cognitive architecture of knowledge influences learning by doing. The "walking is how you learn to walk" proves more effective as practitioners shared a sense of belonging, a common repertoire and a mutual engagement towards a clear set of CCM objectives and activities.

8.3   Conclusion

Epistemes and practices are mutually reinforcing, as the latter enables ideas to become dominant and expand to new practices. Dominance is achieved when ideas are rooted in a net which includes practices and power sources. Dominance arises when paradigm innovation is embed-ded in a consensual understanding of the causal beliefs, when this embeddedness is complemented by a shared notion of the field resulting in formal or informal network ties between professionals, and when a powerful champion of change provides interest-based support for the new policy enterprise.

Knowledge, practices and power are interlinked and mutually rein-forcing drivers of the diffusion of ideas, and that learning communities are more likely to be persuasive (towards decision-makers) and impactful (towards institutions) when epistemic communities and communities of practice overlap, or to be more precise, the latter support the formation of the former as this positively affects the overall robustness of learning communities. For instance, institutional isomorphism is generally rein-forced by the presence of a community of practice as demonstrated by NATO-CSDP relations (Lachmann 2010). Similarly, experiential learn-ing by doing, as the comparative evolution of CCM and SSR has shown, is facilitated by cognitive proximity, shared tacit knowledge, shared rep-ertoire, sustained mutual engagement and working routines, in other words the features that form a community of practice (Cohendet et al. 2001: 14).

NOTES

1. Interviews with CCM experts and practitioners, various locations (Spring 2011).
2. Brussels Interviews, *EU Council Secretariat* (Spring 2011).
3. Brussels Interview, *European Think-Tank* (March 2011).
4. Stockholm Interview, *Swedish Ministry of Foreign Affairs* (March 2012).
5. Stockholm Interview, *Swedish Ministry of Foreign Affairs* (March 2012).
6. According to Cross, "common culture is an encompassing concept that is typically a key part of the identity, heritage, symbolism and sense of purpose shared by a group of individuals. It includes esprit de corps—a sense of camaraderie, and devotion to the goals of the group—but is also more. Some transnational networks, bureaucratic committees or nascent epistemic communities rest only on esprit de corps, but a strong epistemic community is also characterized by a shared culture" (2011: 28–29).
7. I am grateful to Mark Rhinard for his precious comments on this point.

CHAPTER 9

Conclusion: Lessons Learned and Future Challenges

Social and institutional learning theories, including the practice turn, do not fully account for change in the EU security and defence policy. They fail to acknowledge the complex cognitive architecture producing learning by doing. Over fifteen years (2001–2016) of steady evolution of the European security discourse, new crisis-management tools were introduced and tested in the field. By visualising the CSDP as a social field where knowledge and practice-based learning communities operate, one can elaborate a new theory explaining how organisations change, driven by cognitive and ideational stimuli.

Institutional change has to do with the re-interpretation of past events designing the future, as the link between policy failure and policy innovation shows. Such interpretation denotes the emergence of a *consensual* and *dominant* view of a changing social reality, in which old responses are adapted to new needs.

The link between epistemic knowledge formation and practices, and their overlap producing dominance, clarifies the relationship between two different, though mutually supportive types of ideational forces, which underpin institutional learning. First, the epistemic act of norm/paradigm innovation, whereby new shared causal and principled beliefs and notions of validity are fashioned and embedded into a common policy enterprise: this is what characterises epistemic communities. Second, the daily re-elaboration of the shared sense of the past across the changing

© The Author(s) 2017
G. Faleg, *The EU's Common Security and Defence Policy*,
DOI 10.1007/978-3-319-41306-8_9

morphology of the field in which the actors' background knowledge has blossomed, leading to the reiteration and, where necessary, the renovation of practices: this is what communities of practice are built on. Revisiting learning as a product of evolving knowledge and practices bears significant potential for social sciences, since "the progress of knowledge presupposes progress in our knowledge of the conditions of knowledge" (Bourdieu 1990: 1).

This book has demonstrated that a sense of the past, understood as *habitus*, has influenced the shape of the CSDP to fit a more civilian vision of security. One could go as far as to argue that the 1975 Helsinki Final Act has been more influential on the current design and activities of the CSDP than the St Malo Declaration itself, insofar as the latter does not contain any reference to comprehensiveness or the development of joint civilian-military tools for crisis management and conflict prevention. In the same way a new episteme is generated out of a critical appraisal of previous knowledge, or following a technological upgrade, an evolving *habitus* draws from a set of elements that constitute a heritage in individuals' mindsets and within international organisations' codes of conduct: the notions of national interest, strategic cultures, but also education and early work experiences influencing the practitioners' professional path.

The communities that are responsible for learning shall not be limited to geographical or political boundaries: for instance, the OECD's International Network on Conflict and Fragility, where much of the thinking on SSR and on other issues relevant for CSDP was produced, cannot be detected by using the theoretical lenses of "Brusselsisation", which only cover Brussels-based institutional structures.

Against this backdrop, the claim that the EU has "learned" to become a security actor implies that the CSDP's institutional format and activities have been the result of learning from policy failure, which produced policy innovation, as well as learning by doing, which in turn generated evolution. In particular, when epistemic policy innovation is rooted in the re-elaboration of past practices, and hence when a community of practice sustains the learning process, the ideas diffused by transnational communities are likely to be more persuasive and impactful on decision-making. On the contrary, nascent epistemic communities that are not bound to a common practice struggle to become dominant, although some degree of consensus can still be reached. The reason is that, when the first scenario occurs, new ideas feed back into pre-existing consensual knowledge and are reinforced by shared practices; when the second scenario occurs, instead, an emerging consensual knowledge hits bureaucratic or cultural barriers, which are hard to overcome if none or loose network-ties between actors, organisations or policy fields are present.

On the basis of these considerations, let us now conclude with three sets of remarks. The first set outlines the explanatory power of this book vis-à-vis the alternative theories of European security, in light of the empirical findings. It summarises the contribution of a learning communities approach, based on the articulation of practice and episteme, to the academic debate. The second set suggests future trajectories of research on EU and international security, expanding the role of learning theories and sociological institutionalism. Finally, the last set presents the normative implications and their relevance for the future of EU security cooperation, especially in times of deep transformations caused by austerity cuts, emerging threats and growing instability in the Southern and Eastern neighbourhood.

9.1   Explanatory Power

In his preface to *The Order of Things*, Michel Foucault refers to the tension between the "exotic charm of another system of thought" and "the limitation of our own" (Foucault 1970: xvi).

Since they originate in other systems of thought, epistemic communities are prone to fragmentation, due to cultural, ideological and political divides. Knowledge proceeds from its fundamental arrangement, which lies at the crossroad between the encoded, culturally-rooted understanding of the empirical order and its scientific explanations. As Foucault put it, "between the already encoded eye and reflexive knowledge there is a middle region which liberates order itself" (Foucault 1970: xxi). That "arrangement of knowledge" paves the way for the authoritative claim that learning builds upon. It stems from the recognition of the consensus surrounding knowledge and the dominance emanating from it. The explanatory power of this book finds in Foucault's "middle region" its biggest strength and, at the same time, its main source of weakness.

By addressing the blind spots between the epistemic notion of learning, theorised by Ernst Haas and Emanuel Adler, and its evolution through the practice witnessed by Adler himself, the book has sought to elucidate the dynamics and overlap between expertise-based and practice-based communities, and the way the mutually supportive relationship between *habitus* and *episteme* reinforces the diffusion and impact of ideas and, as a result, the prospects for international (European) security cooperation. As a matter of fact, as Bourdieu himself stated, the *habitus* "a product of history, produces individual and collective practices – more history – in accordance with the scheme generated by history" (Bourdieu 1990: 54). It is this system of dispositions that, in Bourdieu's theorisation, allows the continuity and regularity that objectivism sees in social practices without being able to account for it, and ensures the active presence of past experiences, which guarantee the correctness of practice and their constancy over time.

In this regard, the creative act of producing new principled beliefs pertaining to epistemic communities is naturally reinforced if it is lodged into the set of dispositions, habits of mind and regularities that form a community of practice, by means of which the authoritative claim leading to a new arrangement of knowledge is more likely to overcome cultural and structural barriers.

This theorisation has implications for IR Theory and the study of international cooperation—particularly integration processes—which can be summarised in three points.

9.1.1   Follow Ideas, Track Practices

Empirical investigations of European security have over-emphasised the role of bureaucratic structures as agents of socialisation. This approach presents some advantages in operational terms, since bureaucracies tend to have clear boundaries and mandates, making them fit for research. However, learning communities are seldom confined to a single entity.

The process leading to the institutionalisation of a norm, to the creation of a policy framework and finally, to its implementation is a highly complex one. It entails intense consultation between bureaucratic units, institutions, states and other relevant international organisations. An analysis of the EUMC as an epistemic community (Cross 2011), or the COREU network as a community of practice (Bicchi 2011), provides interesting findings in terms of how these structures influence agenda-setting. They are, however, incomplete: it would be like investigating the diffusion and impact of *tiki-taka* soccer by looking at the Spanish national team only, thereby failing to consider how this thinking emerged in the first place as an evolution of Total Football in Barcelona, The Netherlands and other national leagues.[1] To understand how concepts develop, it is therefore necessary to follow ideas, from the moment they are generated down to the processes of diffusion and institutionalisation, hence looking at how cognitive content flows and evolves across (not within) institutional structures.

A main conclusion of this book is that the expansion of a pre-existing practice (CCM) has more power, in terms of persuasiveness and influence, than the epistemic attempt to bridge separated areas of security cooperation into a single framework (SSR). In one case, the rationale behind the formulation of CCM rested on the enhancement of a "know-how asset", shared by a community of practitioners, which was expected to provide CSDP with a niche role in international security. In the other case, instead, the SSR enterprise was linked to the generation of new avenues of knowledge, which openly called into question the existing practices of security. It can hence be concluded that, in order to follow the ideas that successfully influenced the construction of European security, the related practices associated should be tracked down.

9.1.2   Limitations and lex parsimoniae

This work presents several limitations. First of all, it only analysed two empirical cases, making it difficult to draw robust conclusions regarding the typology of learning communities, their interactions and the extent to which this learning approach can be replicated in other environments— for instance, security cooperation in other institutional or regional contexts. There is clearly a need for further empirical research, in particular with a comparative perspective across different international organisations. Moreover, this analysis did not sufficiently explore the possibility that a form of community might evolve into another, for instance how an epistemic community might succeed in becoming a community of practice. Transformative interactions between communities are also a promising research avenue in this respect.

Other limitations of this book relate to the technique used to map learning communities. The choice of applying a qualitative research design was motivated by the need to capture the dynamic flow of knowledge. This choice, however, went to the detriment of a quantitative assessment of network relationships, in other words the structures upon which social interactions occur. The use of a set of criteria drawn from social network analysis, in order to detect relations among actors, could only partially address the problem. Furthermore, some filters through which membership of the communities is selected could not be covered by the framework, such as other pertinent indicators: education and cultures, which concur in the definition of the predominant system of thought in a given sector of cooperation (for instance, the liberal notion of peacebuilding, or the debate over the Western and other understandings of the notion of Responsibility to Protect; cf. also a deeper investigation of the role of language); individual leadership and the way it affects the diffusion of some ideas over others (see, for instance, the Ruggie's agenda on business and human rights).

To abide by the law of parsimony, this work singled out three drivers of learning: (1) the actors, who carry the cognitive content producing learning; (2) the cognitive architecture within which they operate; (3) the power-based enablers (the constituencies), who elevate ideas from being a small boat in a great sea to the domain of political relevance.

9.1.3   The Making of CSDP and Its Relevance for IR Theory

The findings of this book are highly relevant for the agency-structure debate that has haunted IR Theory for decades. Based on the "turn to ideas" (Schmidt 2010) and the basic logics of constructivist sociological institutionalism outlined by Adler, human actions and the world's reality are mutually constitutive and depend on "dynamic normative and epistemic interpretations of the material world" (Adler 1997: 322).

CSDP's learning by doing demonstrates that interactions, socialisation and learning, influence and constitute the identity of actors as well as their interests, but also stresses the role of power in terms of creating the conditions for ideas to become authoritative—or dominant. Learning communities complement sociological perspectives on CSDP and push forward the research agenda in the wider fields of international security and international relations in three ways.

First, they mediate between the internalisation of norms through socialisation, understood as the shaper of agents' preferences, and the presence of power within institutions, which sways socialisation processes. The latter become a mutualisation of influence: views are intrinsically linked to the interests of those who "view" and their desire to influence the mindset of their interlocutors.

Second, learning communities move the analytical focus into human agency, as they emphasise the capacity of actors to shape responses to changed structural circumstances. In this respect, this framework avoids the return of a structuralist institutional account (Menon 2011a), and rejects explanations based on predictability and path-dependency orienting decision-makers' actions. But it also contrasts the growing literature on principal-agent rational-choice theories, which take all consequences as intended and pre-determined.

Third, a learning communities approach shows that international security cooperation can be constructed by the agents' interpretation or reinterpretation of consensual knowledge (*episteme*) and of the schemes of perceptions and actions that are derived from interaction within a social field over a long period (*habitus*) (Mérand 2012). This act delivers a new know-how, making what is to be done self-evident or commonsensical (Pouliot 2008). The making of the CSDP in its formative years is a creative, concerted, isomorphic, multi-layered and evolutionary act. Structural and agential elements are therein combined: actors build on their expertise and/or on practical background knowledge they accumulated which in the end, result in institutional constructions. Mérand (2012) conceives this process as *bricolage*. It can also be compared to the practice of building construction, which entails a collective effort between a real estate developer, who secures funds (the EU); investors, who provide the funding (member states); construction managers, who coordinate the efforts of different groups of participants (networks, such as INCAF); the architects, who provide the building design (epistemic communities); and the engineers (communities of practice), who ensure the link between planning and implementation thanks to their know-how rooted in practical experience.

9.2 Theoretical Implications and Future Trajectories of Research

As the previous section has shown, not all ideas produce international cooperation, but influential ideas certainly do. This section identifies future research avenues with respect to (1) the contribution of a learning community approach vis-à-vis institutional learning, sociological institutionalism and the research agenda on practice/knowledge-based communities; (2) security cooperation in Europe.

9.2.1 Learning Communities and IR Theory

A first, key lesson to be learned for future research is that institutional bodies and transnational bureaucracies cannot be investigated in isolation from one another. The circumstances under which socialisation takes place, and norms are internalised by actors should lead to a renewed, comprehensive research programme, devoted to explain which norms matter in international cooperation and what are the communities involved in their diffusion and their impact on institutional outcomes.

The research agenda on norm diffusion could be refined so as to stress that (1) sources of change are both within and outside the institutional arena as norms transcend institutional borders, and (2) unexpected consequences are part of institutional development,[2] and policies evolve through multiple, non-linear stages. This justifies a deeper understanding of the *praxis* and epistemological origins of social interactions determining the way actors mobilise ideas and use them to foster policy change. A future research agenda could therefore explain how changes in the international system impact on agencies and what accounts for policy-makers' agreement over a certain type of cooperation pattern; and also what explains the emergence of policy consensus (or the lack thereof) at critical junctures, especially when experiences of policy failure are no longer considered as acceptable. In this regard, research should make pre-eminent the analysis of macro-structures (e.g. an international organisation, such as the EU or the International Monetary Fund) and their interactions (e.g. EU-NATO or EU-UN relations), in addition to micro-bureaucratic units (e.g. EUMC, COREU). For instance, comparative research could look at how specific norms, such as state-building, develop across institutions (e.g. OECD and EU approaches to state-building) and explain possible variations in outcomes or patterns of inter-institutional co-operation.

Furthermore, it would be extremely beneficial to our understanding of international affairs if future research agendas could explain the conditions under which a practice becomes stronger or weaker, hence more or less influential, and whether specific types of institutional design (e.g. the EU multi-level governance) facilitate or hamper the emergence of practices. It should also explain the relative weight of cultural factors in explaining experts or practitioners' consensus. This could produce important practical recommendations as international systems move towards multi-polarity and emerging powers can exert a political and cultural counterweight to the West. In a global order in which Western liberal values are increasingly called into question, because of the relative decline in Western hegemony, the question arises as to how the framework of learning communities can be applied to explain multi-polar/multi-lateral patterns of cooperation. The dominance of the liberal peace agenda in the global discourse and the practice of peace making depends, in fact, on the material (Waltz 1979), ideational (Nye 2004) and discursive (Foucault 1970) power of the "Global North" (Peterson et al. 2012). With the transition towards multi-polarity, these power balances worldwide are shifting. These changes take different shapes across different policy and geographical areas. The influence of emerging powers on dominant peace norms has not been explored. Peacebuilding and the notion of the Responsibility to Protect (Kuperman 2008; Bellamy 2011; Weiss 2011) are important cases in point. Research efforts should then be directed towards understanding how ideas become consensual and dominant in a multi-polar system. How can emerging *epistemes* or connecting habits be affected by multiple cultural gaps? In other words, what factors can be considered as more relevant to explain resistance to knowledge formation and practices' expansion as the balance of power is reconfigured—and new security regimes emerge?

9.2.2 Learning Communities and EU Security Studies

Updating the research agenda on security cooperation in Europe is perhaps a more challenging task. CSDP is a very recent research field and scholars, likewise policy-makers, are "learning by writing". Since Christopher Hill's capability-expectations gap (1993), the intensification of studies on EU foreign and security have reduced a theoretical deficit that was considered relatively high in the mid-2000s (Howorth 2002; Bono 2002; Tonra and Christiansen 2004). Theories of CFSP/CSDP may still be uncoordinated, but competing mainstream explanations have emerged, such as rationalist and institutionalist approaches.

This book calls for the development of a social epistemology of the CSDP and, to a wider extent, of European integration. Thus far, research has mostly gone ontological (what constitutes EU security identity) and normative (how does the EU CSDP relate to external challenges, actors and threats). More recently, sociological accounts were brought to the fore of academic debate. What has been neglected is, using Bourdieu's formulation, the knowledge of the knowledge: a systematic and thorough focus on the types of knowledge acquired by the EU security system and their effects.

In a highly interdependent international system characterised by technological and social change proceeding at unprecedented pace, academic research should be able to explain what type of knowledge makes headway into decision-making, what are the cognitive beliefs rooted in expertise and practices that shape discussions about security and defence and what factors facilitate/hamper cooperative outcomes. If we start conceiving EU institutions as maximising the cognitive impact of knowledge and practice-driven learning, future research should then show how the construction of principled and causal beliefs is structured in the first place. Accordingly, it would be interesting to see how other security frameworks have evolved, and how the EU relates to other international organisations with which it shares the same or a contiguous practice field (e.g. NATO, the OECD and the UN).

Moving on from the practice turn, a research agenda on learning communities could explore empirical case studies (for instance, cyber security) in which different types of communities may co-exist and produce a complex cognitive architecture. This may eventually lead to a more robust analytical framework for addressing the major issues surrounding the future of security governance, possibly drawing from the education literature (Feger and Arruda 2008).

Security and defence cooperation in Europe is producing a highly technical, innovative and, from an institutional standpoint, increasingly sophisticated policy field. It is by understanding how ideas, in the form of technical knowledge and practical know-how, are interpreted and channelled into the decision-making that it would be possible to explain the identity and determine the causes of CSDP. The notion of learning communities defines the multiple processes through which actors come together to achieve learning goals in a specific field. By further exploring the explanatory potential of this concept in IR Theory, and by applying it to other policy areas, the gap between knowledge generation and practical implementation may finally be bridged.

9.3   Normative Implications: Towards a Comprehensive CSDP?

In fifteen years of the operational existence of the CSDP, the EU has become a global crisis manager and strengthened its role as a regional security actor, by serving as a partner of the United Nations and finding a relatively stable coexistence with NATO. Since 2012, operational requirements have become more onerous as the demand for security provision increased, due to upheaval in the neighbourhood (cf. the Arab Spring and the 2014 Ukrainian revolution), transformations to global security in a multi-polar world, the growing threat posed by Islamist terrorism, and, last but not least, defence budget restrictions caused by the Eurozone crisis. These new operational experiences are already spurring a new wave of lessons learned (Tardy 2015), which will produce CSDP institutional learning in the ten/fifteen years that will follow the publication of this book. It is of course still premature to draw meaningful conclusions on what lessons have been learned as new crises unfold, and whether and how those lessons will turn into security practices. Although the CSDP is just at the onset of a new policy evolution cycle, some key trends can already be detected.

Early lessons from Libya, Mali, Ukraine, Syria and the Mediterranean show that the EU is politically and militarily impotent whenever a response is needed and the deployment of high-intensity operations is called for. Authors have referred to a period of CSDP existential crisis (Howorth 2014) between 2012 and 2014, marked by slow response to humanitarian tragedies and exacerbated by three factors: the US disengagement from Europe and the "pivot to Asia"; the Eurozone crisis; doubts about the future of the European project, namely the impact of Brexit on security and defence integration in the EU. Yet, there have been signs of revival. The launch of new missions since 2012, and their extension in subsequent years until present (cf. EUCAP Nestor in the Horn of Africa, EUCAP Niger, last but not least EUNAVFOR MED Sophia off the coast of Libya) has been designed to turn the CA into comprehensive action and let the EU assume its global responsibilities in high-risk theatres (Faleg and Blockmans 2012). These initiatives constitute important and concrete steps to tackle insecurity in a comprehensive manner, following the strategic roadmap defined by the regional strategies for the Sahel (EEAS 2012) and the Horn of Africa (Council of the European Union 2011).[3] Furthermore, since the December 2013 European Council, actions have been systematically undertaken to enhance the CSDP operational preparedness and effectiveness, launch new military capability projects through pooling and sharing, move faster towards the creation of a European defence market and redefine the EU security strategy, which the High Representative is expected to deliver by the Summer of 2016.

Notwithstanding these initiatives, CSDP evolution continues to face important challenges. Beyond rhetoric, member states are still reluctant to agree on a common vision for the CSDP, as their strategic cultures and interests still differ significantly (Fiott 2015). This deficit can be best defined as a "governance gap", which reveals the lack of a strong core of states driving integration forward and the absence of an agreement on the model of governance that would satisfy common operational requirements and achieve convergence of national interests (Faleg 2013). Without this core of winning and able member states, governance dynamics cannot steer policy evolution or initiate ambitious reforms in the long-term. Closing the governance gap and rebalancing the CSDP towards a truly comprehensive, civil-military security actor will be an important challenge for future institutional learning processes. A new governance system is needed to boost convergence of strategic cultures, increasing solidarity and trust in national defence planning, revamping strategy-making to attain a clearer level of ambition and last but not least move towards deeper integration (Faleg 2013; Blockmans and Faleg 2015).

These considerations point directly to the great dilemma surrounding the future of EU security cooperation. Acknowledging ten years of progressive institutionalisation and development of shared practices, the Lisbon Treaty has formalised structures and procedures to reinforce the CA, hence integrating military with civilian tools for long and short term crisis response capacity. However, this new arrangement was characterised by scarce resources (worsened in the wake of the Eurozone crisis), lukewarm political underpinning (due to differences in member states preferences resulting in political sensitivities and stumbling blocks, such as the issue of a permanent operational headquarter), and loose strategic direction. How could this stalemate be overcome?

The answer to that is neither in the withdrawal of the state to the benefit of right-minded Brussels-based civil servants controlling policy-making due to their positional power (Dijkstra 2012), nor in the *directoire* of a core group of member states (e.g. the Franco-British) providing the authority for legitimacy and ignition, while at the same time retaining the control over the red button.

The right recipe lies somewhere in the middle. It resides in the formation and consolidation of an empowered community of like-minded agenda-setters belonging to different backgrounds (Commission officers, military officials, Brussels-based diplomats and seconded national experts), but sharing a common sense of practice reinforcing their conviction that a CA to security represents the future of crisis management and conflict prevention. The normative vision and practical aspects of the EU's crisis response should become mutually reinforcing and feed into the strategic discourse. In an integrated approach, the reinforcement of a common *esprit de corps* (Garcia and Pomorska 2015) must necessarily become integrative, breaking the walls between competing cultures and previously separated organisational routines. This process can only work if a series of conditions apply: the presence of constituencies agreeing on the need to provide a strong political and financial backing to this cause—for instance, the German-Swedish initiative to intensify military pooling and sharing in Europe through the implementation of the "Ghent Framework"[4]; a rationale for action justifying the greater push towards deeper integration and greater comprehensiveness—e.g. the austerity measures imposing to "do more with less"; the search for complementarities between NATO's and the EU's pooling and sharing agendas; an empirical validation of the policy enterprise—e.g. emulation of successful operational models and best practices, such as the EU comprehensive efforts in the Horn of Africa and their application to Mediterranean security (Faleg and Blockmans 2015), entailing a co-existence of multi-dimensional and inter-operating missions; finally, the emergence of a consensual/dominant understanding of the strategic way forward, fostered by stronger and accountable leadership.

The bottom line is that the learning communities approach to CSDP reinforces the claim that the power-based representation of technical knowledge and experiential know-how concur in explaining the design and activities of the CSDP as we see it today. As a consequence, these factors are crucial to estimate the trajectories of security cooperation as they will unfold tomorrow. Arguably, the construction of a comprehensive CSDP depends on the capacity of EU leaders to develop a consensual and dominant vision of the changing nature of security affairs. Such vision is imposed by exogenous factors, such as a changing security environment. It is also rooted in practice, through learning by doing, and supported by a sizeable group of member states, who perceive the integrated approach as a common denominator. If theory must serve the practical purpose of making predictions about future scenarios, I would therefore argue that while the first decade of the 2000s was marked by the civilian aspects of CSDP, reflected in the civilian deployments outnumbering military ones, the second decade will be focused on the construction of a comprehensive vision of CSDP out of the design sketched over the past ten years, possibly leading to integrated structures, missions and capabilities. The CSDP has already started its transformation from a civilian to a comprehensive actor. A generational shift is needed to produce a cultural shift, as individuals need to live through and experience new policies.[5] The underlying idea of the CA (that things are done better if done together) was implausible ten years ago and still finds some resistance in certain environments. What makes the difference now is that integrated policies implemented in the Balkans or in the Horn of Africa, through learning by doing and the constitution of nascent professional networks, will plausibly create the practices that will, in turn, back up paradigm innovation.[6]

The number of lessons to be learned to transform the CSDP, at a crucial stage of its development, is considerable. To give new impetus to EU security and defence, there is no other way but learning from past mistakes. As this book has shown, empowering and reinforcing transnational communities is a key step to create a thriving learning environment, step up cooperation among member states and relaunch integrative efforts, which can ultimately lead to a safer and more secure Europe.

NOTES

1. I am grateful to Roberto Roccu for his comments on the limits of a bureaucratic approach to learning communities, as well as for spending countless hours talking academically about soccer, including discussions on the evolution of "Total Football" as an example of norm diffusion in sports tactics.
2. Policy outcomes might be different from what is expected, as shown by the development of a civilian, as opposed to military, CSDP.
3. Cf. also European Parliament (2012).
4. Cf. "Pooling and sharing, German-Swedish initiative", Food for Thought Document, Berlin and Stockholm, November 2010.
5. London Interview, Foreign and Commonwealth Office (December 2012).
6. I am grateful to Mary Martin for her input on the broader relation between theory development and empirical back-up.

References

Abrahamsen, R., and M. Williams. 2006. Security sector reforms: Bringing the private in. *Conflict, Security and Development* 6(1): 2–23.

Adebahr, C. 2009. *Learning and change in European foreign policy: The case of the EU special representatives.* Baden Baden: Nomos.

Adler, E. 1997. Seizing the middle ground: Constructivism in world politics. *European Journal of International Relations* 3(3): 319–367.

Adler, E. 2005. *Communitarian international relations: The epistemic foundations of international relations.* London/New York: Routledge.

Adler, E. 2008. The spread of security communities: Communities of practice, self-restraint, and NATO's Post-Cold War transformation. *European Journal of International Relations* 14(2): 195–230.

Adler, E., and M. Barnett (eds.). 1998. *Security communities.* Cambridge: Cambridge University Press.

Adler, E., and S. Bernstein. 2005. Knowledge in power: The epistemic construction of global governance. In *Power in global governance*, ed. M. Barnett and R. Duvall. Cambridge: Cambridge University Press.

Adler, E., and B. Crawford (eds.). 1991. *Progress in postwar international relations.* New York: Columbia University Press.

Adler, E., and P.M. Haas. 1992. Conclusion: Epistemic communities, world order and the creation of a reflective research program. *International Organization* 46(1): 367–390.

Adler, E., and V. Pouliot. 2011a. International practices. *International Theory* 3(1): 1–36.

Adler, E., and V. Pouliot. (eds.). 2011b. *International practices.* Cambridge Studies in International Relations, October 2011.

© The Author(s) 2017
G. Faleg, *The EU's Common Security and Defence Policy,*
DOI 10.1007/978-3-319-41306-8

Albrecht, P., F. Stepputat, and L. Andersen. 2010. Security sector reform. The European Way. In *The future of security sector reform*. Waterloo: Center for International Governance Innovation.

Allen, D. 1998. Who speaks for Europe? The search for an effective and coherent external policy. In *A common foreign policy for Europe? Competing visions of the CFSP*, ed. J. Peterson and H. Sjursen. London: Routledge.

Allen, D., W. Wessels, and R. Reinhardt (eds.). 1982. *European political cooperation: Towards a foreign policy for Western Europe*. London: Butterworths European Studies.

Allison, G.T. 1971. *Essence of decision: Explaining the Cuban missile crisis*. Boston: Little Brown.

Anastasiou, H. 2007. Securing human rights through war and peace: From paradox to opportunity. In *Philosophical perspectives on the war on terrorism*, The philosophy of peace series, ed. M.P. Gail. Amsterdam: Rodopi Press.

Andréani, G. 2000. Why institutions matter. *Survival* 42(2): 81–95.

Andreatta, F. 2005. Theory and European Union's international relations. In *International relations and the European Union*, ed. C. Hill and M. Smith. Oxford: Oxford University Press.

Argyris, C. 1999. *On organizational learning*, 2nd ed. Malden: Blackwell Publishing.

Argyris, C., and D.A. Schon. 1978. *Organizational learning: A theory of action perspective*. Reading: Addison-Wesley Publishing Company.

Aspinwall, M.D., and G. Schneider. 2000. Same menu, separate tables: The institutionalist turn in political science and the study of European integration. *European Journal of Political Research* 38: 1–36.

Bahnson, C. 2010. The European Union and SSR in Guinea-Bissau. In *The politics of security sector reform: Challenges and opportunities for the European Union's global role*, ed. M. Ekengren and G. Simons, 259–272. Farnham: Ashgate.

Bailes, A.J. 2006. The European defence challenge for the Nordic countries. In *The Nordic countries and the European security and defence policy*, ed. A.J. Bailes, G. Herolf, and B. Sundelius. Oxford: Oxford University Press.

Ball, N. 1998. *Spreading good practices in security sector reform: Policy options for the British government*. London: Saferworld.

Ball, N. 2002. *Enhancing security sector governance: A conceptual framework for UNDP*. New York: UNDP.

Ball, N., and D. Hendrickson. 2009. *Trends in Security Sector Reform (SSR): Policy, practice and research*. CSDG paper no. 20, March 2009.

Ball, N., T. Bouta, and L. van de Goor. 2003. *Enhancing democratic governance of the security sector. An institutional assessment tool*. The Hague: Clingendael Institute.

Barbé, E. 1995. *La seguridad en la Nueva Europa*. Madrid: Catarata.

Barnett, M.N., and M. Finnemore. 1999. The politics, power and pathologies of international organizations. *International Organization* 53(4, Autumn): 699–732.

Barnett, M., H. Kim, M. O'Donnell, and L. Sitea. 2007. Peacebuilding: What is in a name? *Global Governance* 13(1): 36–53.

Barry, L. 2012. *European Security in the 21st century: The EU's comprehensive approach.* Institute of International and European Affairs 17 July 2012.

Batt, J. 2006. *EU Presidency conference on security sector reform in the Western Balkans.* EU Institute for Security Studies, Report 06–03. Available from: http://www.iss.europa.eu/uploads/media/rep06-03.pdf. Accessed 28 June 2011.

Baun, M. 2005. How necessary is a common strategic culture? *Oxford Journal on Good Governance* 2(1): 33–37.

Bausback, I. 2010. The European Union and security sector reform in the democratic Republic of Congo. *International Journal of Rule of Law, Transitional Justice and Human Rights* 1: 154–163.

Beyers, J. 2007. Multiple Embeddedness and Socialization in Europe: The Case of Council Officials. In Checkel, J. T. (ed.) *International Institutions and Socialization in Europe*, Cambridge University Press.

Bellamy, A. 2011. *Global politics and the responsibility to protect: From words to deeds.* New York: Routledge.

Benner, T., A. Binder, and P. Rotmann. 2007. *Learning to build peace? Developing a research framework.* GPPi research paper no. 7.

Bennett, A. 1999. *Condemned to repetition? The rise, fall and reprise of Soviet-Russian military interventionism, 1973–1996.* Cambridge: MIT Press.

Betts, R.K. 1996. The delusion of impartial intervention. In *Managing global chaos*, ed. C. Crocker, F. Hampson, and P. Aall. Washington, DC: US Institute of Peace.

Biava, A., M. Drent, and G.P. Herd. 2011. Characterizing the European Union's strategic culture: An analytical framework. *Journal of Common Market Studies* 49(6): 1227–1248.

Bicchi, F. 2011. The EU as a community of practice: Foreign policy communications in the COREU network. *Journal of European Public Policy* 18(8): 1115–1132.

Bickerton, C.J., B. Irondelle, and A. Menon. 2011. Security co- operation beyond the nation- state: The EU's common security and defence policy. *Journal of Common Market Studies* 49(1): 1–21.

Biehl, H., B. Giegerich, and A. Jonas (eds.). 2013. *Strategic cultures in Europe: Security and defence policies across the continent.* Wiesbaden: Springer.

Biscop, S. 2004. Able and willing? Assessing the EU's capacity for military action. *European Foreign Affairs Review* 9(4): 509–527.

Biscop, S. 2005. *The European security strategy: A global agenda for positive power.* Aldershot: Ashgate.

Biscop, S., and J. Coelmont. 2010. *A strategy for CSDP, Europe's ambitions as a global security provider*, Egmont paper no 37. Gent: Academia Press.

Björkdahl, A., O. Richmond. and S. Kappler. 2009. *The EU peacebuilding framework: Potentials and Pitfalls in the Western Balkans and the Middle East.* JAD-PbP working paper no. 3, June 2009.

Blair, S., and G. Gya. 2010. The two faces of civilian in civilian crisis management: An opportunity to bring them together in the Lisbon era. *Studia Diplomatica* LXIII(1): 105–131.

Bloching, S. 2010. *EU SSR Guinea-Bissau: Lessons identified.* Brussels: International Security Information Service, Europe, 22 November 2010.

Bloching, S. 2011. *Security sector reform missions under CSDP: Addressing current needs.* Brussels: International Security Information Service, Europe.

Blockmans, S. (ed.). 2008. *The European Union and crisis management: Policy and legal aspects.* The Hague: T.M.C-Asser Press.

Blockmans, S., and G. Faleg. 2015. *More Union in European Defence.* Report of a CEPS Task Force chaired by Javier Solana, Centre for European Policy Studies (CEPS), February 2015.

Bono, G. 2002. *European Security and Defence Policy: Theoretical approaches, the Nice Summit and hot issues.* Research and Training Network: Bridging the accountability gap in European security and defence policy, ESDP and Democracy Project, February 2002.

Bono, G. 2004. The EU's military doctrine: An assessment. *International Peacekeeping* 11: 439–456.

Bossong, R. 2012. *EU civilian crisis management and organisational learning,* Economics of security working paper 62. Berlin: Economics of Security.

Bourdieu, P. 1990. *The logic of practice.* Stanford: Stanford University Press.

Breslauer, G.W., and P.E. Tetlock (eds.). 1991. *Learning in US and Soviet foreign policy.* Boulder: Westview Press.

Breuer, F. 2012. Sociological institutionalism, socialisation and the brusselisation of CSDP. In *Explaining the EU's CSDP: Theory in action,* ed. X. Kurosawa and F. Breuer. New York: Palgrave.

Brown, J.S., and P. Duguid. 1998. Organizing knowledge. *California Management Review* 40(3): 90–111.

Bryden, A. 2011. International coherence in security sector reform, *DCAF Horizon 2015 working paper series,* 6, Geneva.

Brzoska, M. 2000. The concept of security sector reform. In *Security sector reform,* Brief 15, ed. H. Wulf, 6–13. Bonn: BICC.

Brzoska, M. 2006. *"Security sector reform in peace support operations", special issue of International peacekeeping.* London: Routledge.

Brzoska, M., and A. Heinemann-Gruder. 2004. Security sector reform and post-conflict reconstruction under international auspices. In *Reform and reconstruction of the security sector,* ed. A. Bryden and H. Hänggi. Münster: Lit Verlag.

Bull, H. 1977. *The anarchical society.* New York: Columbia University Press.

Bull, H., and A. Watson. 1984. *The expansion of international society.* Oxford: Clarendon Press.

Buxton, I. 2008. A First Pillar Perspective on EU and SSR: The development of a comprehensive EU approach. In *The European Union and security sector reform*, ed. P. Fluri and D. Spence. London: John Harper Publishing.

Buzan, B. 1993. From international system to international society: Structural realism and regime theory meet the English school. *International Organization* 47: 327–352.

Cameron, F. 1999. *The foreign and security policy of the European Union: Past, present and future*. Sheffield : Sheffield Academic Press.

Caporaso, J.A. 2000. *The European Union: Dilemmas of regional integration*. Boulder: Westview Press.

Chandler, D. 2007. The security-development nexus and the rise of "anti-foreign policy". *Journal of International Relations and Development* 10: 365–386.

Checkel, J.T. 1999. Social construction and integration. *Journal of European Public Policy* 6(4): 545–560.

Checkel, J.T. 2001. Why comply? Social learning in European identity change. *International Organization* 55(Summer): 553–588.

Checkel, J.T. 2005. International institutions and socialization in Europe. Special issue of *International Organization* 59(4, Fall): 801–1079.

Checkel, J.T. 2007. *International institutions and socialization in Europe*. Cambridge: Cambridge University Press.

Checkel, J.T. 2008. Process tracing. In *Qualitative methods in international relations: A pluralist guide*, ed. A. Klotz and D. Prakash, 114–127. Basingstoke: Palgrave MacMillan.

Chivvis, C.S. 2010. *EU civilian crisis management: The record so far*. Santa Monica: RAND National Defense Research Institute.

Christiansen, Thomas. 2001. *The social construction of Europe*. London: Sage.

Christiansen, T., K.E. Jorgensen, and A. Wiener. 1999. The social construction of Europe. *Journal of European Public Policy* 6(4): 528–544.

Chuter, D. 2006. Understanding security sector reform. *Journal of Security Sector Management* 4(2): 1–21.

Clément, C. 2009a. EUSEC RD Congo. In *European security and defence policy: The first ten years (1999–2009)*, ed. G. Grevi, D. Helly, and D. Keohane, 243–254. Paris: EU Institute for Security Studies.

Clément, C. 2009b. Security sector reform in the DRC: Forward to the past. In *Security sector reform in challenging environments*, ed. H. Born and A. Schnabel, 89–117. Geneva: Centre for the Democratic Control of Armed Forces (DCAF).

Coate, S., and S. Morris. 1999. Policy persistence, in *American economic review*. *American Economic Association* 89(5): 1327–1336.

Cockell, J.G. 2000. Conceptualising peacebuilding: Human security and sustainable peace. In *Regeneration of war-torn societies*, ed. M. Pugh. London: Palgrave Macmillan.

Cohendet, P., Créplet, F. and Dupouet, O. 2001. Organisational Innovation, Communities of Practice and Epistemic Communities: the Case of Linux, in

Kirman, A. and Zimmermann, J.B. (eds) *Economics with Heterogeneous Interacting Agents*, Berlin-Heidelberg: Springer, 303–326.

Cooper, R. 2003. *The breaking of nations: Order and chaos in the twenty first century*. New York: Atlantic Monthly Press.

Cornish, P., and G. Edwards. 2005. The strategic culture of the European Union: A progress report. *International Affairs* 81(4): 801–820.

Council of the European Union. 1999a. Non-military instruments of crisis management. Doc. 11044/99, 16 September 1999.

Council of the European Union. 1999b. Non-military crisis response instruments available in EU member states. Doc. 12323/99, 24 November 1999.

Council of the European Union. 2002a. CIMIC concept for EU-led crisis management operations. Doc. 7106/02, 18 March 2002.

Council of the European Union. 2002b. Action plan for further strengthening of civil-military coordination in EU crisis management. Doc. 13480/1/02, 29 October 2002.

Council of the European Union. 2002c. Crisis management concept: Template. Doc. 14940/02, 28 November 2002.

Council of the European Union. 2002d. Follow-up to the action plan for the further strengthening of civil-military co-ordination in EU crisis management: Crisis management concept: Template. Doc. 14940/02, 28 November 2002.

Council of the European Union. 2003. Civil-Military Co-ordination (CMCO). Doc. 14457/03, 7 November 2003.

Council of the European Union. 2004. Civilian headline goal 2008. Doc. 15863/04, 7 December 2004.

Council of the European Union. 2005a. Civilian headline goal 2008: Proposals by the Council Secretariat on the management of the process during 2005. Doc. 5761/05, 26 January 2005.

Council of the European Union. 2005b. Implementation of the EU training concept in ESDP: Analysis of training requirements in the field of ESDP. Doc.7774/1/05 REV 1, 12 April 2005.

Council of the European Union. 2005c. Civil military cell: Terms of reference. Doc. 10580/1/04 REV 1, 8 September 2005.

Council of the European Union. 2005d. EU concept for ESDP support to Security Sector Reform. Doc. 12566/4/05, 13 October 2005.

Council of the European Union. 2006a. Civil-Military Coordination: Framework paper of possible solutions for the management of EU crisis management operations. Doc.8926/06, 2 May 2006.

Council of the European Union. 2006b. Draft council conclusions on a policy framework for security sector reform. Doc. 9967/06, 6 June 2006.

Council of the European Union. 2006c. Council conclusions on a policy framework for security sector reform. 2736th General Affairs Council meeting—Luxembourg, 12 June 2006.

Council of the European Union. 2006d. Civil-Military Co-ordination (CMCO): Possible solutions for the management of EU crisis management operations: Improving information sharing in support of EU crisis management operations. Doc. 13218/5/06 REV 5, 31 October 2006.

Council of the European Union. 2007a. Draft Aceh Monitoring Mission AMM: Lessons identified and recommendations. Doc. 6596/2/07, 13 April 2007.

Council of the European Union. 2007b. New civilian headline goal 2010. Doc. 14823/07, 9 November 2007.

Council of the European Union. 2007c. Lessons: Reporting process. Doc. 15812/07, 27 November 2007.

Council of the European Union. 2007d. Civilian Response Teams CRT: Follow-up of the implementation process. Doc. 15939/07, 29 November 2007.

Council of the European Union. 2008a. Towards an architecture for evaluation of civilian ESDP missions. Doc. 11207/08, 16 June 2008.

Council of the European Union. 2008b. Guidelines for identification and implementation of lessons and best practices in civilian ESDP missions. Doc. 15987/08, 19 November 2008.

Council of the European Union. 2009a. EU Concept for Civil-Military Co-operation (CIMIC) for EU-led military operations. Doc. 11716/08 REV 1, 3 February 2009.

Council of the European Union. 2009b. Abstract of 2009 annual report on the identification and implementation of lessons and best practices in civilian CSDP missions. Doc. 17487/09, 11 December 2009.

Council of the European Union. 2010a. EU civilian and military capability development beyond 2010. Doc. 17127/10, 7 December 2010.

Council of the European Union. 2010b. Annual report on the identification and implementation of lessons and best practices in civilian CSDP missions in 2010. Doc. 17386/10, 8 December 2010.

Council of the European Union. 2011. "A strategic framework for the Horn of Africa", Annex to the annex of the Council conclusions on the Horn of Africa. Doc. 16858/11, 14 November 2011.

Council of the European Union. 2014. Council conclusions on the EU's comprehensive approach. Foreign Affairs Council meeting, Brussels, 12 May 2014.

Council of the European Union. 2015. Council conclusions on the EU Horn of Africa regional action plan 2015–2020. General Secretariat of the Council, Doc 13200/15, 26 October 2015.

Créplet, F., O. Dupouet, and E. Vaast. 2003. Episteme or practice? Differentiated communitarian structures in a biology laboratory. In *Communities and technologies: Proceedings of the first international conference on communities and technologies*, ed. M. Huysman, E. Wenger, and V. Wulf, 43–63. Amsterdam: Springer.

Cross, M.K. 2007. An EU homeland security? Sovereign vs. supranational order. *European Security* 16(1): 79–97.

Cross, M.K. 2008. A European epistemic community of diplomats. In *The diplomatic corps as an institution of international society*, ed. P. Sharp and G. Wiseman. Basingstoke: Palgrave Macmillan.

Cross, M.K. 2010. *Cooperation by committee: The EU military committee and the committee for civilian crisis management*. Paris: EU Institute for Security Studies, Occasional Paper, February 2010.

Cross, M.K. 2011. *Security integration in Europe: How knowledge-based networks are transforming the European Union*. University of Michigan Press.

Crossan, M., H. Lane, and R. White. 1999. An organizational learning framework: From intuition to institution. *Academy of Management Review* 24(3): 522–537.

D'Urso, D. (2008) *Oltre il learning by doing? La questione della valutazione delle missioni PESD*. Centro Studi di Politica Internazionale (CESPI), Working paper 44/2008.

Dalgaard-Nielsen, A. 2008. Half full, half empty, Review essay. *Survival*, 50: 1, Roudteldge.

DCAF. 2006. *Intergovernmental approaches to security sector reform*. Background paper for the workshop on "Developing a SSR concept for the United Nations", held on 7 July 2006 in Bratislava and co-hosted by the Ministry of Foreign Affairs and the Ministry of Defence of the Slovak Republic, with the assistance of DCAF.

DCAF. 2009 Security sector governance and reform. DCAF Backgrounder, Geneva Centre for the Democratic Control of Armed Forces (DCAF), May 2009.

De Vore, M. 2013. Explaining European armaments cooperation: Interests, institutional design and armaments organizations. *European Foreign Affairs Review* 18(1): 1–28.

De Zwaan, J.W. 2008. Foreign policy and defence cooperation in the European Union: Legal foundations. In *The European Union and crisis management: Policy and legal aspects*, ed. S. Blockmans. The Hague: TCM Asser Press.

Derks, M., and S. More. 2009. The European Union and internal challenges for effectively supporting security sector reform. Clingendael Institute, Security and Conflict Programme, Conflict Research Unit, June 2009.

Deutsch, K. 1963. *The nerves of government*. New York: Free Press.

Deutsch, K.W., Burrell, S.A., Kann. R.A., Lee, M. 1957. *Political Community and the North Atlantic Area: International Organization in the Light of Historical Experience*. Princeton University Press.

Dierkes, M., A. Berthoin Antal, J. Child, and I. Nonaka. 2001. *Handbook of organizational learning and knowledge*. Oxford: Oxford University Press.

Dijkstra, H. 2008. The Council Secretariat's role in the common foreign and security policy. *European Foreign Affairs Review* 13(2): 149–166.

Dijkstra, H. 2010. Explaining variation in the role of the EU Council Secretariat in first and second pillar policy-making. *Journal of European Public Policy* 17(4): 527–544.

Dijkstra, H. 2012. The influence of EU officials in European security and defence. *European Security* 21(3): 311–327.

Dijkstra, H. 2013. *Policy-making in EU security and defense: An institutional perspective.* Basingstoke: Palgrave Macmillan.

Dobbins, J., et al. (eds.). 2008. *Europe's role in nation-building from the Balkans to the Congo.* Santa Monica: RAND Corporation.

Doelle, P., and A. Gouzée de Harven. 2008. Security sector reform and EU development policy. In *The European Union and security sector reform*, ed. P. Fluri and D. Spence. London: John Harper Publishing.

Dolowitz, D., and D. Marsh. 1996. Who learns from whom? *Political Studies* 44(2): 343–357.

Dolowitz, D., and D. Marsh. 2000. Learning from abroad: The role of policy transfer in contemporary policy making. *Governance* 13(1): 5–24.

DOS, DOD, USAID. 2009. *Security Sector Reform*, February 2009.

Downie, R.D. 1998. *Learning from conflict: the US military in Vietnam, El Salvador and the drug war.* Westport: Praeger.

Downs, A. 1967. *Inside bureaucracy.* Boston: Little Brown and co.

Drake, W.J., and K. Nicolaidis. 1992. Ideas, interests and institutionalization: Trade in services and the Uruguay round. *International Organization* 46(1): 37–100.

Drent, M. 2011. The EU's comprehensive approach to security: A culture of coordination? *Studia Diplomatica* LXIV(2): 3–18.

Duke, S. 1999. *The elusive quest for European security: From EDC to CFSP.* Basingstoke: Macmillan.

Duke, S. 2005. *The Linchpin COPS: Assessing the workings and institutional relations of the political and security committee.* Working paper 2005/W/05. European Institute for Public Administration, Maastricht.

Duke, S. 2008. The future of EU-NATO relations: A case of mutual irrelevance through competition? *Journal of European Integration* 30(1): 27–43.

Duke, S., and A. Courtier. 2010. EU peacebuilding: Concepts, players and instruments. In *The European Union and peacebuilding: Policy and legal aspects*, ed. S. Blockmans, J. Wouters, and T. Ruys. The Hague: TMC Asser Press.

Duke, S., and H. Ojanen. 2006. Bridging internal and external security: Lessons from the European security and defence policy. *Journal of European Integration* 28(5): 477–494.

Duke, S., and S. Vanhoonhacker. 2006. Administrative governance in the CFSP: Development and practice. *European Foreign Affairs Review* 11(2): 163–182.

Dunlop, C.A. 2014. The possible experts: How epistemic communities negotiate barriers to knowledge use in ecosystems services policy. *Environment and Planning C: Government and Policy* 32(2): 208–228.

Dursun-Ozkanca, O. (ed.). 2014. *The European Union as an actor in security sector reform*. London: Routledge.

Dursun-Ozkanca, O., and A. Vandemoortele. 2012. The European Union and the security sector reform practices: Challenges of implementation. Special issue of *European Security* 21(2): 139–160.

Dwan, R. 2002. EU Policing for peace operations: What does it mean?. *Discussion paper* no. 23. European Interdependence Research Unit.

Dwan, R. 2006. Civilian tasks and capabilities in EU operations. In *A human security doctrine for Europe: Project, principles, practicalities*, ed. M. Glasius and M. Kaldor. New York: Routledge.

Ehrhart, H.G. 2007. *Civil-military cooperation and coordination in the EU an in selected Member States, Policy Department External Policies*. European Parliament, October.

Ekengren, M., and G. Simons. 2011. *The politics of security sector reform. Challenges and opportunities for the European Union's global role*. Farnham: Ashgate.

Emerson, M., and Gross, E. (ed.). (2007) *Evaluating the EU's crisis missions in the Balkans*. Brussels: Centre for European Policy Studies (CEPS).

ENTRi. 2013. In control: A practical guide for civilian experts working in crisis management missions. Handbook of Europe's New Training Initiative for Civilian Crisis Management (ENTRI). Berlin: Center for International Peace Operations.

EPLO. 2011. *Power analysis: The EU and peacebuilding after Lisbon*. European Peacebuilding Liaison Office (EPLO).

Erikson, J., and M. Rhinard. 2009. The internal—external security nexus: Notes on an emerging research agenda. *Cooperation and Conflict* 44: 243–267.

Etheredge, L.S. 1985. *Can governments learn? American foreign policy and Central American revolutions*. New York: Pergamon Press.

European Commission. 2004. *Annual report 2004 on the European Community's development policy and the implementation of external assistance in 2003*.

European Commission. 2006. A concept for European Community support for security sector reform. Doc. COM(2006) 253, 24 May 2006.

European Commission. 2013. EU enhances its comprehensive approach to external conflicts and crises. Brussels: Press Release, 11 December 2013.

European Commission and HR/VP. 2013. Joint communication to the European Parliament and the Council: The EU's comprehensive approach to external conflicts and crises. Doc. JOIN(2013) 30 final, 11 December 2013.

European External Action Service. 2012. *Strategy for security and development in the Sahel*.

European Parliament. 2010. Consolidating the EU's crisis management structures: Civil-military coordination and the future of the EU OHQ. Study for the Directorate-General for External Policies of the Union, Directorate B, Doc. PE 433.822, March 2010.

European Parliament. 2012. CSDP Missions and operations: Lessons learned processes. Study for the Directorate-General for External Policies of the Union, Directorate B, Doc. PE 457.062, April 2012.

European Security Strategy. 2003. A secure Europe in a better world, adopted by the Heads of States and Government on 12 December 2003.

European Union. 2008. European security and defence policy: The civilian aspects of crisis management. Doc n. civ/02, June 2008.

Faleg, G. 2012. Between knowledge and power: Epistemic communities and the emergence of security sector reform in the EU security architecture. *European Security* 21(2): 161–184.

Faleg, G. 2013. The governance gap in European security and defence. *CEPS Commentary*, 17 December 2013.

Faleg, G. 2014. Between knowledge and power: Epistemic communities and the emergence of security sector reform in the EU security architecture. In *The European Union as an actor in security sector reform*, ed. O. Dursun-Ozkanca. New York: Routledge.

Faleg, G., and S. Blockmans. 2012. The EU's re-engagement as a security actor: Fresh start or still sleepwalking?. *CEPS Commentary*, 12 July 2012.

Faleg, G., and S. Blockmans. 2015. EU Naval Force EUNAVFOR MED sets sail in troubled waters. *CEPS Commentary*, 26 June 2015.

Faleg, G., and A. Giovannini. 2012. The EU between pooling & sharing and smart defence: Making a virtue of necessity?. *CEPS Special Report*, Centre for European Policy Studies (CEPS), May 2012.

Faria, F. 2014. What EU comprehensive approach?. *Briefing Note*, no. 71, European Centre for Development Policy Management, October 2014.

Farkas, A. 1998. *State learning and international change*. Ann Arbor: University of Michigan Press.

Feger, S., and E. Arruda. 2008. Professional learning communities: Key themes from the literature. Report, The Education Alliance, Brown University.

Finnemore, M. 1996. Norms, culture and world politics: Insights from sociology's institutionalism. *International Organization* 50: 325–347.

Finnemore, M., and K. Sikkink. 1998. International norm dynamics and political change. *International Organization* 52(4): 847–917.

Finnemore, M., and K. Sikkink. 2001. Taking stock: The constructivist research program in international relations and comparative politics. *Annual Review of Political Science* 4: 391–416.

Finnish Government. 2008. *Finland's national strategy for civilian crisis management*. Approved by the Finnish Government on 28 August 2008.

Fiott, D. (ed.). 2015. *The common security and defence policy: National perspectives*, Egmont paper, vol. 79. Gent: Academia.

Forster, A., and W. Wallace. 2000. Common foreign and security policy. From shadow to substance? In *Policy making in the European Union*, 4th ed, ed. H. Wallace and W. Wallace, 461–492. Oxford: Oxford University Press.

Foucault, M. 1970. *The order of things: An archaeology of the human sciences.* London: Tavistock.

Froitzheim, M., and F. Soderbaum. 2013. Building peace from the outside: The role of the EU in the Democratic Republic of the Congo. In *Globalization and development: Rethinking interventions and governance*, ed. A. Bigsten, 171–192. London: Routledge.

Fukuda-Parr, S., and C. Messineo. 2012. *Human security: A critical review of the literature.* Centre for Research on Peace and Development (CRPD), Working paper no. 11, KU Leuven.

Fullan, M. 2005. *Leadership and sustainability: System thinkers in action.* San Francisco: Corwin Press.

GAERC, General Affairs and External Relations Council. 2005. *GAERC conclusions.* 269st Council Meeting, Brussels, 21–22 November.

Gaigals, C., and M. Leonhardt. 2001. *Conflict sensitive approaches to development: A review of practice.* London: Saferworld, International Alert, and IDRC.

Galtung, J. 1976. Three approaches to peace: Peacekeeping, peacemaking, and peacebuilding. In *Peace, war and defense: Essays in peace research*, vol. II. Copenhagen: Ejlers.

Garcia, A.E.J. and Pomorska, K 2015. Attitudes, identities and the emergence of an esprit de corps in the EEAS. In Batora, J. and Spence, D. (eds) *The European External Action Service: European Diplomacy Post-Wesphalia.* Basingstoke: Palgrave, 373–391.

George, A.L., and A. Bennett. 2005. *Case studies and theory development in the social sciences.* Cambridge: BCSIA.

Gibbons, L. 1998. CHAD replaces EMAD. In *Humanitarian Exchange Magazine*, Issue 11. Available from: http://www.odihpn.org/report.asp?id_1095. Accessed 7 Sept 2011.

Giegerich, B. 2006. *European security and strategic culture: National responses to the EU's security and defence policy*, Duesseldorfer Schriften zu internationaler Politik und Voelkerrecht 1. 1st ed Baden-Baden, Nomos.

Giegerich, B., and E. Gross. 2006. Squaring the circle? Leadership and legitimacy in European security and defence cooperation. *International Politics* 43(4): 500–509.

Ginsberg, R.H. 2001. *The European Union in international politics: Baptism by fire.* Lanham, MD: Rowman & Littlefield.

Ginsberg, R.H. 2010. *Demystifying the European Union: The enduring logic of regional integration.* Lanham: Rowman & Littlefield.

Gladwell, M. 2002. *The tipping point: How little things can make a big difference.* Boston: Little, Brown.

Glasius, M., and M. Kaldor. 2005. Individuals first: A human security strategy for the European Union. *Internationale Politik und Gesellschaft* 01: 62–82.

Gong, G. 1984. *The standard of "civilisation" in international society.* Oxford: Clarendon Press.

Göteborg European Council. 2001. Presidency Conclusions, Doc. 200/1/01, 15 and 16 June 2001.

Gourlay, C. 2004. European Union procedures and resources for crisis management. *International Peacekeeping* 11(3): 404–421.

Gray, C.S. 2007. *War, peace and international relations: An introduction to strategic history.* London: Routledge.

Greif, A. 2006. *Institutions and the path to modern economy. Lessons from medieval trade.* Cambridge: Cambridge University Press.

Grevi, G. 2007. *Pioneering foreign policy: The EU special representatives,* Chaillot paper 106. Paris: EU Institute for Security Studies, October.

Grevi, G., D. Helly, and D. Keohane. 2009. *European security and defence policy: The first 10 years (1999–2009).* Paris: EU Institute for Security Studies.

Gross, E. 2008. EU Crisis Management in the Western Balkans, in Blockmans, S. (ed) *The European Union and Crisis Management: Policy and Legal Aspects.* The Hague: TMC Asser Press, 311–328.

Gross, E. 2009. *The Europeanization of national foreign policy: Continuity and change in European crisis management.* Basingstoke: Palgrave Macmillan.

Gross, E., and Jacob, M. 2013. Assessing the EU's approach to security sector reform (SSR). Study for the European Parliament, Directorate-General for External Policies of the Union, January 2013.

Gross, E., and A. Juncos (eds.). 2011. *EU conflict prevention and crisis management: Roles, institutions and policies.* New York/London: Routledge.

Guay, T. 1998. *At arm's length: The European Union and Europe's defence industry.* New York: Macmillan Press/St. Martin's Press.

Haas, E.B. 1980. Why collaborate? Issue-linkage and international regimes. *World Politics* 32: 357–405.

Haas, E.B. 1990a. *When knowledge is power: Three models of change in international organizations.* Berkeley: University of California Press.

Haas, P.M. 1990b. *Saving the Mediterranean: The politics of international environmental cooperation.* New York: Columbia University Press.

Haas, P.M. 1992. Introduction: Epistemic communities and international policy coordination. *International Organization* 46(1): 1–35.

Haas, E.B. 1997a. *Nationalism, liberalism and progress: The rise and decline of nationalism.* Ithaca: Cornell University Press.

Haas, P.M. 1997b. *Knowledge, power and international policy coordination.* Columbia: University of South Carolina Press.

Hafner-Burton, E.M., M. Kahler, and A.H. Montgomery. 2009. Network analysis for international relations. *International Organization* 63: 559–592.

Hall, P. 1993. Policy paradigms, social learning, and the state: The case of economic policymaking in Britain. *Comparative Politics* 25(3): 275–296.

Hall, P., and R. Taylor. 1996. Political science and the three new institutionalisms. *Political Studies* 44(5): 936–957.

Hancké, Bob. 2009. *Intelligent research design: A guide for beginning researchers in the social sciences*. Oxford: Oxford University Press.

Hanggi, H., and F. Tanner. 2005. *Promoting security sector governance in the EU's Neighbourhood*, Chaillot paper no. 80. Paris: EU ISS.

Hansen, L. 2011. Performing practices: A poststructuralist analysis of the Muhammad cartoon crisis. In *International practices*, ed. E. Adler and V. Pouliot, 280–309. Cambridge: Cambridge University Press.

Headline Goal 2010, approved by General Affairs and External Relations Council on 17 May 2004 endorsed by the European Council of 17 and 18 June 2004.

Heclo, H. 1974. *Modern social politics in Britain and Sweden*. New Haven: Yale University Press.

Helly, D. 2009. EU SSR Guinea-Bissau. In *European security and defence policy: The first ten years (1999–2009)*, ed. G. Grevi, D. Helly, and D. Keohane, 369–378. Paris: EU Institute for Security Studies.

Helsinki European Council. 1999. Presidency report on non-military crisis management of the European Union, Annex 2 to Annex IV of the Presidency Conclusions, 10 and 11 December 1999.

Hemmer, C. 2000. *Which lessons matter? American foreign policy decision making in the Middle East, 1979–1987*. New York: State University of New York Press.

Hendrickson, D. 1999. A review of security sector reform. Working paper no. 1, Centre for Defence Studies, King's College, University of London.

Hendrickson, D. 2000. Security sector reform: A work in progress. *Humanitarian Exchange Magazine*, October 17. Available from: http://www.odihpn.org/report.asp?id2231. Accessed 25 Aug 2011.

Héritier, A. 2007. *Explaining institutional change in Europe*. Oxford: Oxford University Press.

Hill, C. 1993. The capability-expectations gap, or conceptualizing Europe's international role. *Journal of Common Market Studies* 31(3): 305–328.

Hill, C. 1998. Closing the capability-expectations gap? In *A foreign policy for Europe?* ed. J. Peterson and H. Sjursen. London: Routledge.

Hoffmeister, F. 2008. Inter-pillar coherence in the European Union's civilian crisis management. In *The European Union and crisis management: Policy and legal aspects*, ed. S. Blockmans. The Hague: TMC Asser Press.

Hoffmann, S. 1966. Obstinate or Obsolete? The Fate of the Nation-State and the Case of Western Europe. In *Daedalus*, 95(3): 862–915.

Hofmann, S. 2009. Overlapping institutions in the realm of international security: The case of NATO and the ESDP. *Perspectives on Politics* 7(1): 45–52.

Howorth, J. 2000. *European integration and defence: The ultimate challenge?* Paris: WEU-ISS.

Howorth, J. 2002. The CSDP and the forging of a European security culture. In *Chaillot paper 43*. Paris: EU Institute for Security Studies.

Howorth, J. 2004. Discourse, ideas, and epistemic communities in European security and defence policy. *West European Politics* 27(2): 211–234.

Howorth, J. 2007. *Security and defence policy in the European Union*, European Union series. Basingstoke: Palgrave Macmillan.

Howorth, J. 2011. *Decision making in security and defence policy: Towards supranational intergovernmentalism?* KFG working paper no 25, March 2011.

Howorth, J. 2014. European security post-Libya and post-Ukraine: In search of core leadership. In *Imagining Europe: Towards a more united and effective EU*, IAI research papers no 15, ed. N. Tocci. Edizioni Nuova Cultura.

Howorth, J., and A. Menon. 2009. Still not pushing back: Why the European Union is not balancing the United States. *Journal of Conflict Resolution* 53(5): 727–744.

Huber, G.P. 1991. Organizational learning: The contributing processes and the literatures. *Organization Science* 2(1): 88–115.

Hyde-Price, A. 2007. *European security in the twenty-first century: The challenge of multipolarity*, Contemporary security studies. New York: Routledge.

Ifestos, P. 1987. *European political cooperation: Towards a framework of supranational diplomacy?* Aldershot: Ashgate.

Ikenberry, G.J. 1990. The international spread of privatization policies: Inducements, learning and policy bandwagoning. In *The political economy of the public sector reform and privatization,* ed. E.N. Suleiman and J. Waterbury. Boulder: Westview Press.

Ikenberry, G.J., and C. Kupchan. 1990. Socialization and hegemonic power. *International Organization* 44(3): 283–315.

Ioannides, I. 2006. *EU police reform in Macedonia: "Learning by doing?".* CFSP Forum 4(4), July 2006.

Ioannides, I. 2010. EU civilian capabilities and cooperation with the military sector. In *EU crisis management: Institutions and capabilities in the making*, Quaderni IAI no. 19, ed. E. Greco, N. Pirozzi, and S. Silvestri. Rome: Istituto Affari Internazionali, November 2010.

Italian Presidency Paper on "European defence: NATO/EU consultation, planning and operations", December 2003.

Jacobs, A. 2011. EU civilian crisis management: A crisis in the making? *CSS analysis in security policy*, no 87. Zurich: Centre for Security Studies, February 2011.

Joint Declaration issued at the British-French Summit, Saint-Malo, France, 3–4 December 1998.

Jones, S.G. 2007. *The rise of European security cooperation.* Cambridge: Cambridge University Press.

Jopp, M., and U. Diedrichs. 2009. Learning from failure: The evolution of the EUS's foreign, security and defence policy in the course of the Yugoslav crisis. In *Crises in European integration: Challenges and responses, 1045–2005*, ed. L. Kuhnhardt. New York/Oxford: Berghahn Books.

Jordan, A., and A. Schout. 2006. *The coordination of the European Union: Exploring the capacities for networked governance*. Oxford: Oxford University Press.

Jorgensen, K.E. 1998. The European Union's performance in world politics: How should we measure success? In *Paradoxes of European foreign policy*, ed. J. Zielonka. The Hague: Kluwer Law International.

Jorgensen, K.E. 1999. Possibilities of a "Nordic" influence on the development of the CFSP? In *European security integration: Implications for non-alignment and alliances*, eds. M. Jopp and H. Ojanen. Programme on the Northern Dimension of the CFSP.

Juncos, A.E. 2006. Learning by doing: Civil-military co-ordination in EU crisis management policies. Paper presented at the Third Pan-European Conference of the ECPR Standing Group on EU Politics, Istanbul, 21–23 September 2006.

Juncos, A.E. 2010. The other side of EU crisis management: A sociological institutionalist analysis. In *EU conflict prevention and crisis management: Roles, institutions and policies*, ed. E. Gross and A.E. Juncos. New York: Routledge.

Juncos, A.E. 2015. Manufacturing Esprit de Corps: The case of the European external action service. *Journal of Common Market Studies* 52: 302.

Juncos, A.E., and K. Pomorska. 2006. *Playing the Brussels game: Strategic socialisation in the CFSP Council Working Groups*. European Integration Online papers, vol. 10.

Juncos, A., and K. Pomorska. 2010. Secretariat, facilitator or policy entrepreneur? Role perceptions of the officials of the Council Secretariat. *European Integration Online Papers* 14: 1–26.

Juncos, A.E., and C. Reynolds. 2007. The political and security committee: Governing in the shadow. *European Foreign Affairs Review* 12(2): 127–147.

Jupille, J., and J.A. Caporaso. 1999. Institutionalism and the European Union: Beyond international relations and comparative politics. *Annual Review of Political Science* 2: 429–444.

Kagan, J. 2004. *Paradise & power: America and Europe in the new world order*. London: Atlantic Books.

Kaldor, M., M. Martin, and S. Selchow. 2007. Human security: A new strategic narrative for Europe. *International Affairs* 83(2): 273–288.

Katzenstein, P.J. 1996. *The culture of national security: Norms and identity in world politics*. New York: Columbia University Press.

Katzenstein, P.J. 2010. A world of plural and pluralist civilizations: Multiple actors, traditions and practices. In *Civilizations in world politics: Plural and pluralist perspectives*, ed. P.J. Katzenstein, 1–40. New York: Routledge.

Kay, A. 2005. A critique of the use of path dependency in policy studies. *Public Administration* 83(3): 553–571.

Keohane, R.O. 1988. *Neorealism and its critics*. New York: Columbia University Press.

Keohane, R.O. 1989. *International institutions and state power. Essays in international relations theory*. Boulder: Westview Press.

Keohane, D. 2008. *Willing and able? EU defence in 2020*. London: Centre for European Reform.

Keohane, D. 2011. Lessons from EU peace operations. *Journal of International Peacekeeping* 15: 200–217.

Keukeleire, S. 2010. European security and defence policy: From taboo to spearhead of EU foreign policy. In *The foreign policy of the European Union: Assessing Europe's role in the world*, ed. F. Bindi. Washington, DC: Brookings Institution Press.

Khol, R. 2006. Civil-military coordination in EU crisis management. In *Civilian crisis management: The EU way*, Chaillot paper no. 90, ed. A. Nowak, 123–138. Paris: EU Institute for Security Studies.

King, G., and C.J.L. Murray. 2001. Rethinking human security. *Political Science Quarterly* 116(4): 585–610.

Kirchner, E., and J. Sperling. 2007. *EU security governance*. Manchester: Manchester University Press.

Knoke, D. 1990. *Political Networks: The Structural Perspective*. New York: Cambridge University Press.

Knopf, J.W. 2003. The importance of international learning. *Review of International Studies* 29: 185–207.

Koenig, N. 2012. EU conflict prevention and crisis management: Looking back to look ahead. *The International Spectator* 47(3): 130–132.

Kohler-Koch, B. 2002. European networks and ideas: Changing national policies? *European Integration Online Papers* 6(6): 158.

Kohler-Koch, B., and B. Rittberger. 2006. Review article: The "governance turn" in EU studies. *Journal of Common Market Studies* 44(1): 27–49.

Koops, J. 2012. NATO's influence on the evolution of the European Union as a security actor. In *The influence of international institutions on the European Union*, ed. O. Costa and K.E. Jørgensen. Basingstoke: Palgrave MacMillan.

Korski, D., and R. Gowan. 2009. Can the EU rebuild failing states? A review of Europe's civilian capacities. *ECFR*, October 2009.

Krahmann, E. 2005. Security governance and networks: New theoretical perspectives in transatlantic security. *Cambridge Review of International Affairs* 18(1): 19–34.

Krasner, S.D. (ed.). 1983. *International regimes*. Ithaca: Cornell University Press.

Kratochwil, F.V. 1989. *Rules, norms, and decisions. On the conditions of practical and legal reasoning in international relations and domestic affairs*. Cambridge: Cambridge University Press.

Kriesi, H., and M. Jegen. 2001. The Swiss energy policy elite: The actor constellation of a policy domain in transition. *European Journal of Political Research* 39(2): 251–287.

Kupchan, C.A. 2003. *The end of the American era: US foreign policy and the geopolitics of the twenty-first century.* New York: Vintage Books.

Kuperman, K. 2008. The moral hazard of humanitarian intervention. *International Studies Quarterly* 52(1): 49.

Lachmann, N. 2010. *NATO-CSDP-EU relations: Sketching the map of a community of practice.* CEPSI, University of Montreal, FALL 2010.

Ladzik, J. 2009. *EU military and civilian crisis management operations: The first six years,* European Policy Brief. London: The Global Policy Institute, April 2009.

Lavenex, S., and F. Schimmelfennig (eds.). 2009. EU external governance. Special issue of *Journal of European Public Policy* 16(6): 791–949.

Law, D.M. 2006. *The post-conflict security sector,* DCAF policy paper 14. Geneva, June 2006.

Law, D.M. 2007. Intergovernmental organizations and their role in security sector reform. In *Intergovernmental organizations and security sector reform,* ed. D.M. Law. Geneva: DCAF.

Law, D.M., and O. Myshlovska. 2008. The evolution of the concepts of security sector reform and security sector governance: The EU perspective. In *The European Union and security sector reform,* ed. P. Fluri and D. Spence. London: John Harper Publishing.

Le Sage, A. 1998. Engaging the political economy of conflict: Towards a radical humanitarianism. *Civil Wars* 1(4): 27–55.

Lederach, J.P. 1997. *Building peace: Sustainable reconciliation in divided societies.* Washington, DC: U.S. Institute of Peace Press.

Legro, J.W. 1997. Which norms matter? Revisiting the "failure" of internationalism. *International Organization* 51(1): 31–63.

Leng, R.J. 2000. *Bargaining and learning in recurring crises: The Soviet-American, Egyptian-Israeli, and Indo-Pakistani Rivalries.* Ann Arbor: University of Michigan Press.

Levitt, B., and J.G. March. 1988. Organizational learning. *Annual Review of Sociology* 14: 319–340.

Levy, J.S. 1994. Learning and foreign policy: Sweeping a conceptual minefield. *International Organization* 48: 279–312.

Lindborg, C. 2002. European approaches to civilian crisis management. *BASIC special report.* Washington, DC, March 2002.

Liotta, P.H., and T. Owen. 2006. Why human security? *The Whitehead Journal of Diplomacy and International Relations* 7(1): 37–54.

MacFarlane, S.N., and Y.F. Khong. 2006. *Human security and the UN: A critical history.* Indianapolis: Indiana University Press.

Major, C., and C. Molling. 2009. More than wishful thinking? The EU, UN NATO and the comprehensive approach to military crisis management. In *Military crisis management: The challenge of inter-organizationalism*, ed. J.A. Koops. Studia Diplomatica, vol. LXII(3).

March, J.G., and J.P. Olsen. 1984. The new institutionalism: Organizational factors in political life. *American Political Science Review* 78: 734–749.

March, J.G., and J.P. Olsen. 1989. *Rediscovering institutions: The organizational basis of politics*. New York: Free Press.

March, J.G., and J.P. Olsen. 2004. *The logic of appropriateness*. Oslo: ARENA Working papers, WP 04/09.

Marier, P. 2009. The power of institutionalized learning: The uses and practices of commissions to generate policy change. *Journal of European Public Policy* 16(8): 1204–1223.

McNamara, K. 1998. *The currency of ideas*. Ithaca: Cornell University Press.

Mearsheimer, J.J. 1990. Correspondence: Back to the future, Part II: International relations theory and post-Cold War Europe. *International Security* 15(2): 194–199.

Meharg, S., A. Arnusch, and S. Merrill. (eds.). 2010. Security sector reform: A case study approach to transition and capacity building. PKSOI papers, US Army Peacekeeping and Stability Operations Institute, January 2010.

Menkhaus, K. 2004. *Impact assessment in post-conflict peacebuilding challenges and future directions*. Interpeace.

Menon, A. 2006. The limits of comparative politics: International relations in the European Union. In *Comparative federalism: The European Union and the United States in comparative perspective*. Oxford: Oxford University Press.

Menon, A. 2009. Empowering paradise? The ESDP at ten. *International Affairs* 85: 2227–2246.

Menon, A. 2011a. Power, institutions and the CSDP: The promise of institutionalist theory. *Journal of Common Market Studies* 49(1): 83–100.

Menon, A. 2011b. European defence policy from Lisbon to Libya. *Survival* 53(3): 75–90.

Menon, A., and U. Sedelmeier. 2010. Instruments and intentionality: Civilian crisis management and enlargement conditionality in EU security policy. *West European Politics* 33(1): 75–92.

Menon, A., K. Nicolaïdis, and J. Welsh. 2004. In defence of Europe: A response to Kagan. *Journal of European Affairs* 3(2): 5–14.

Mérand, F. 2008. *European defence policy: Beyond the nation state*. Oxford: Oxford University Press.

Mérand, F. 2012. Bricolage: A sociological approach to the making of CSDP. In *Explaining the EU's common security and defence policy: Theory in action*, ed. X. Kurosawa and F. Breuer. Basingstoke: Palgrave-Macmillan.

Mérand, F., S. Hofmann, and B. Irondelle. 2011. Governance and state power: A network analysis of European security. *Journal of Common Market Studies* 49(1): 121–147.

Merlingen, M. 2006. *European Union peacebuilding and policing: Governance and the European security and defence policy*, Routledge advances in European politics 40. London: Routledge.

Merlingen, M., and R. Ostrauskaite. 2005. ESDP police missions: Meaning, context and operational challenges. *European Foreign Affairs Review* 10(2): 215–235.

Meyer, C.O. 2006. *The quest for a European strategic culture: Changing norms on security and defence in the European Union.* Basingstoke: Palgrave Macmillan.

Moravcsik, A. 1998. *The choice for Europe: Social purpose and state power from Messina to Maastricht*, Cornell studies in political economy. Ithaca: Cornell University Press.

More, S. and M. Price. 2011. The EU's support to security sector reform in the Democratic Republic of Congo: Perceptions from the field in Spring 2010. Clingendael Conflict Research Unit, May 2011.

Mostl, M. 2011. Civil-military coordination in the common security and defence policy of the European Union. In *Sustainable peacebuilding, human security perspective*, eds. W. Benedek et al. Special Focus vol. 1:2011.

Mouritzen, H. 1991. Tensions between the strong and the strategies of the weak. *Journal of Peace Research* 28(2): 217–230.

Nadelmann, E. 1990. Global prohibition regimes: The evolution of norms in international society. *International Organization* 44(4): 479–526.

Nelsen, B.F., and A. Stubb (eds.). 2003. *The European Union. Readings on the theory and practice of European integration.* Houndmills: Palgrave Macmillan.

Non-paper by the United Kingdom, Austria and Finland for a seminar on CMCO, London, 17 October 2005.

Norheim-Martinsen, P.M. 2010. Beyond intergovernmentalism: European security and defence policy and the governance approach. *Journal of Common Market Studies* 48(5): 1351–1365.

North, D.C. 1990. *Institutions, institutional change and economic performance.* Cambridge: Cambridge University Press.

Nowak, A. (ed.). 2006. Civilian crisis management: The EU way. *Chaillot paper* no 90. EU Institute for Security Studies, June 2006.

Nuttall, S. 2000. *European political cooperation.* Oxford: Clarendon Press.

Nye, J.S. 1987. Nuclear learning and US-Soviet security regimes. *International Organization* 41: 371–402.

Nye J. 2004. *Soft Power: The Means to Success in World Politics.* New York: Public Affairs.

OECD. 1997. Conflict, peace and development co-operation on the threshold of the 21st century. DAC Policy Statement, May 1997.

OECD 2001. Conflict, Peace and Development Cooperation. In *The DAC Guidelines: Helping Prevent Violent Conflict.* Paris: OECD Publishing.

OECD. 2001a. Security issues and development cooperation: A conceptual framework for enhancing policy coherence. In *Conflict Prevention and Development Cooperation Papers, The DAC Journal* 2(3): 31–71.

OECD. 2001b. Helping prevent violent conflict. *DAC guidelines and references series.* Paris: OECD Publishing.

OECD 2004. *Security system reform and governance*, DAC guidelines and reference series. Paris: OECD Publishing.

OECD. 2005. *Security system reform and governance*, DAC guidelines and references series. Paris: OECD Publishing.

OECD. 2007. *OECD-DAC handbook on security system reform: Supporting security and justice.* Paris: OECD Publishing.

Øhrgaard, J.C. 1997. 'Less than supranational, more than intergovernmental': European political cooperation and the dynamics of intergovernmental integration. *Millenium: Journal of International Studies* 26: 1.

Ojanen, H. 2000. The EU and its Northern Dimension: An actor in search of a policy, or a policy in search of an actor? *European Foreign Affairs Review* 5: 359–376.

Ojanen, H. 2008. Finland and the ESDP: "Obliquely forwards"?. In *New security issues in Northern Europe: The Nordic and Baltic States and the ESDP*, ed. C. Archer. UACES Contemporary European studies series. Abingdon: Routledge.

Olsen, J.P. 2002. *The many faces of Europeanization.* Working paper no. 1, ARENA Centre for European Studies, Oslo.

Olsen, G.R., and J. Pilegaard. 2005. The cost of non-Europe? Denmark and the common security and defence policy. *European Security* 14(3): 339–350.

OSCE. 1990. *Charter of Paris for a New Europe*, 19–21 November 1990.

OSCE. 1994. Code of conduct on politico-military aspects of security. Doc. FSC/1/95, 3 December 1994.

OSCE. 1999. *Charter for European Security.* Istanbul Summit, November 1999.

Pape, R. 2005. Soft balancing against the United States. *International Security* 30(1): 7–45.

Paris, R. 2002. International peacebuilding and the 'mission civilisatrice'. *Review of International Studies* 28: 637–656.

Peake, G., A. Horn, and F. Olonisakin. 2006. United Kingdom-Led security sector reform in Sierra Leone. *Civil Wars* 8(2): 109–123.

Perruche, J.P. 2006. The European security strategy and the future of the European security and defence policy. Public Hearing, European Parliament, 13 July.

Peterson, J., R. Alcaro. and N. Tocci. 2012. Multipolarity and transatlantic relations. *Transworld working paper*, no 1. Istituto Affari Internazionali.

Pierson, P. 1996. The path to European integration: A historical institutionalist analysis. *Comparative Political Studies* 29(2): 123–163.

Pijpers, A., E. Regelsberger, and W. Wessels. (eds.). 1988. *European political cooperation in the 1980s: A common foreign policy for Western Europe?* Martinus Nijhoff Publishers/Trans European Policy Studies Association (TEPSA). Dordrecht: Martinus Nijhoff Publishers.

Pirozzi, N. 2013. *The EU's comprehensive approach to crisis management.* Geneva Centre for the Democratic Control of Armed Forces, EU Crisis Management Papers Series, June 2013.

Pirozzi, N., and S. Sandawi. 2009. *Military and civilian ESDP missions: Ever growing and effective?* Documenti IAI 09/29. Rome: Istituto Affari Internazionali.

Pollack, M.A. 2003. *The engines of European integration: Delegation, agency, and agenda setting in the EU.* Oxford: Oxford University Press.

Pond, E. 1999. Kosovo: A catalyst for Europe. *Washington Quarterly* 22(4): 77–92.

Pond, E. 2002. *The rebirth of Europe,* 2nd ed. Washington, DC: Brookings Institution Press.

Posen, B. 2006. European Union security and defense policy: Response to unipolarity? *Security Studies* 15(2): April-June 2006, 149–186.

Pouliot, V. 2008. The logic of practicality: A theory of practice of security communities. *International Organization* 62(2): 257–288.

Pouliot, V. 2010. The materials of practice: Nuclear warheads, rhetorical commonplaces and committee meetings in Russian-Atlantic relations. *Cooperation and Conflict* 45(3): 294–311.

Powell, W.W., and P.J. DiMaggio (eds.). 1991. *The new institutionalism in organizational analysis.* Chicago: University of Chicago Press.

Price, R., and C. Reus-Smit. 1998. Dangerous liaisons? Critical international relations theory and constructivism. *European Journal of International Relations* 4(2): 59–94.

Pullinger, S. 2006. Developing EU civil military co-ordination: The role of the new civilian military cell. *Joint Report by ISIS Europe and CeMiSS,* Brussels, June 2006.

Quille, G., G. Gasparini, R. Menotti, and N. Pirozzi. 2006. *Developing EU civil military co-ordination: The role of the new civilian military cell.* Brussels: Cemiss.

Radaelli, C.M. 1995. The role of knowledge in the policy process. *Journal of European Public Policy* 2(2): 159–183.

Radaelli, C.M. 2000. Policy transfer in the European Union: Institutional isomorphism as a source of legitimacy. *Governance* 13(1): 25–43.

Radaelli, C.M. 2009. Measuring policy learning: Regulatory impact assessment in Europe. *Journal of European Public Policy* 16(8): 1145–1164.

Raemmler, S. 2010. Organisational learning in CSDP. Paper presented at the 7 Pan-European International relations Conference (SGIR), Stockholm, 9–11 September 2010.

Rehrl, J., and H.B. Weisserth. (eds.). 2010 *Handbook on CSDP. The common security and defence policy of the European Union.* Publication of the Federal Ministry of Defence and Sports of the Republic of Austria.

Report on the implementation of the European Security Strategy. 2008. "Providing security in a changing world", approved by the European Council held in Brussels on 11 and 12 December 2008 and drafted under the responsibilities of the EU High Representative Javier Solana.

Reynolds, C. 2007. Governing security in the European Union: Institutions as dynamics and obstacles. In *Dynamics and obstacles of European governance*, ed. D. de Bievre and C. Neuhold. Cheltenham: Edward Elgar.

Richmond, O. 2001. Human security, the 'rule of law,' and NGOs: Potentials and problems for humanitarian intervention. *Human Rights Review* 2(4), July–September 2001.

Richmond, O. 2004. The globalisation of responses to conflict and the peace-building consensus. *Cooperation and Conflict* 39(2): 129.

Rieff, D. 2002. Humanitarianism in crisis. *Foreign Affairs* 81(6): 111–121.

Rieker, P. 2004. Europeanization of Nordic security: The European Union and the changing security identities of the Nordic States. *Cooperation and Conflict* 39: 369–392.

Risse-Kappen, T. 1994. Ideas do not float freely: Transnational coalitions, domestic structures, and the end of the Cold War. *International Organization* 48(2): 185–214.

Risse-Kappen, T. 1995. *Co-operation among democracies*. Princeton: Princeton University Press.

Rochon, T.R. 1998. *Culture moves: Ideas, activism, and changing values*. Princeton: Princeton University Press.

Rogers, E. 1983. *Diffusion of innovations*, 3rd ed. New York: The Free Press.

Rose, N., and P. Miller. 1992. Political power beyond the state: The problematics of government. *British Journal of Sociology* 43: 173–205.

Rosenau, J. 1992. Governance, order and change in world politics. In *Governance without government: Order and change in world politics*, ed. J. Rosenau and E. Czempiel. Cambridge: Cambridge University Press.

Ruggie, J.G. 1975. International responses to technology: Concepts and trends. *International Organizations* 29(3): 557–583.

Rynning, S. 2011. Realism and the common security and defence policy. *Journal of Common Market Studies* 49(1): 23–42.

Sabatier, P. 1998. The advocacy coalition framework: Revisions and relevance for Europe. *Journal of European Public Policy* 5(1): 98–130.

Sabatier, P., and H.C. Jenkins-Smith. 1993. *Policy change and learning. An advocacy coalition approach*. Boulder: Westview Press.

Sabiote, M.A. 2010. New tasks for peace operations? The interlinkage between SSR and integrated peace missions. In *Multilateral security and ESDP operations*, ed. F. Attina' and D. Irrera. Burlington: Ashgate.

Santa Maria da Feira European Council. 2000. Presidency Conclusions, 19 and 20 June 2000.

Santopinto, F., and M. Price (eds.). 2013. *National visions of EU defence policy: Common denominators and misunderstandings.* Brussels: Center for European Policy Studies.

Sartori, G. 1970. Concept misinformation in comparative politics. *American Political Science Review* 64(4): 1033–1053.

Scannell, D. 2004. Financing ESDP military operations. *European Foreign Affairs Review* 9(4): 529–549.

Schatzki, T.R., K. Knorr Cetina, and E. von Savigny (eds.). 2001. *The practice turn in contemporary theory.* New York: Routledge.

Schmidt, V.A. 2010. Taking ideas and discourse seriously: explaining change through discursive institutionalism as the fourth 'new institutionalism'. In *European Political Science Review*, vol. 2 no. 1 pp. 1–25.

Schnabel, A. and Ehrhart, H.G. (eds) 2005. *Security Sector Reform and Post-Conflict Peacebuilding.* New York: United Nations University Press.

Schroeder, U. 2007. Governance of EU Crisis Management. In Emerson, M. and Gross, E. (eds) *Evaluating the EU's Crisis Management Missions in the Balkans.* Brussels: Centre for European Policy Studies.

Schurman, R., and W.A. Munro. 2010. *Fighting for the future of food: Activists versus agribusiness in the struggle over biotechnology.* Minneapolis: University of Minnesota Press.

Schuyer, J. 2008. The civilian headline goal 2008: Developing civilian crisis management capabilities for the EU. In *The European Union and crisis management: Policy and legal aspects,* ed. S. Blockmans. The Hague: T.M.C. Asser Institute Press.

Scott, W.R., and J.W. Meyer (eds.). 1994. *Institutional environment and organizations: Structural complexity and individualism.* Thousand Oaks: Sage.

Searle, J. 1995. *The construction of social reality.* New York: Free Press.

Sedra, M. 2006. Security sector reform in Afghanistan: The slide towards expediency. *International Peacekeeping* 13(1): 94–110.

Sheriff, A. 2007. Security sector reform and EU norm implementation. In *Intergovernmental approaches to security sector reform,* ed. D.M. Law. Geneva: DCAF.

Short, C. 2000. Security sector reform and military expenditure. Speech to the security sector reform and military expenditure symposium, London, 17 February. Available from: http://www.clareshort.co.uk/speeches/DFID/17%20Feb%202000.pdf. Accessed 1 Sept 2011.

Sikkink, K. 1998. Transnational politics, international relations theory and human rights. *Political Science and Politics* 31(3): 518.

SIPRI Yearbook. 1996. *Armaments, disarmament and international security.* Oxford: Oxford University Press.

SIPRI Yearbook 2006. Armaments, Disarmament and International Security. Stockholm International Peace Research Institute.

Sira, I.H., and J. Gräns. 2010. *The promotion of human security in EU security policies.* INEX policy brief no 7, March 2010.

Sjursen, H. 2003. Understanding the common foreign and security policy: Analytical building blocks. In *Understanding the European Union's external relations,* ed. M. Knodt and S. Princen. London: Routledge.

Smith, M.E. 2003. Institutional moments, policy performance and the future of EU security/defense policy. *EUSA Review* (European Union Studies Association) 16(1).

Smith, M.E. 2004a. *Europe's foreign and security policy: The institutionalization of cooperation.* Cambridge: Cambridge University Press.

Smith, M.E. 2004b. Institutionalization, policy adaptation and European foreign policy cooperation. *European Journal of International Relations* 10(1): 95–136.

Smith, M.E. 2005. CFSP and ESDP: From idea to institution to policy? In *Common foreign and security policy,* ed. M. Holland. London: Continuum.

Smith, K.E. 2008. *European Union foreign policy in a changing world.* Cambridge: Polity.

Smith, K.E. 2010. The European Union in the world: Future research agendas. In *Research agendas in EU studies: Stalking the elephant,* ed. M. Egan, N. Nugent, and W. Paterson. Basingstoke: Palgrave.

Smith, M.E. 2011. Developing a 'comprehensive approach' to international security: Institutional land the CSDP. Paper presented at the 2011 meeting of the European Union Studies Association (EUSA).

Spence, D., and P. Fluri. 2008. *The European Union and security sector reform.* London: John Harper Publishing.

Stein, J.G. 1994. Political learning by doing: Gorbatchev as an uncommitted thinker and motivated learner. *International Organization* 48: 155–183.

Stein, J.G. 1996. Deterrence and learning in an enduring rivalry: Egypt and Israel, 1948-73. *Security Studies* 6: 104–152.

Steinmo, S., K. Thelen, and F. Longstreth (eds.). 1992. *Structuring politics: Historical institutionalism in comparative analysis.* Cambridge: Cambridge University Press.

Stoett, P. 1999. *Human and global security: An exploration of terms.* Toronto: University of Toronto Press.

Stone Sweet, A., W. Sandholtz, and N. Fligstein (eds.). 2001. *The institutionalization of Europe.* Oxford: Oxford University Press.

Sudgen, J. 2006. Security sector reform: The role of epistemic communities in the UK. *Journal of Security Sector Management* 4(4): 1–20.

Suhrke, A. 1999. Human security and the interests of states. *Security Dialogue* 30(3): 265–276.

SWP/ZIF. 2012. *The crisis management toolbox.* Berlin: German Institute for International and Security Affairs, Center for International Peace Operations.

Tadjbakhsh, S., and A. Chenoy. 2007. *Human security: Concepts and implications*. London: Routledge.

Tardy, T. 2005. EU-UN cooperation in peacekeeping: A promising relationship in a constrained environment. In *The EU and the UN: Partners in effective multilateralism*, Chaillot paper 78, ed. M. Ortega. Paris: EU Institute for Security Studies.

Tardy, T. 2011. *Cooperating to build peace: The UN-EU inter-institutional complex*, Geneva papers research series, 2 (May 2011). Geneva: Geneva Centre for Security Policy (GCSP).

Tardy, T. 2015. *CSDP in action: What contribution to international security?*, Chaillot Paper no. 134, EU Institute for Security Studies, May 2015.

Tocci, N. 2008. *The European Union, civil society and conflict transformation*, MICROCON policy briefing 3, June.

Tonra, B. 2001. *The Europeanisation of national foreign policy: Dutch, Danish and Irish foreign policy in the European*. Union: Ashgate.

Tonra, Ben, and Thomas Christiansen. 2004. *Rethinking European Union foreign policy*. Manchester: Manchester University Press.

Tschirgi, N. 2003. Peacebuilding as the link between security and development: Is the window of opportunity closing? *Studies in Security and Development*. New York: International Peace Academy. December 2003.

UNDP. 1994. *Human development report 1994*. Oxford: Oxford University Press.

United Nations. 1992. An agenda for peace: Preventive diplomacy, peacemaking and peace-keeping. Report of the Secretary-General pursuant to the statement adopted by the Summit Meeting of the Security Council on 31 January 1992.

United Nations. 2009. Human security and peacebuilding in Africa: The need for an inclusive approach. Report, December 2009.

US Agency for International Development (USAID), US Department of Defense (DOD), US Department of State (DOS) 2009. *Security Sector Reform*. Policy Guidelines, February 2009.

Van Eekelen, W. 2006. *From words to deeds: The continuing debate on European security*, CEPS-DCAF Joint publication. Brussels: Centre for European Policy Studies.

Vanhoonacker, S., and A. Jacobs. 2010. ESDP and institutional change: The case of Belgium. *Security Dialogue* 41(5): 559–581.

Vanhoonacker, S., H. Dijkstra, and H. Maurer. 2010. Understanding the role of bureaucracy in the European Security and defence policy: The state of the art. In *Understanding the role of bureaucracy in the European Security and defence policy*, ed. Vanhoonacker, S. et al. European Integration online Papers (EIoP), Special Issue 1, Vol. 14, http://eiop.or.at/eiop/texte/2010-004a.htm

Vennesson, P. 2010. Competing visions for the European Union grand strategy. *European Foreign Affairs Review* 15: 57–75.

Verdun, A. 1999. The role of the Delors Committee in the creation of EMU: An epistemic community? *Journal of European Public Policy* 6(2): 308–328.

Wallace, H., W. Wallace, and M.A. Pollack. 2005. *Policy-making in the European Union*, The New European Union series, 5th ed. Oxford: Oxford University Press.

Waltz, K.N. 1979. *Theory of international politics*. Reading: Addison-Wesley Publishers.

Webber, M., S. Croft, J. Howorth, T. Terriff, and E. Krahmann. 2004. The governance of European security. *Review of International Studies* 30: 3–26.

Wedin, L. 2008. Northern Europe and the ESDP: The case of Sweden. In *New security issues in Northern Europe: The Nordic and Baltic States and the ESDP*, ed. Archer, C. UACES Contemporary European studies series.

Weiler, Q. 2009. The European Union and security sector reform in Africa: A leader in theory, a laggard in reality? Bruges Regional Integration and Global Governance Papers, 1, United Nation University CRIS.

Weiss, T.G. 1999. *Military-civilian interactions: Intervening in humanitarian crises*. Lanham: Rowman & Littlefield.

Weiss, T.G. 2011. RtoP alive and well after Libya. *Ethics & International Affairs* 25(3): 287–292.

Wendling, C. 2010. The comprehensive approach to civil-military crisis management: A critical analysis and perspective. *Institut de Recherche Stratégique de l'Ecole Militaire (IRSEM)* 1: 154–166.

Wendt, A. 1992. Anarchy is what states make of it: The social construction of power politics. *International Organization* 46(2): 391–425.

Wendt, A. 1999. *Social theory of international politics*. Cambridge: Cambridge University Press.

Wenger, E. 1998. *Communities of practice: Learning, meaning and identity*. Cambridge: Cambridge University Press.

Wenger, E., R. McDermott, and W.M. Snyder. 2002. *Cultivating communities of practice: A guide to managing knowledge*. Boston: Harvard Business Press.

Wessels, W. 1982. European political cooperation: A new approach to European foreign policy. In *European political cooperation: Towards a foreign policy for Western Europe*, ed. D. Allen, R. Reinhardt, and W. Wessels. London: Butterworths.

Whiteneck, D. 1996. The industrial revolution and birth of the anti mercantilist idea: Epistemic communities and global leadership. *Journal of World-Systems Research* 2(1): 40–57.

Wiener, A. 2008. *The invisible constitution of politics: Contested norms and international encounters*. New York: Cambridge University Press.

Williams, R. 2002. Development agencies and security-sector restructuring. *Conflict, Security & Development* 2(1): 145–149.

Wouters, J., and T. Ruys. 2008. EU-UN. In *The European Union and crisis management: Policy and legal aspects*, ed. S. Blockmans. The Hague: TMC Asser Press.

Young, O. 1989. *International cooperation: Building regimes for natural resources and the environment*. Ithaca: Cornell University Press.

Zito, A.R. 2001. Epistemic communities, collective entrepreneurship and European integration. *Journal of European Public Policy* 8(4): 585–603.

Zito, A.R. 2009. European agencies as agents of governance and EU learning. *Journal of European Public Policy* 16(8): 1224–1243.

Zito, A.R., and A. Schout. 2009. Learning theory reconsidered: EU integration theories and learning. *Journal of European Public Policy* 16(8): 1103–1123.

INDEX

A

Aceh monitoring mission, CSDP missions and operations, 59

Action Plan for non-military crisis management, 90

adaptation, 3, 5, 7, 18, 20, 37n4, 38n6

Afghanistan, 18, 44, 117, 123, 147, 149, 150, 159n24

Africa, 4, 42, 44, 59, 60, 67, 83, 112, 115, 160n24, 187, 189, 190

African Security Sector Network (ASSN), 112, 115

African Union (AU), 42, 83

Agency-structure debate, 182

an Agenda for Peace, 44, 45

Amsterdam Treaty, 86, 90

Anna Lindh, 167

Anti-federalists member states, 87

arrangements of knowledge, 62, 72

Article 17 TEU, 88

Asia, 4, 58, 187

ASSN. *See* African Security Sector Network (ASSN)

Atlanticists, 18, 27, 87, 161n43

AU. *See* African Union (AU)

Austria, 57, 62n7, 63n17, 87, 107, 108, 114, 115, 132, 134, 152, 153, 160n41

Austrian Study Center for Peace and Conflict Resolution, 107, 153

B

background knowledge, 8, 21, 23, 25, 26, 38n12, 136, 165, 171, 174, 178, 183

balance of power, 6, 15, 65, 70–2

Balkans, 4, 16, 17, 31, 56, 58, 86, 87, 90, 91, 96n6, 101, 104, 114, 115, 129, 136, 141, 144, 147, 168, 190

Benelux, 120

Berlin Plus Agreement, 4

Berlin wall, unification of Germany, 136

Bosnia, 58, 60, 87, 91, 94, 97n30, 117, 141, 148, 152

Boutros Boutros-Ghali, 44, 45

Brusselsisation, 8, 17, 67, 178

Note: Page numbers followed by 'n' refer to footnotes.

© The Author(s) 2017
G. Faleg, *The EU's Common Security and Defence Policy*,
DOI 10.1007/978-3-319-41306-8

constituencies, 3, 7, 9, 10, 29, 30, 87, 109, 112, 125, 126, 130, 131, 137, 157, 166, 172, 182, 189

constructivism, 18, 37n4

content analysis, 37, 85, 126n1

COREPER. *See* Committee of Permanent Representatives (COREPER)

Council Secretariat, 6, 33, 57, 66, 68, 72, 73, 78, 85, 88, 90, 94, 96n15, 108, 117, 118, 122, 123, 126n1, 134, 158n1, 175n2

CPDC. *See* Conflict Prevention and Development Co-operation Network(CPDC)

Cranfield University, 111

Crisis Management and Planning Directorate (CMPD), 67, 68, 74, 75n2, 94, 108, 122, 134, 147

Crisis Management Board EEAS, 67

Crisis Management Center (Finland), 154

Crisis Management GOALKEEPER, 148

critical communities, 21

Critical Maritime Routes Programme, 59

CSDG. *See* Conflict, Security and Development Group (CSDG)

CSDP. *See* Common Security and Defence Policy (CSDP)

cyber security, 186

D

DDR. *See* Disarmament, demobilization and reintegration (DDR)

Delors Committee, 164

Democratic control of armed forces, 95n4, 102, 107, 113, 132

Democratic Republic of Congo, 46, 147

Department for International Development (DFID), 107, 110, 115, 132

Deployable European Expert Teams, 124

DEVCO. *See* International Cooperation and Development (DEVCO)

Development assistance, 44, 80, 95, 103, 104, 111

Development Assistance Committee (DAC)-OECD, 80, 84, 109, 111, 112, 114–16, 118, 120, 127n9, 168

DFID. *See* Department for International Development (DFID)

DFID's Conflict and Humanitarian Affairs Department (CHAD), 46, 110, 115

Disarmament, demobilization and reintegration (DDR), 82

dominance, 3, 30, 117, 164, 172–4, 177, 179, 184

durability, Legro's criteria for norm robustness, 30, 34, 124, 125, 155, 156

E

Eastern Europe, 31, 92, 103, 104, 115, 136, 146

East Timor, 46

Economic Community of West African States, ECOWAS, 83

EDA. *See* European Defence Agency (EDA)

EEAS. *See* European External Action Service (EEAS)

EEAS Strategy for Security and Development in the Sahel, 42

effective multilateralism, 47, 55, 149

ELMA. *See* European Lessons
Management Application
(ELMA)

EMU. *See* European Monetary Union
(EMU)

emulation, 6, 29–32, 37, 39n13, 100,
109, 112, 130, 136, 143–5, 155,
167–9, 189

English school, 31, 39n14

enlargement, 31, 84, 86n6, 103, 104,
146, 160n41

ENTRi. *See* New Training Initiative for
Civilian Crisis Management
(ENTRi)

Episteme, 2, 8, 22, 25, 101, 125, 136,
157, 164–7, 171, 174, 178, 179,
183, 185

Epistemic communities, 2, 9, 15, 19,
21–4, 25–8, 33, 99, 101, 102,
106, 107, 109, 112, 123, 125,
138, 142, 172, 174, 175n6,
177–80, 183

EPLO. *See* European Peacebuilding
Liaison Office (EPLO)

Erkki Tuomioja, 139

Ernst Haas, 22–5, 179

ESDC. *See* European Security and
Defence College (ESDC)

ESS. *See* European Security Strategy
(ESS)

EUAM Ukraine, CSDP missions and
operations, 117

EUBAM Libya, CSDP missions and
operations, 145, 159n24

EUBAM Rafah, CSDP missions and
operations, 145, 150, 159n24

EUCAP Mali, CSDP missions and
operations, 42, 59, 145,
159n24, 187

EUCAP Nestor, CSDP missions and
operations, 42, 59, 145,
159n24, 187

EUCAP Niger, CSDP missions and
operations, 187

EUFOR Althea, CSDP missions and
operations, 58, 60

EUFOR Concordia, CSDP missions
and operations, 4

EUFOR RD Congo, CSDP missions
and operations, 59

EU Horn of Africa Action Plan
2015-2020, 59

EU Horn of Africa Strategic
Framework, 42

EU Institute of Security Studies, 37n1,
69, 113, 114

EUJUST-LEX Iraq, CSDP missions
and operations, 117

EULEX Kosovo, CSDP missions and
operations, 145, 149, 151,
159n24, 160n26

EU Military Staff, 59, 67

EU Military Staff (EUMS), 67

EUMM Georgia, CSDP missions and
operations, 145, 149, 150,
159n24

EUMS. *See* EU Military Staff (EUMS)

EUNAVFOR Atalanta, CSDP missions
and operations, 42, 59

EU Operation Centre (OPCEN), 67

EUPAT Macedonia, CSDP missions
and operations, 151

EUPM Bosnia and Herzegovina
(BiH), CSDP missions and
operations, 117

EUPOL Afghanistan, CSDP missions
and operations, 117, 149, 150,
159n24

EUPOL COPPS (Palestine), CSDP
missions and operations, 117

EUPOL DRC, CSDP missions and
operations, 117

EUPOL Kinshasa, CSDP missions and
operations, 59, 60